'Professor Raj Kumar, a leading educational reformer in India, is a prominent voice in the new generation of human rights thinkers and doers. His reflections on the pervasive plague of corruption in developing countries are certain to illuminate the subject, which is among the greatest obstacles to human progress in the world, not just in India.'

—**Professor Peter H. Schuck**
*Simeon E. Baldwin Professor Emeritus of Law, Yale Law School*

'Professor Raj Kumar is one of the boldest and most innovative figures in legal education. In this book he addresses corruption in India, a major issue that must be solved if India is to reach its potential as a democratic and economic leader in the world. Professor Raj Kumar's insight is to treat freedom from corruption as a human right, thereby bringing legal frameworks beyond those of the criminal law to address the problem. Persons interested in human rights and economic development, as well as the rule of law, will find this book insightful and even inspiring.'

—**Professor Stewart J. Schwab**
*Allan R. Tessler Dean & Professor of Law, Cornell Law School*

'Professor Raj Kumar broadly examines the pervasive impact of corruption on human rights in India and offers a thoughtful framework for reducing this barrier to human and commercial development. He shows that corruption is not just an economic phenomenon, but pervasively undermines the promise of Indian democracy. This is a brave and important book.'

—**Professor Ronald J. Gilson**
*Meyers Professor of Law and Business, Stanford Law School
& Stern Professor of Law and Business, Columbia Law School*

'This wise work takes us fully beyond the conventional public policy and law reform discourse concerning controlling corruption. It pioneers some new ways of understanding governance and public service corruption as constituting an ongoing, gross, and flagrant violation of some of the most cherished constitutionally enshrined and internationally articulated human rights values, norms, and standards. While guiding us to a rich comparative understanding, Professor C. Raj Kumar engages the distinctively distressing details of the Indian context, within the promise of Indian judicial activism as a resource for the re-democratisation of India. Human rights and social movement activists, conscientious political and bureaucratic actors, as well as public intellectuals everywhere will benefit a great deal by a constant recourse to this germinal text.'

—**Professor Upendra Baxi**
*Emeritus Professor of Law, University of Warwick &
Former Vice Chancellor, University of Delhi*

'Pointing out that pervasive corruption inhibits access to justice and denies people the realization of a wide range of educational, economic, and social rights, Vice Chancellor Raj Kumar makes a powerful case for replacing the current criminal law approach to corruption with a broader human rights-based approach. The human rights approach would, in addition to enforcing the criminal law, place the victims of corruption rather than the corrupt officials at the centre, empower them to realise their rights through transparent systems and accountable institutions, and shift the focus to the prevention of corruption.'

—**N. Ravi**
*Editor, The Hindu*

'This book is an important and timely contribution to building a tipping point of cultural change against corruption in India. Professor Raj Kumar's lucid and comprehensive review of the problem, its history, and the strategic options for reducing it will be indispensable reading for all those who love India.'

—**Professor Lawrence W. Sherman**
*Wolfson Professor of Criminology, University of Cambridge*

'In this important new work, Professor Raj Kumar urges us to reframe India's corruption challenge—to understand it not as a set of transgressions of a simple criminal prohibition but rather as a structural violation of the human rights of citizens to a government that is devoted to their well-being. This different view of the problem generates a new set of approaches to solving it. If ordinary Indian citizens are recognized as corruption's victims, then they should be given access to the tools they need to protect themselves. Professor Raj Kumar draws from the successes of jurisdictions such as Hong Kong and Singapore to outline a comprehensive set of such tools—from community education to a strengthened right to information to judicial training to the establishment of a new independent commission against corruption. Everyone who is committed to the continued development of the world's largest democracy has much to learn from this thoughtful and provocative book.'

—**Professor Jeffrey S. Lehman**
*Professor of Law and Former President, Cornell University &*
*Chancellor and Founding Dean Peking University School of Transnational Law*

'Professor Raj Kumar offers us important insight about Indian society and about the Indian legal system and, through the lens of India's experience, he conveys broader lessons about transparency and good governance.'

—**Professor David M. Schizer**
*Dean and the Lucy G. Moses Professor of Law, Columbia Law School*

'Professor Raj Kumar has done something really terrific here. This groundbreaking book on the intersection of the rule of law, corruption, and human rights is a much needed contribution to the fields of comparative law, law and society, and law-in-India. Not only does Professor Raj Kumar address the current state of the literature, he is also fluent in the various policy debates and historical and international developments that have occurred on the subjects of law and corruption. In my view, this book has multiple purposes—it will be extremely important for students, scholars, and policy officials; and given how accessible it is to read, I have no doubt that this text will become a permanent fixture for future investigators on corruption as well. We have all long known about Professor Raj Kumar's superb academic and institution-building skills, and this most recent book resoundingly reconfirms this point in full.'

—**Professor Jayanth K. Krishnan**

*Charles L. Whistler Faculty Fellow & Professor of Law*
*Director, India Initiative, Center on the Global Legal Profession*
*Co-Director, Center on Law, Society, and Culture*
*Indiana University Maurer School of Law*

'For those looking for models and strategies to fight corruption, here is a book which gives insights on experiences across Asia and elsewhere. A Rights-based approach with the involvement of civil society and an independent commission supported by political will can, it is argued, bring about a decisive change in the level of corruption. A timely book which is likely to make an impact in policy development and institutional reform.'

—**Professor N.R. Madhava Menon**

*Former Director, National Law School, Bangalore &*
*Former Director, National Judicial Academy, Bhopal*

'Professor Raj Kumar provides an important new perspective on global corruption by viewing it through the prism of human rights rather than criminal law. He demonstrates that corruption impedes the implementation of fundamental civil, political, economic, social and cultural rights. Taking India as his case study, Professor Raj Kumar's research shows that the effects of corrupt government are most deeply felt by the poorest and least empowered in Indian society. This well researched and lucid book makes a powerful argument for legislative and constitutional reforms in India and for transparent governance under the rule of law.'

—**Professor Gillian Triggs**

*Challis Professor of International Law & Dean, Sydney Law School*

'Professor Raj Kumar makes a compelling case that battling corruption in India is much more than a criminal justice issue—it is fundamental to the empowerment of the Indian people and the establishment of the rule of law in the world's largest democracy. This book is not only a careful scholarly treatment of a pervasive problem; it is a provocative call to action.'

—**Professor Curtis J. Milhaupt**

*Parker Professor of Comparative Corporate Law & Vice Dean, Columbia Law School*

'Corruption justifiably receives a bad press. Professor Raj Kumar intelligently, significantly and forcefully adds to that bad press by emphasising its effects on human rights (both involving specific violations of rights and governments' abilities to create the conditions under which human rights can be fulfilled) and the rule of law. Prof.

Kumar's proposed measures to address corruption warn against over reliance on criminal law and emphasise the need for an Indian ICAC and measures that empower citizens to recognize and combat corruption. I commend this book to citizens of any state who are offended by corruption within it.'

—**Professor Charles Sampford**
*Director, The Institute for Ethics, Governance and Law (IEGL)*
*President, International Institute for Public Ethics*

'For more than a decade, Professor Raj Kumar has impressed me with his passion for fighting corruption and his insistence that it is a critical problem of governance that violates the human right to justice and undermines development. This book is thus the result of over a decade's research and reflections and marries his impassioned belief in the right of citizens to corruption-free governance to a dispassionate analysis of the causes of corruption and institutional solutions to it. It brings to bear a broad comparative analysis to the focus on India. Professor Raj Kumar is surely right to emphasise the legal framework, the institutional mechanisms, the investigation and prosecution machinery, the public awareness and education strategy, and civil society empowerment approaches in their inter-connectedness. Extremely valuable to students of development, law, human rights, politics and governance. And perfectly timed to capture and give intellectual shape and direction to the growing rage and revulsion of Indians to daily revelations of mega-corruptions.'

—**Professor Ramesh Thakur**
*Professor of International Relations, Australian National University,*
*Former Senior Vice Rector, United Nations University & UN Assistant Secretary-General*

'This book makes a signal contribution to the understanding and, it is hoped, the mitigation of corruption, a serpent that threatens civil society around the world. Professor Raj Kumar brilliantly combines an original theoretical analysis, which demonstrates the many human rights effects of corruption, with proposed concrete remedies that will require political will and courage to be implemented. The book focuses on India, but it will resonate wherever corruption exists.'

—**Professor Norman Dorsen**
*Stokes Professor of Law, New York University School of Law*
*President, American Civil Liberties Union (1976–91)*

'Corruption corrodes the fabric of any civilised society. Once it takes root it is very difficult to eradicate. The fight against corruption is therefore both urgent and vital if we are to maintain the rule of law and promote public welfare. Professor Raj Kumar's book on the subject promotes this objective.'

—**Professor Adrian Zuckerman**
*Professor of Civil Procedure, University of Oxford*

'There could hardly be a more timely question in the governance studies, than how corruption debases human rights. There could hardly be a more representative case study, than India. There could hardly be a better scholar to write a book on this, than Professor Raj Kumar.'

—**Dr Vesselin Popovski**
*Senior Academic Programme Officer,*
*Institute for Sustainability and Peace, United Nations University*

'Professor Raj Kumar's book breaks welcome new ground in highlighting the relationship between corruption and human rights in India, rather than confining himself to the traditional examination of corruption as criminal activity alone. His recommending the creation of an independent commission against corruption, bringing together all relevant institutions, will certainly help address corruption more effectively. In keeping with the times, the book underscores the importance of civil society activism and the right to information as crucial aspects of the fight against corruption in India. Prof. Kumar impressively marshals his knowledge and writes with admirable lucidity. Transparency and accountability are crying needs in our democracy. The book's description of international and comparative perspectives in the fight against corruption is salutary. This book is a must-read for those who wish to eliminate the danger posed by corruption to the very foundations of democracy and the rule of law, which are fundamental to the society that India aspires to build.'

—**Dr Shashi Tharoor**
*Member of Parliament, Former Under-Secretary-General, United Nations,*
*& Trustee, Fletcher School of Law & Diplomacy, Tufts University*

'At a time when the whole nation is engaged in an animated discussion on why India has failed to check the enormous corruption in high places, Professor Raj Kumar makes a timely and meaningful contribution to the debate. He brings a new perspective to the problem that should gladden the hearts of those who stand unequivocally for protecting the human rights of the whole community. The author's lucid prose makes him highly readable for the lay man ... a landmark in the history of literature on a burning issue.'

—**Dr R.K. Raghavan**
*Former Director, Central Bureau of Investigation (CBI), India*

'This book is an authentic, comprehensive and sensitive study of the problem of corruption and its human rights dimension in India. It is not confined to the restatement of the problem; it offers some thought-provoking solutions as well. Authored by an accomplished, dynamic and forward-looking scholar of modern India, the study is a rich contribution to literature. It is also an invaluable guide to policymakers. It enriches the contemporary debate on the curse of corruption. It appears to be a compulsory reading for those who seek riddance from corruption in order to achieve good governance.'

—**Professor Yogesh K. Tyagi**
*Professor of International Law and Director,*
*Centre for Promotion of Human Rights, Teaching and Research*
*School of International Studies, Jawaharlal Nehru University*

'It is no secret that the governmental institutions of the emerging economies of Asia are rife with corruption that threatens their continued growth and stability. To date, most of the analyses of the effects and cures for corruption have focused upon reforms of the criminal justice systems of these societies. Professor Raj Kumar's book is the first study that takes as its theme the notion that corruption is most profitably viewed through the lens of human rights. While the book concentrates its attention primarily upon the problem of corruption in India, this ground-breaking study should be essential reading for all those in academia, government, business and the human rights community who want to understand the effects of corruption on the rights of the masses of the poor and disenfranchised who have been left out of the astonishing economic growth over the last decade in India, China, Vietnam and other parts of Asia. Professor Raj Kumar's insightful recognition of the connection between corruption and human rights allows him to offer fresh solutions that go beyond the institutions of the past and present, which have failed miserably in the fight against corruption.'

—**Professor Barbara Holden-Smith**
*Vice Dean and Professor of Law, Cornell Law School*

'This book is a good introduction to a legal approach to fight corruption. It has a wealth of comparative references. Even if you disagree with the institutional approach, you will not fail to benefit from the rich analysis in this book.'

—**Professor Pratap Bhanu Mehta**
*President & Chief Executive, Centre for Policy Research, New Delhi*

'Corruption is one word that encompasses many worlds, the author tells us. It will take many words to indicate, even in small measure, the many merits and usefulness of this book. Amidst the vast and ever-growing literature on corruption, this book, with its focus on human rights as the key to unlock a formidable combination of moral indifference and legal laxity in the fight against corruption, is unique and timely. It makes a compelling case with a comparative perspective for a crusade against corruption as a violation of human rights.'

—**R. Sudarshan**
*Policy Advisor-Legal Reform and Justice,*
*UNDP Asia-Pacific Regional Centre, United Nations Development Programme*

'An ambitious and timely study of one of the critical human rights issues of our time.'

—**Jacqueline Bhabha**
*Executive Director, Harvard University Committee on Human Rights Studies*
*Carr Center for Human Rights Policy, Harvard Kennedy School*

# Corruption and Human Rights
## in India

# Corruption and Human Rights
## in India

Comparative Perspectives
on Transparency and
Good Governance

## C. Raj Kumar

OXFORD
UNIVERSITY PRESS

# OXFORD
UNIVERSITY PRESS

Oxford University Press is a department of the University of Oxford.
It furthers the University's objective of excellence in research, scholarship,
and education by publishing worldwide. Oxford is a registered trademark of
Oxford University Press in the UK and in certain other countries

Published in India by
Oxford University Press
YMCA Library Building, 1 Jai Singh Road, New Delhi 110001, India

ISBN 13: 978-0-19-807732-9
ISBN 10: 0-19-807732-7

Typeset in 11/13.4 Minion Pro
By Excellent Laser Typesetters, Pitampura, Delhi 110 034
Printed in India at Artxel, New Delhi 110 020

*This book is dedicated to my parents
who instilled in me a sense of honesty and integrity; my
wife who believed in my intellectual abilities and
empowered me to undertake this work; and my
children who quietly supported me and provided
happiness at all times with their smiles.*

# Contents

*Acknowledgements*                                                              xv

*Foreword by Justice V.R. Krishna Iyer*                                         xix

1. **Introduction**                                                             1

   Corruption: Introducing the Problem                                          2

   Overview of Corruption in India                                             15

   Corruption and its Relationship with Human Rights                           28

   Corruption and its Implications for the Rule of Law                         30

2. **Corruption and its Impact on Human Rights**                               40

   Corruption and the Human Rights Framework                                   40

   Corruption and its Relationship with Specific
   Human Rights                                                                49

   Sovereignty in the Context of Globalization, Human
   Rights, and Development                                                      57

3. **Corruption and its Consequences for Governance
   in Asia: A Comparative Perspective**                                         64

   The Proliferation of Corruption in Asia:
   Problematizing the Issue                                                     64

   Models for Combating Corruption in Asia                                      71

   Linkages between Violations of Human Rights and
   Corruption in Asia                                                           80

**4. Existing Framework for Combating Corruption in India**    **94**

Constitutional Framework for Promoting Transparency
in Governance                                                      94

Legal and Institutional Framework for Fighting Corruption     108

**5. New Legislative and Institutional Reforms for**           **128**
**Eliminating Corruption in India**

Legislative Measures Required                                     128

Institutional Measures: National Human Rights
Commission                                                        139

Institutional Measures: Central Information
Commission and the Right to Information                           162

**6. The Way Forward: Establishing an Independent**            **171**
**Commission Against Corruption**

Creating the Right Political Environment for
Combating Corruption                                              171

Towards Establishing an Independent Commission
against Corruption                                                188

ICAC and its Relationship with Other Institutions—
Formal and Informal                                               197

The Way Forward: A Cohesive Approach to
Combating Corruption                                              200

*Postscript*                                                      214

*Index*                                                           225

# Acknowledgements

———————————— ∾ ∿ ————————————

I would like to thank the School of Law of City University of Hong Kong, where I spent a good part of my academic career for all the institutional support that I received over the years. I would also like to thank the National Human Rights Commission, for having provided the necessary help and assistance in obtaining key information relating to this book.

I would like to thank the Faculty of Law of the University of Hong Kong and a number of faculty members for their strong encouragement and support all these years in helping me complete this work. In particular, I would like to thank Professor Yash Ghai, Professor Hurst Hannum, Professor Tony Carty, and Professor Fu Hualing for their valuable suggestions over the years in writing this book. During the several years of my stay in Hong Kong, I have had the opportunity to interact with Professor Johannes Chan and Professor Albert Chen; and I appreciate their encouragement and support.

I had undertaken the writing of this book while holding a full time faculty and administrative position at the O.P. Jindal Global University. There are a number of scholars in India and Hong Kong who helped me shape my thinking and perspectives on this issue and I appreciate their time, help, and assistance. I have richly benefitted from the opportunity of discussing certain core issues relating to this book with Professor Wang Guiguo, Dean, School of Law, City University of Hong Kong, Professor Richard Cullen, formerly, Visiting Professor,

Faculty of Law, the University of Hong Kong and Professor Michael
C. Davis of the Chinese University of Hong Kong. I would also like
to thank my former Research Associates/Assistants Professor Amit
Bindal, Professor Yugank Goyal, Ms Stephanie Hays, and Mr Aditya
Singh for their help and assistance in completing this book. I would
like to acknowledge the contribution of my current Research Associ-
ates, Ms Ruchira Goel and Ms Latika Vashist.

This book was shaped by my many years of work relating to the
problems and challenges of establishing a rule of law society in
India. My understanding and perspectives relating to the problems
of the Indian legal system and the challenges and opportunities
that are available to respond to the crisis of governance have been
shaped by my interaction with my teachers, Professor M.P. Singh,
Vice Chancellor, National University of Juridical Sciences, Kolkata;
Professor Parmanand Singh, Former Dean, Faculty of Law, University
of Delhi; and Professor B.B. Pande, formerly Professor of Law, Faculty
of Law, University of Delhi.

I would like to place on record the encouragement and support
rendered by Mr Naveen Jindal, Chancellor, O.P. Jindal Global
University (JGU); Dr Sanjeev P. Sahni, Head, Education Initiatives,
Jindal Group; Professor D.K. Srivastava, former Pro Vice Chancellor
(Academic), JGU; Dr A. Francis Julian, Chief Legal Advisor, JGU;
and Mr Aman Shah, Registrar, JGU. I would like to thank Ms Neha
Phull, Manager and International Relations Officer, JGU, for her help
and assistance.

I appreciate the competence and professionalism of the entire
team at the Oxford University Press for support in producing this
book in a very short time.

I am grateful to Justice V.R. Krishna Iyer, former Judge of the
Supreme Court of India, for his generous Foreword to the book. I
am truly humbled by his words of appreciation and thank him for
agreeing to write this Foreword at the age of 96.

I would like to express my heartfelt gratitude to my parents,
Professor K. Chockalingam and Dr Vijayalakshmi Chockalingam for
shaping my character to enable me to appreciate the importance of
integrity in public and private life. The importance of honesty and

rectitude were deeply embedded during the formative years of my life by my parents, which shaped my thinking on these issues from a law and public policy perspective. I am grateful to them for continuously encouraging me to complete this work.

This book is seeing the light of the day because of my wife, Mrs Pratibha Jain, former Vice President and Head of Legal, Goldman Sachs India, who motivated me all along and encouraged and supported me in every respect so that I was able to complete this work. I am grateful to her for inspiring me to do this as she took upon herself the responsibility of taking care of our home, while herself, pursuing a responsible legal career. I would like to express my sincere apologies to our children, Abhimanyu J. Kumar (7 years) and Avantika J. Kumar (3½ years) for the time that I was away from them and thank them for their love and affection even when I have ignored them, while working on this book.

12 June 2011

# Foreword

It is a matter of great pleasure and pride to write a foreword to the book, *Corruption and Human Rights in India Comparative Perspectives on Transparency and Good Governance* authored by Professor C. Raj Kumar. Professor Raj Kumar is a remarkable crusader of human rights with professional excellence and soulful commitment.

I have known Professor Raj Kumar since his days as a student of law in the University of Delhi. He is brilliant, volcanic, and prodigiously devoted to his law research and human rights jurisprudence. He is a fine public speaker and a leader among scholars. I have always encouraged him to pursue human right studies and was delighted to witness his many achievements over the years, including the award of the Rhodes Scholarship to study at the University of Oxford. He successfully completed his studies at Oxford and then later at the Harvard Law School with a specialization in human rights.

Within a short span of time, he established an international reputation as a prolific scholar and a sound thinker in the field of human rights in all its dimensions. His work relating to national human rights commissions is most significant and extremely relevant for understanding the role of human rights institutions in protecting and promoting human rights in India and elsewhere. In more recent years, he has been working on understanding the human rights implications of corruption, and has advised the United Nations Development Programme and the United Nations University

on fighting corruption and promoting good governance. Throughout
his career, Professor Raj Kumar's multifaceted contributions have
been admirable and his commitment has been profound for human
rights and access to justice. There are many votaries of human rights
jurisprudence I know, but Professor Raj Kumar has been a foremost
activist in the field. He envisioned the creation of a global University
in India and is the Vice Chancellor of this unique University near
New Delhi with characteristics trans-global.

The fact that the Oxford University Press is publishing this work of
Professor Raj Kumar is in itself a great recognition of the excellence
of the book. I am delighted that he chose to write this book following
up on an earlier theme covered by his previous book, *Human Rights,
Justice and Constitutional Empowerment*, which was also published
by the Oxford University Press.

India's major menace in public life is corruption. When our
nation became free from British imperialism, we made a tryst
with destiny to wipe every tear from every eye—the elimination of
poverty and eradication of corruption. But during the last 60 odd
years of independence, corruption in our public life has mounted.
Different dimensions of it have been dealt with in this book. Corruption has become an all-pervasive phenomenon and all wings of
the government have been affected by it. Never in the 60 years of
judicial history in India have such serious charges been made against
judges as have been made in recent times. Nowadays, high courts
are not free from moral violations. Extraordinary defences by judges
in hiding their wealth or in promoting to the Bench their close relations were not so common earlier as they are now. The people of our
Republic have truly become victims to such vagaries of corruption.
The robed brethren are accused of robbing wealth and yet no inquiry,
no action by the Cabinet and no inquiry by Parliament into the judicial jejuneness has taken place.

The time has come for a democratic revolt against the judiciary
and a demand for an appointment commission, a performance
commission, and an anti-corruption commission to keep a constant
watch over judges and the respect they command. If judges fail in
their moral fibre, the rule of law and the rule of life would collapse

and open the route to military rule and functional chaos. 'Power tends to corrupt and absolute power corrupts absolutely' said Lord Acton. Long ago, Britain, an imperial power and India, as one of its largest colonies, was one of the victims of corrupt administration. When the British trampled over India and every British ruler amassed wealth by corruption, it provoked independence by statutory enactment. The notoriously exploitative Warren Hastings who was impeached for corruption demonstrated how public power not accountable to even the great office of Viceroy led to impeachment and produced eloquent speeches by men like Edmund Burke who in his address of the impeachment of Warren Hastings orated:

'I impeach him in the name of the people of India, whose rights he has trodden under foot, and whose country he has turned into a desert. Lastly, in the name of human nature itself, in the name of both sexes, in the name of every age, in the name of every rank, I impeach the common enemy and oppressor of all!'

So when India became free Jawaharlal Nehru in his historic tryst with destiny speech stated:

Long years ago we made a tryst with destiny and now the time comes when we shall redeem our pledge not wholly or in full measure but very substantially. The service of India means the service of the millions who suffer, it means the ending of poverty and ignorance and disease and inequality of opportunity. The ambition of the greatest man of our generation has been to wipe every tear from every eye.

The millions of the poverty stricken people of India were condemned to suffering because their imperial masters robbed India of its wealth. Despite this disastrous experience of corruption by the British rulers in India, free India did not have a clean administration. Indians, instead, were in the words of Winston Churchill, 'rogues, rascals and freebooters'. During the 60 years of *swaraj*, corruption has been ubiquitous and universal. One of the inevitable consequences of corruption is terrorism, communalism, and the suppression of human rights.

The greatest menace to the human rights of the Indian people is not the lack of constitutional grandeur with dignity and divinity enshrined in the paramount parchment. In the abandonment of integrity, fraternity, unity, and humanity, the greatest challenge of the statesmen of India is to make its politics straight and beyond pollution. Professor Raj Kumar has highlighted this factor. If 'We, the People of India' are to be true to its cultural heritage, we must struggle to win *swaraj* and jettison corruption. Our contribution is great but our administrators have betrayed our supreme cultural past. What was that sublime value-system in the words of Max Mueller:

If we were to look over the whole world to find out the country most richly endowed with all the wealth, power, and beauty that nature can bestow—in some parts a very paradise on earth—I should point to India. If I were asked under what sky the human mind has most fully developed some of its choicest gifts, has most deeply pondered over the greatest problems of life, and has found solutions of some of them, which will deserve the attention even of those who have studied Plato and Kant—I should point to India. And If I were to ask myself from what literature we here in Europe, we who have been nurtured almost exclusively on the thoughts of Greeks and Romans, and of one Semitic race, the Jewish, may draw the corrective which is most wanted in order to make our inner life more perfect, more comprehensive, more universal, in fact more truly human a life, not for this life only, but a transfigured and eternal life—again I should point to India.

This book written by Professor Raj Kumar is an extraordinary contribution to the understanding of the relationship of corruption and human rights and its deeper impact on access to justice and rule of law. I sincerely hope that all politicians, bureaucrats, judges, and members of civil society read this book as it is intellectually enriching and empowering to the citizenry for pursuing various struggles against corruption and lack of good governance.

12 June 2011                                                     V.R. KRISHNA IYER

# 1

# Introduction

'Just as it is impossible not to taste the honey or the poison that finds itself at the tip of the tongue, so it is impossible for a government servant not to eat up at least a bit of the king's revenue. Just as fish under water cannot possibly be found out either as drinking or not drinking water, so government servants employed in the government work cannot be found out taking money.'

Kautilya, 300 BCE[1]

'Corruption and hypocrisy ought not to be inevitable products of democracy, as they undoubtedly are today.'

Mohandas Karamchand Gandhi (1869–1948)

'[Corruption] deepens poverty; it debases human rights, it degrades the environment; it derails development, including private sector development; it can drive conflict in and between nations; and it destroys confidence in democracy and the legitimacy of governments. It debases human dignity and is universally condemned by the world's major faiths.'

The Durban Commitment to Effective Action against Corruption[2]

---

[1] R. Shama Sastry, *Kautilya's Arthasastra* 71 (1967). (Bangalore: Government Press) See also Upendra Thakur, *Corruption in Ancient India* (1979) (Delhi: Abhinav Publications).

[2] The Commitment was signed by 1,600 delegates from 135 countries at the Anti-corruption Conference sponsored by Transparency International in October 1999.

## CORRUPTION: INTRODUCING THE PROBLEM

Corruption in India is a problem that has serious implications for both protecting the rule of law and ensuring access to justice. Corruption is pervasive in the system of governance in India, undermining the effectiveness of all institutions of governance. Since independence successive governments have attempted to take numerous measures to reduce the levels of corruption in the country, including legislative and institutional measures. However, due to an absence of political will and sincerity in taking concrete steps to eliminate corruption, most of these measures have not achieved the results that were intended.

The present work intends to examine the human rights implications of corruption in India. It will discuss the existing legal and institutional frameworks for controlling corruption in India and in particular the implications of corruption for protecting and promoting human rights. The purpose of the study is to provide a new framework for legislative and institutional reforms in India with a view to addressing corruption. While proposing this framework, the author is mindful of the inherent weaknesses of legislative reforms in Indian society, as well as of the crisis of law enforcement, a challenge faced in all sectors of administration in the country. The effectiveness of legislative and institutional reforms to fight corruption will depend upon a number of factors, and there is a need for other initiatives, as well as civil society empowerment to ensure that these initiatives are effective. The challenge of establishing a rule-of-law society is writ large in India. The existing governmental machinery across the state and Central Governments has not been able to inspire confidence among the people of India as far as eliminating corruption is concerned.

The present analysis argues that corruption in India is not merely a law enforcement issue where the existing laws of the state are violated and which can be remedied merely by more stringent law enforcement. Rather, corruption in India is a much more fundamental problem that undermines the very social fabric, and the political and bureaucratic structure of the Indian society. Thus, while it is necessary for the law enforcement machinery to be empowered, the larger issue concerning corruption in India is how it violates human rights, in particular the constitutional rights guaranteed under the Constitution of India. Further, corruption in India violates the constitutional foundations of Indian democracy, on the basis of which a rule-of-law society in India was meant to be established. However, the promises made by the Constitution makers have been broken over the years by the scourge of corruption in every institution, which has led to a scourge in the governance apparatus from top to bottom.

Before the issue of corruption is discussed, it is important to provide some perspective on the definitions of corruption. There have been numerous debates and controversies surrounding the exact meaning of corruption. The generally accepted definition in contemporary literature focuses on the abuse of a public office or power for private gain.[3] This definition has also been adopted by institutions like the World Bank.[4] However, this definition is quite broad in its ambit and generic in nature. There is no global consensus over the specific elements that constitute corruption, leading most scholars to argue that attempting to define 'corruption' in general is a futile exercise.[5] Thus, while the 2003 UN Convention Against Corruption (UNCAC)[6] uses the word 'corruption' in a number of places, it does not actually

[3] Asian African Legal Consultative Org., Combating Corruption: A Legal Analysis 9 (2005), available at http://www.aalco.int/Special%20study%201%20 contents%202005.pdf (last visited 11 May 2011).

[4] Ian Bannon, The Fight against Corruption: A World Bank Perspective, workshop on Transparency and Government (25–8 May 1999), Stockholm, Sweden, available at http://www.iadb.org/regions/re2/consultative_group/groups/transparency_workshop6.htm (last visited 11 May 2011).

[5] See, for example, S.L. Joseph et al., Castan Centre for Human Rights, Human Rights Translated: A Business Reference Guide (2008), available at http://humanrights.unglobalcompact.org/doc/human_rights_translated.pdf; David Kinley, Human Rights and Corporations (2009) (Australia: Ashgate).

[6] United Nations Convention Against Corruption, Art. 2, 31 October 2003, 2349 UNTS 41. India ratified the UNCAC in May 2011. See 'India Ratifies UN Convention Against Corruption', The Hindu (12 May 2011), available at http://www.thehindu.com/news/national/article2012804.ece (last visited 11 May 2011).

define corruption itself. Rather, it defines and criminalizes certain *acts* of corruption, such as bribery, money laundering, abuse of power, and embezzlement.[7] At the same time, it must be recognized that this definition excludes corruption by non-state actors and, in particular, the role of multinational corporations and other business enterprises, as well as NGOs in fomenting the problem of corruption. The main argument advanced for this exclusion is that official corruption poses particular challenges to governance and affects the access to justice, thereby undermining the protection and promotion of human rights, a problem that may not be so prevalent in cases of private corruption. However, institutions like the Asian Development Bank have factored in the role of private players in corruption, as will be seen below.

The ADB has been spearheading a number of initiatives in the fight against corruption. As early as 1998, the anti-corruption policy of the ADB[8] articulated that, as an institution, it intends to reduce the burden that corruption puts on governments and economies in the Asia–Pacific region.[9] Further, in November 2004, the ADB clarified that fraud and corruption under the anti-corruption policy include corrupt, fraudulent, collusive, and coercive practices, and defined those terms. For the ADB, corrupt and fraudulent practices under the anti-corruption policy comprise of the following acts:

(i)   corrupt practice, which is the offering, giving, receiving, or soliciting, directly or indirectly, of anything of value to improperly influence the actions of another party;
(ii)  fraudulent practice, which is any action, including misrepresentation, to obtain a financial or other benefit or avoid an obligation by deception;
(iii) coercive practice, which is impairing or harming, or threatening to impair or harm, directly or indirectly, any party or persons closely related to a party, to improperly influence the actions of that party; and

[7] Ibid.
[8] See Asian Development Bank, 'Anticorruption Policy: Harmonized Definitions of Corrupt and Fraudulent Practices' (1998), available at http://www.adb.org/Documents/Policies/Anticorruption/definitions-update.pdf ('ADB Harmonized Definitions') (last visited 11 May 2011).
[9] Ibid.

(iv) collusive practice, which is an arrangement between two or more entities without the knowledge, but designed to improperly influence the actions, of another party.[10]

The ADB, unlike the World Bank, has included the private sector in the framework for fighting corruption. Thus, for the ADB, '[c]orruption involves behaviour on the part of officials in the public and private sectors, in which they improperly and unlawfully enrich themselves and/or those close to them, or induce others to do so, by misusing the position in which they are placed.'[11] To that extent, ADB's definition is more inclusive in scope.

Article 1 of the Organisation for Economic Co-operation and Development Convention on Combating Bribery of Foreign Public Officials in International Business Transactions (henceforth 'OECD Convention') has defined the offence of bribery of foreign public officials as the voluntary giving (promising or offering) of something of value to a foreign public official in order to obtain or retain business or other improper advantage in the conduct of international business.[12] This convention focuses on the person who offers, promises, or gives a bribe (termed 'active' bribery), but does not focus on the recipient of the bribe (so-called 'passive' bribery).[13]

---

[10] Ibid., pp. 1–2. For an insightful analysis of the variegated forms that corruption acquires, see Upendra Baxi, *The Future of Human Rights* 291–2 (2008) New York: Oxford University Press; Joel S. Hellman, Geraint Jones, and Daniel Kaufman, 'Size the State, Seize the Day: State Capture, Corruption and Influence in Transition', *World Bank Policy Research Working Paper* No. 2444 (Washington DC, 2000).

[11] Asian Development Bank, 'Anticorruption: Policies and Strategies' 9–10 (1998), available at http://www.adb.org/Documents/Policies Anticorruption/anticorruption.pdf (last visited 11 May 2011).

[12] Organization for Economic Cooperation and Development (OECD), Convention on Combating Bribery of Foreign Public Officials in International Business Transactions, Art. 1(1–2), 18 December 1997, 37 I.L.M. 1 (1998).

[13] OECD, 'Fighting Bribery and Corruption: Frequently Asked Questions', available at http://www.oecd.org/document/18/0,3343,en_2649_34859_35430226_1_1_1_1,00.html (last visited 13 March 2008).

Corruption also promotes mis-governance as it affects the integrity of the legal, judicial, and administrative apparatus. The World
Bank has observed:

Governance is the process and institutions by which authority in a country is
exercised: (i) the process by which governments are selected, held accountable, monitored, and replaced; (ii) the capacity of governments to manage
resources efficiently, and to formulate, implement, and enforce sound policies and regulations; and, (iii) the respect for the institutions that govern
economic and social interactions among them.[14]

The existing anti-corruption framework in India places far too
much emphasis on the criminal justice system for dealing with corruption, a system that is itself facing a crisis due to corruption and
other problems. Thus, fighting corruption is also essential for restor-
ing the people's faith in the Indian criminal justice system. That said
however, legal controls relating to corruption should focus more
on the promotion of transparency and accountability in governance.
Empowerment of the citizenry needs to be the foundation for legal
and institutional reforms to address corruption. Generally, the initiatives that have been undertaken so far in this regard have not met
with success. However, the development of the right to information
in India with the objectives of empowering the citizens of India and
ensuring transparency in governance is worth mentioning, given its
positive outcomes. This work will thus provide a critical analysis of
the right to information law and the workings of the Central Information Commission (CIC) and the State Information Commissions
(SICs). These institutions are new initiatives in India that are carving their own political space, with the power to create transparency
and accountability, and to enforce the right to information. This
book will throw light on some decisions taken by the CIC that have
direct implications for strengthening the legal framework for fighting
corruption.

---

[14] World Bank Institute, 'Governance: A Participatory Action-oriented
Program' 2 (2001), available at http://info.worldbank.org/etools/docs/library/
205639/fy02_brief.pdf (last visited 11 May 2011).

The need to establish an independent commission against corruption in India in order to provide a stronger and effective legal and institutional framework for fighting corruption will be examined. That establishing 'independent' institutions in India is a major challenge is well recognized. This work will confront some of these challenges and provide the necessary reasons and justifications for establishing such an institution. Experiences from other countries, particularly Asian countries (where such institutions have yielded positive results), will be appropriately used to bring home the fact that independent institutions can indeed succeed in fighting corruption. Of course, any comparative analysis has its own limitations, as all reforms that need to take place in a particular country will depend upon the social, legal, and political context of that nation. Nevertheless, it is extremely useful to draw upon the experiences of other countries in the fight against corruption, as there are large similarities among countries, particularly Asian countries, when it comes to the impact of corruption on governance.

In the context of the human rights implications of corruption, the right to access to justice and its linkages with corruption will be examined. At the core of the notion of access to justice lie the rights of an individual to have access, and the obligations of the government to provide it. A society that fails to recognize and effectively implement access to justice cannot establish the rule of law. Access to justice, like the rule of law, is not merely a matter of form without substance. Just as the enactment of any law does not by itself satisfy the requirement of the rule of law, the mere existence of any means for seeking justice does not actually ensure access to justice. Access to justice depends on, among other things, the availability, suitability, efficiency, and convenience of the forum, and the capacity—economic, social, physical, or otherwise—of the person seeking access to justice. These issues will therefore be addressed in detail in this book.

What needs to be recognized is that the fundamental problem of empowering the citizenry in the fight against corruption has been largely neglected in India. Understanding the linkages between corruption and access to justice involves recognizing that certain acts of corruption are human rights violations. Thus, what is significant about the recognition of corruption as a human rights violation needs to be examined closely. One may ask that, as numerous human rights violations take place in India everyday, even if corruption were recognized as a human rights violation, how would it help in the larger fight against corruption? Thus, the central question becomes: To what extent does the recognition of corruption as a violation of human rights help in the fight against corruption? Human rights violations have assumed great significance and received attention in societies around the world. With reference to the enforcement of economic and social rights, Audrey Chapman has argued that 'A "violations approach" is more feasible precisely because it does not depend on the availability and public release of extensive and appropriate statistical data or on major improvements in states' statistical systems. The monitoring of human rights is not an academic exercise; it is intended to ameliorate human suffering resulting from violations of international human rights standards...'[15]

The mere recognition of human rights violations followed by actions that will help in the enforcement of human rights could itself be an effective tool in the fight against corruption. Corruption needs to be recognized not only as a violation of specific human rights, but also as an issue that undermines the ability of governments to create conditions for the fulfillment of *all* human rights. Under this paradigm, the focus of the efforts to eliminate corruption would be on the people who are affected by acts of corruption.

In a background note for the UN Conference on Anti-corruption Measures, Good Governance and Human Rights held in Warsaw during 8–9 November 2006, prepared by the United Nations Office of the High Commissioner for Human Rights in 2006, it was observed:

The corrupt management of public resources compromises the government's ability to deliver an array of services, including health, educational and

---

[15] Audrey R. Chapman, 'A "Violations Approach" to Monitoring the International Covenant on Economic, Social and Cultural Rights', *Human Rights Dialogue*, 1 (10) (Fall 1997), available at http://www.carnegiecouncil.org/resources/publications/dialogue/1_10/articles/580.html (last visited April 2011).

welfare services, which are essential for the realization of economic, social and cultural rights. Also, the prevalence of corruption creates discrimination in access to public services in favour of those able to influence the authorities to act in their personal interest, including by offering bribes ... Importantly, corruption in the rule-of-law system weakens the very accountability structures which are responsible for protecting human rights and contributes to a culture of impunity, since illegal actions are not punished and laws are not consistently upheld.[16]

The focus of the rights-based approach to fighting corruption is to recognize the importance of transparency and accountability in governance. It also underscores the need for the empowerment of the citizens through the recognition of a human right against corruption. This framework of understanding corruption in India as a human rights issue departs from the existing approach in many ways. First, the existing approach of merely strengthening the criminal law enforcement mechanisms has not addressed the question of victimization due to acts of corruption. The human rights approach, on the other hand, places the victims of corruption and their human rights at the centre of anti-corruption efforts. It recognizes that corruption in India has enormous consequences for the delivery of justice across different institutions of government, leading to people losing faith in the legal system and the state apparatus.

Second, the human rights approach to anti-corruption efforts seeks accountability for acts of corruption[17] (something that has been a fundamental problem in the case of India), and places emphasis on the empowerment of people, as they are the ultimate victims of acts of corruption. The difference between the criminal law enforcement approach to recognizing criminal culpability, and the human rights approach to seeking accountability for corruption lies in the *apparatus*

---

[16] UN Office of the High Comm'r for HR (OHCHR), Background Note for UN Conference on Anti-corruption Measures, Good Governance and Human Rights, ¶6, Doc. HR/POL/GG/SEM/2006/2 (Warsaw, 8–9 November 2006).

[17] L. Cockroft, 'Corruption and Human Rights: A Crucial Link', Working Paper (Berlin, 1998).

through which such accountability is sought. In the former, one must entirely depend on the state apparatus to ensure accountability, whereas through the latter, the victims themselves are empowered to ensure transparency, which in turn leads to accountability in governance in addition to their ability to seek justice through judicial remedies. This departs from the existing criminal law enforcement framework in that it addresses one of the most serious consequences of corruption in India—its adverse impact on disempowering people, particularly the poor and the vulnerable. The inherent weaknesses of the criminal justice system are in fact manifested through its unsuccessful efforts to seek criminal accountability for acts of corruption. In a society that is struggling to uphold the rule of law, where the criminal justice system is facing a crisis, it becomes a far more challenging task to use criminal justice as the sole approach to fight corruption. However, the human rights approach focuses on the victims of corruption, so that instead of depending upon the state machinery to seek accountability, the citizens are empowered to ensure transparency in governance. The right to information, thus, becomes a vital tool in the fight against corruption, as it allows for the creation of a vigilant citizenry that is not willing to accept corruption as an established reality in India.

Third, the human rights approach examines the human rights impact of acts of corruption, thus ensuring that policy makers are in a position to develop strategies that protect and promote human rights, including the right to corruption-free governance. This relationship, between public policy reform and the improvement of governance with respect to ensuring a corruption-free administration, is a critical component of understanding the human rights implications of corruption. The institutional frameworks of courts and commissions that deal with acts of corruption are best suited to enforce laws that protect and promote human rights, including the laws that prohibit corruption. However, for these institutional frameworks to be effective, there is a need for enhancing the communication and interaction between the human rights institutions, anti-corruption institutions and civil society, which is what the human rights approach focuses on.

Fourth, the human rights approach to studying corruption recognizes the vulnerability of the impoverished people in India, where the problem of corruption under conditions of poverty and lack of social security poses profound difficulties for protecting the basic human rights. In fact, one of the core rationales for using human rights tools in the fight against corruption is to recognize that the victims of corruption in impoverished communities are vulnerable, and are not in a position to seek any other remedy. In a society where corruption is rampant, in order to access the resources of the state, people obviously need to pay bribes, and since they are not in a position to do so due to their economic status, they are adversely affected in their ability to seek redress. Corruption, thus, affects the poor in such a manner that they are left with no alternatives, and the policies and resources allocated by the state for empowering the poor and vulnerable do not reach them due to corruption.

Fifth, the human rights approach formulates strategies to deal with corruption bearing in mind that empowering the people in the fight against corruption is the key to addressing corruption. Thus, it focuses on ensuring transparency in governance and accountability of the government as the primary tools for fighting corruption. In addition to the empowerment of institutions in the fight against corruption, this approach also uses civil society and people to expose acts of corruption.

Sixth, the existing institutional machinery that deals with corruption has placed far too much emphasis on reactive policies—the investigation, prosecution, and conviction of perpetrators of acts of corruption. While this is critical for ensuring the rule of law, access to justice involves placing emphasis on the people who are affected by corruption and ensuring that acts of corruption do not take place in the future. Thus, in the human rights-based approach to fighting corruption, the institutional framework of the Central Information Commission (CIC) and the legal framework provided by the legislation on the right to information, assume considerable significance. The right to information creates a new venue for asserting greater transparency on the part of the government and ensures greater public vigilance with a view to reducing acts of corruption.

Corruption has a profound impact on the implementation of civil, political, economic, social, and cultural rights. The normative framework of law and the institutional apparatus that it creates for enforcing the rule of law is critical for ensuring access to justice. Access to justice encompasses a variety of aspects, but it primarily deals with the ability of people in a society to have proper systems in place that can ensure justice. These systems can be created by the civil and criminal justice systems, administrative regulations and institutions, and by the judiciary and other quasi-judicial apparatuses. However, the key factor that will ensure access to justice to people in a society is the effectiveness of these institutions. It is in this context that corruption and its elimination becomes critical for ensuring access to justice. Access to justice cannot be achieved in Indian society without eliminating corruption, as the role of the state and its instrumentalities continues to be significant when it comes to formulating and implementing policies. The Indian citizenry continues to be largely dependent upon the government and the power that it exercises, which is inevitably characterized by corruption. The role of the state, thus, needs to be assessed in the context of how effectively it is discharging its duties and responsibilities for ensuring good governance.

It is important to interpret governance in India in the context of a renewed understanding of sovereignty. If the Government of India exercises powers to assert its sovereignty, these powers cannot be exercised in an isolated and value-neutral manner. These powers ought to be exercised with a view to creating a governance system that will ensure that sovereignty rests with the people and that the state exercises its powers in a responsible manner. In the Indian context, the recognition that sovereignty rests with the people of India has long been established. The Supreme Court of India in an important judgment way back in 1964 in the case of *State of West Bengal* v. *Union of India* held, 'Legal sovereignty of the Indian nation is vested the people of India who as stated by the preamble have solemnly resolved to constitute India into a Sovereign Democratic Republic for the objects specified therein. The political sovereignty is distributed between ... the Union of India and the States with greater weightage in favour of the Union...'[18]

The *New Webster's International Dictionary* defines the term governance as 'act, manner, office, or power of governing'; 'government'; 'state of being governed'; or 'method of government or regulation.'[19] However, these explanations do not fully capture the contemporary understanding of governance and its relationship to sovereignty. To understand this, it may be useful to refer to the report of the Council of Rome, which observed:

We use the term governance to denote the command mechanism of a social system and its actions that endeavour to provide security, prosperity, coherence, order and continuity to the system... Taken broadly, the concept of governance should not be restricted to national and international systems but also should be used in relation to regional, provincial and local governments as well as to other social systems such as education and the military, to private enterprises and even to the microcosm of the family.[20]

In order to understand the conceptual underpinnings of sovereignty from a governance perspective, it is important to recognize that sovereignty hinges on state responsibility.[21] The 2001 report of the International Commission on Intervention and State Sovereignty,

[18] AIR (1963) SC 1241.

[19] This was referred to in Thomas G. Weiss, 'Governance, Good Governance and Global Governance: Conceptual and Actual Challenges', in Rorden Wilkinson (ed.), *The Global Governance Reader* 68 (2005) (London: Routledge).

[20] Alexander King and Bertrand Schneider, 'The First Global Revolution: A Report of the Council of Rome' 181–2 (1991). See also James N. Rosenau, 'Governance in the Twenty-First Century', in Rorden Wilkinson (ed.), *The Global Governance Reader* 46.

[21] C. Raj Kumar, 'Report of the Consultant for the UNDP Project for Strengthening of the Commission to Investigate Allegations of Bribery or Corruption', Sri Lanka 5 (2000) (referring to the concept as taken from the 'Responsibility to Protect' in the context of humanitarian interventions).

titled *The Responsibility to Protect*, tackles the question of when, if ever, it is appropriate for states to take coercive—and, in particular, military—action against another state for the purpose of protecting people facing a humanitarian crisis in that other state. The report advances the principle of sovereignty-as-responsibility—the idea that the obligation to protect civilians is inherent in state sovereignty.[22]

It argues that in extreme cases, when states are unable or unwilling to protect their own population, responsibility must be borne by the broader community of states. The report has observed the following to be the basic principles of 'the responsibility to protect':

(1) State sovereignty implies responsibility and the primary responsibility for the protection of its people lies with the state itself.
(2) Where a population is suffering serious harm as a result of internal war, insurgency, repression or state failure, and the state in question is unwilling or unable to halt or avert it, the principle of non-intervention yields to the international responsibility to protect.[23]

Further, the responsibility to protect has three elements:

(1) The responsibility to prevent,
(2) The responsibility to react, and
(3) The responsibility to rebuild.[24]

While this concept was discussed in the context of humanitarian intervention, for the purposes of this work, I find it extremely useful to relate it to governance as a core responsibility of sovereignty. It is in this context that the issue of corruption in India comes as a serious obstacle to governance, undermining the sovereignty of a state. Under the basic principles of sovereignty, a population can suffer serious harm due to corruption and lack of transparency, not necessarily physically, but in a number of other ways that hinder the full and

[22] See Int'l Comm'n on State Sovereignty and Intervention (ICISS), 'The Responsibility to Protect' (2001), available at http://www.iciss.ca/pdf/Commission-Report.pdf (last visited 11 May 2011).
[23] Ibid., p. xi (last visited 11 May 2011).
[24] Ibid.

complete development of human potential. [25] Corruption violates the basic principles of sovereignty as responsibility, as the powers of the state are exercised in an irresponsible way due to misallocation of resources resulting in micro and macroeconomic problems.[26]

In the context of widespread corruption in India, the Asian Human Rights Commission in Hong Kong has observed:

Corruption and the concept of a socialist, secular and democratic republic cannot go together. Corruption undermines justice, liberty, equality and fraternity, the core values of India's constitutional framework. Freedom and sovereignty has no purpose or meaning should corruption remain the central cord with which the social fabric of a country is woven and if corruption determines the balance of power in interactions among the people and between the people and their government...[27]

## OVERVIEW OF CORRUPTION IN INDIA

Corruption[28] is a phenomenon that is widely prevalent in the administrative system of India[29] and is one of India's most nagging problems, impeding growth and development.[30] It is institutionalized

[25] Kumar, 'Report of the Consultant for the UNDP Project for Strengthening of the Commission to Investigate Allegations of Bribery or Corruption', p. 14.

[26] Ibid., p. 15.

[27] 'A Responsible Government Will Listen to the People, Says AHRC', (excerpts from the statement issued by the Asian Human Rights Commission, Hong Kong, 11 April 2011). For the full text, please visit http://leagueofindia.com/article/responsible-government-will-listen-people-says-ahrc (last visited 16 May 2011).

[28] For understanding the debates surrounding the definitional issues concerning corruption, see Michael Johnston, 'The Search for Definitions: The Vitality of Politics and the Issue of Corruption', 149 Int'l Soc. Sci. J. 321, 321–36 (1996).

[29] For a very interesting reading on the impact of corruption on the rule of law in India, see Christophe Jaffrelot, 'Indian Democracy: The Rule of Law on Trial', 1 Indian Rev. 17, 17–121 (2002).

[30] See N. Vittal, Corruption in India: The Roadblock to National Prosperity (2003) (New Delhi: Academic Foundation).

in India. Every aspect of the governance apparatus is marred by this problem, with variations only in the level of corruption. It has reached such alarming proportions that the governance[31] structure of India is affected by its social, economic, and political consequences, leading to the misallocation of resources.[32] The statistics relating to corruption in India speak for themselves. The numbers of cases of corruption registered vary from state to state and depend upon a range of factors. For example, between 2000 and 2009, the two states with the highest number of registered cases also had some of the poorest rates of conviction—Maharashtra had the highest number of cases registered (4,566) with a conviction rate of 27 per cent; Rajasthan had the second highest number of registered cases at 3,770, with a conviction rate of one-third.[33] There are huge challenges in relation to investigation, prosecution, and conviction in cases relating to corruption. The criminal justice system is marred by such a degree of uncertainty and inefficiency coupled with corruption that the judicial process of corruption cases ending in a conviction seems to be a distant dream. Justice V.R. Krishna Iyer, former judge of the Supreme Court of India, has observed:

The glory and greatness of Bharat notwithstanding, do we not, even after the braggartly semicentennial noises, behave as a lawless brood, tribal and casteist, meek and submissive when political goons and mafia gangs commit crimes in cold blood, and canny corruption and economic offences ubiquitous? The criminal culture among the higher rungs and creamy layers of society, even when nakedly exposed, does not produce the public outrage one should expect, with no burst of rage from those who must speak ... In this darkling national milieu, the penal law and its merciless enforcement

[31] For understanding the problem of corruption from a governance standpoint, see Hongying Wang and James N. Rosenau, 'Transparency International and Corruption as an Issue of Global Governance', 7 *Global Governance* 25, 25–49 (2001).

[32] See Bhikhu Parekh, 'A Political Audit of Independent India', 362 *Round Table* 701, 701–9 (2001).

[33] This data has been compiled by Venkatesh Nayak at PRS Legislative Research. See 'Corruption Cases in India: 2000-09', available at http://prsindia.org/corruptioncasesindia.php (last visited 11 May 2011).

need strong emphasis. Alas the criminals are on the triumph [sic], the police suffer from 'dependencia syndrome' and integrity is on the decadence [sic] and the judges themselves are activists in acquittals of anti-social felons. Less than ten percent of crimes finally end in conviction and societal demoralization is inevitable.[34]

Procuring accurate data with respect to corruption cases against government officials is complex, as it involves the need for obtaining prior sanction before any prosecution of officials involved in acts of corruption can take place. Thus, the actual number of registered cases cannot accurately reflect the actual instances of corruption by government officials. PRS Legislative Research has noted that as of the end of 2010, the Central Government had not provided responses to 236 requests, of which 155 (66 per cent) had been pending for more than three months; and state governments had not responded to 84 requests, of which 13 (15 per cent) had been pending for more than three months.[35]

Corruption affects India at all levels of decision-making and in the distribution of the state's largesse.[36] According to one of Transparency International's latest Global Corruption Reports, in 2009, India is ranked 85th out of 180 countries in the Corruption Perception Index 2008.[37] Although the social, economic, and political consequences of corruption are immense for India, there is little political consensus on taking serious measures to address this problem. In fact, politicians are perceived to be among the chief perpetrators of this problem.

[34] 'Report of the Committee on Criminal Justice Reforms' (2003) (referring to the article by Justice V.R. Krishna Iyer, published in *The Hindu*, 25 May 1999).

[35] PRS Legislative Research, 'Vital Statistics: Corruption Cases against Government Officials' (8 April 2011), available at http://www.prsindia.org/administrator/uploads/general/1302269425~~Vital%20Stats%20-%20Corruption%20cases%20against%20government%20officials%2008Apr11.pdf (last visited 11 May 2011).

[36] See Mahesh K. Nalla and Korni Swaroop Kumar, 'Conceptual, Legal, Ethical and Organizational Dimensions of Corruption in India: Policy Implications', in H.J. Albrecht (ed.), *Policing Corruption: International Perspectives* 51 (2005) (USA: Rowman and Littlefield).

[37] Transparency Int'l, Global Corruption Report 2009, 258 (2009).

Efforts made by state institutions, and in particular by the judiciary, are invariably met with stiff resistance.[38] An interesting aspect of the cases relating to corruption that have been pursued by the Central Vigilance Commission is their outcome. Between 2005 and 2009, penalties were imposed on 13,061 cases based on the advice of the Central Vigilance Commission, which included 846 cases in which sanction was granted for criminal prosecution. Major penalties were imposed in 4,895 cases including dismissal, reduction to lower rank, and cut in pension.[39] Minor penalties such as censure were imposed in 5,356 cases, and administrative action was taken in 1964 cases.[40]

Corruption in India not only poses a significant danger to the quality of governance; it also threatens in an accelerated manner the very foundation of India's democracy, rule of law, and statehood.[41] Corruption violates human rights as it discriminates against people;[42] it violates the principles of equality and fairness as decisions are taken in an arbitrary manner favouring bribe-givers, as opposed to people who are legally entitled.[43] There have been efforts taken at different levels in India to tackle the problem.[44] Until recently, however, most of these efforts have tended to focus on the problem of corruption from the standpoint of criminal law. Law enforcement agencies have been targeting corruption at different levels of government—central, state,

[38] Salahuddin Aminuzzaman, 'A Regional Overview Report on National Integrity Systems in South Asia' 21 (2004).

[39] PRS Legislative Research, 'Vital Statistics'.

[40] Ibid.

[41] Jaffrelot, 'Indian Democracy'.

[42] For further reading on human rights based approaches to developing corruption-free governance in India, see C. Raj Kumar, 'Corruption and Human Rights: Promoting Transparency in Governance and the Fundamental Right to Corruption-free Service in India', 17 *Colum. J. Asian L.* 31 (2003) vol. 17.

[43] Ibid.

[44] See Sunil Sondhi, 'Combating Corruption in India: The Role of Civil Society' 18–26 (Paper for XVIII World Conference of the Int'l Pol. Sc. Assoc. 2000), available at http://www.sunilsondhi.com/resources/Combating+Corruption. pdf (last visited 11 May 2011).

and local—to punish the wrongdoers.[45] However, as stated earlier, the central premise of this book is that mere reform of law enforcement cannot adequately tackle the problem of corruption in India.

## Legal Systems' Ineffectiveness and Judicial Indifference

One of the central problems in tackling corruption today is that the colonial immunities and privileges for the bureaucracy continue to exist in post-Independence India as well. The post-Independence democratic commitment by the Indian state to the rule of law requires, at the very least, that all persons are considered equal before the law. However, when it relates to the prosecution of offences committed by 'public servants', the colonial vintage of treating such offences in the privileged zone of immunity still continues. Such a power of immunity from criminal prosecution given by colonial law-makers to the public servants in the Code of 1868 still remains inscribed in post-Independence law. Section 197 of the Code of Criminal Procedure (CrPC), 1973, still remains as a bar to prosecuting government servants, with the latest case involving one of the chief ministers of Uttar Pradesh, where the Governor refused to give a sanction under the relevant section.[46]

In corruption-related offences, Section 19 of the Prevention of Corruption Act (PoCA), 1988, requires a similar sanction by the appropriate authority for the cognizance of corruption offences. The definition of the expression 'public servant' is elaborated under Section 2(c) of the PoCA. There also exists enough complexity in the determination of 'competent authority', due to which Subsection (2) provides that in case of any doubt as to the competent authority, only that authority can accord sanction which would have been competent

[45] See Nagarajan Vittal, 'Corruption and the State: India, Technology, and Transparency', *Harv. Int'l Rev.*, 6 May 2006, at 20, 20–5, available at http://hir.harvard.edu/disease/corruption-and-the-state (last visited 11 May 2011).

[46] For discussions on this, see Aditya Swarup, 'Common Men, Uncommon Law: Exploring the Links between Disciplinary Proceedings and Criminal Law' (2007), available at http://papers.ssrn.com/sol3/papers.cfm?abstract_id=1021171 (last visited 23 June 2010).

to remove the public servant from office. This means that the courts in India are burdened with the arduous task of determining that the sanction, once given, is in correct form and given by the appropriate authority, thus creating further problems in the prosecution of acts of corruption by public officials.

It is extremely difficult to appreciate the social good, no matter how one defines it, that is served by the conferment of such a power by any liberal democratic polity. It has been observed that prior sanction provisions have 'shielded murderous police officers, abusive prison officials and corrupt politicians and bureaucrats for decades.'[47] There is enough evidence to suggest that the need for prior sanction has led to the manipulation of the criminal justice process in cases relating to corruption. It is almost compelling to raise the question—why should such a sanction be required at all for prosecution of public servants in relation to charges of corruption? Further, is such a power to accord sanction entirely a discretionary power, or is it coupled with a duty wherein a corresponding right is generated to the prosecution to have such a sanction accorded? The absence of such questions from the contemporary discourse on corruption in India among lawyers, judges, scholars, and law reformers has resulted in a failure to formulate a proper perspective on the jurisprudence of corruption in India and the potential of law to combat corruption in public life.

The Supreme Court of India in *Prakash Singh Badal* v. *State of Punjab*[48] held that the protection under Section 19 is not available to former public servants. Thus, former public servants are excluded from the zone of immunity provided by Section 19. The court observed that 'the question of obtaining sanction would arise in a case where the offence has been committed by a public servant who is holding the office and by misusing or abusing the powers of the office,

---

[47] Tarunabh Khaitan, 'Parties Should Be Asked to Repeal Impunity Provisions', *The Hindu*, 23 March 2009, available at http://www.hindu.com/2009/03/23/stories/ 2009032351230900.htm (last visited 11 May 2011).

[48] Appeal (civil) 5636 of 2006. The case is available online at http://www. indiankanoon.org/doc/1634320/ (last visited 12 May 2011).

he has committed the offence.'[49] The decision undoubtedly provided a victory, albeit a very limited one, for promoting transparency and accountability to a small extent. However, an attempt was made by the legislature in 2008 to overturn the effects of the judgment of the Supreme Court when it hurriedly passed an amendment bill to the PoCA. The Bill purported to restore the protection to former public servants. Fortunately, the bill lapsed after being blocked by the opposition in the upper house of the Parliament.

The text of the amendment bill, providing justification for the retention of the sanction, reflected a certain degree of reluctance to seek greater transparency and accountability. The Statement of Object and Reasons in the Prevention of Corruption (Amendment) Bill, 2008, states:

The purpose of section 19 of the said Act is to provide a safeguard to a public servant from vexatious prosecution from any bona fide omission or commission in the discharge of his official duties. Presently, this protection is not available for a person who has ceased to be a public servant. The said section is being amended to provide the said protection to the persons who ceased to be public servants on the lines of section 197 of the Code of Criminal Procedure, 1973.[50]

The justification of safeguarding public servants from 'vexatious prosecution' needs to be delved into deeper as it forms the kernel of the existence of such sanction requirements. It is possible to make a case for the need to retain such a sanction due to existing problems in the criminal justice system, as there could be vested interests operating within and without the government, leading to vexatious prosecutions. But the benefits of imposing restrictions on provisions relating to the requirement of prior sanction far outweigh any possible objections. For instance, it is possible that many unscrupulous

[49] Ibid.

[50] Prevention of Corruption (Amendment) Bill, 2003, Statement of Objects and Reasons, ¶2(iv), available at http://www.prsindia.org/uploads/media/ 1229929759/1229929759_The_Prevention_of_Corruption__Amendment__ Bill__2008.pdf (last visited 13 May 2011).

groups or individuals may intimidate and harass conscientious public servants performing their public duties by accusing them of false allegations relating to graft and corruption, and hence this possibility should be inhibited by the law. Therefore, it can be argued that only if the competent authority decides that a good case exists should sanction be accorded to prosecute a public servant. However, a closer look at the existing legal framework will demonstrate that such apprehensions are unfounded. Section 170 of the CrPC requires that there should be existence of 'sufficient evidence or reasonable ground' in order to send a case for judicial cognizance. Further, Section 190 provides discretion to the judicial magistrate to refuse to take cognizance of any case if the same is not merited. In a nutshell, there are enough safeguards that already exist to avoid 'vexatious prosecution' against any person, including public servants.

Further, such a justification also points towards the lack of trust of the government in its own prosecuting agencies. In that case the broader issue that arises is that if the prosecuting agencies are prone to taking recourse to frivolous and vexatious prosecutions, then such agencies must be reformed. One must add to this that if there is a possibility of such 'vexatious prosecutions', then the ordinary citizenry must also be protected from the same. Providing a separate system to public servants hardly gives them any incentive to reform the corrupt and inefficient legal system. It has been rightly pointed out that there is an important democratic virtue in subjecting the public servants to 'the same vulnerabilities of a malfunctioning system as ordinary citizens are subject to.'[51] This is the fundamental premise that must be adhered to by any society that conforms to the rule of law. In a truly democratic state there must necessarily be a higher burden on the state for its actions than on private citizens, and not the other way round. Thus, the existence of an undemocratic and discriminatory requirement of sanction for prosecution undermines the democratic fabric of the Indian Republic. It also affects the efforts to promote greater transparency and accountability in governance.

---

[51] Khaitan, 'Parties Should Be Asked to Repeal Impunity Provisions'.

To sum up the discussion, it is important to recognize that there are glaring gaps within the legal framework in India that not only delay but at times also make it impossible to arrest the corrupt practices of public officials. It is noteworthy that the year that marked the Indian independence from British imperialism also saw the enactment of the law aiming to eradicate corruption. However, the codification of the new and latest corruption law by the Parliament, forty-one years after the enactment of the original legislation, still retains the anachronistic requirement of sanction for prosecuting public servants. Further, there is no time schedule for arriving at a sanction decision, which leads to significant delays in the decision-making process. Incidentally, there is no requirement for speedy disposal of corruption offences in the PoCA. However, the right to speedy trial read into Article 21 of the Constitution by the Supreme Court applies with full force to the anti-corruption statute as well. That explains the vital role that judiciary can play in combating corruption.

## Normalization of Corruption in Sociological Imagination

What the utility of the moral virtue of rectitude is in the exercise of power and to combat corruption remains a pertinent question today. What could be the value of a moral crusade against corruption in the endeavour to eliminate the same? In this context it is useful to point out the fact that substantial public opinion widely prevalent in India as well as societal imagination believes most politicians bureaucrats indulge in corrupt practices. The problem with 'folklore' is that rather than being based upon empirical or scientific evidence, it is a result of guesswork and gossip, which ends up further hampering the social fabric. This point was succinctly advanced as early as 1964 by the Government of India's Santhanam Committee Report in the following terms:

It was represented to us that corruption has increased to such an extent that people have started losing faith in the integrity of public administration. We had heard from all sides that corruption, in recent years, spread even to those levels of administration from which it was conspicuously absent in the past. We wish we could confidently and without reservation assert that the political level ministers, legislators, party officials were free from *malady*. The general impressions are unfair and exaggerated. But the very fact that such impressions are there causes damage to [the] social fabric.[52]

These unfair and exaggerated impressions perpetuate the folklore about corruption, which in turn becomes the constitutive element in the perpetuation of corrupt practices. What is troublesome is the discourse of *normalization* of corruption that exists even at the highest levels of social institutions. The apex court's observations in *A. Wati v. State of Manipur*,[53] wherein the official guilty of corrupt practices was not even given the minimum imprisonment prescribed by the legislature as he was a 'respectable person' in the court's opinion adequately illustrates this normalization in the process of adjudication as well, such that indulging in corrupt practices does not lead to loss of 'respect' in the eyes of society. This also indicates the need for an emphasis on ethics and probity in public life along with decisive legal and policy reforms against corruption in India. This is of paramount importance in order to arrest the endemic of corruption in India.

The effectiveness of a state depends on the quality of its governance. The most important thing about effective governance is that whatever the rules and regulations in society, they should be voluntarily followed. Differently put, for the effective functioning of a society, most of the things in citizens' lives should be self-regulated. Thus, the normative framework of the society should be designed in such a manner as to be widely acceptable to all citizens. This is difficult for economies in transition like India, or for those having large inequalities. Old values are in the process of being given up and new values have not yet evolved, so it becomes difficult to resolve the conflict that arises between the old and the new or the gainers and the losers. For instance, if taxes were evaded in the past, through schemes like Voluntary Disclosure of Income Scheme (VDIS) in 1997, past sins could be washed clean. Tax evasion became legitimate and honest

---

[52] Report of the Committee on the Prevention of Corruption 12–13 (1964).
[53] AIR (1996) SC 361.

taxpayers feel cheated since if they too had evaded taxes they might have benefitted.[54]

There have been many challenges for the judiciary in dealing with corruption. The Constitution of India has entrusted a vast array of powers to the courts. The 'activist' response of the higher judiciary vis-à-vis corruption has remained more or less absent or at best lukewarm. At the same time, we need to acknowledge that the collection of evidence as well as robust prosecution in corruption-related cases has been difficult. The law enforcement machinery is marred with corruption, and hence there are serious issues relating to the independence and integrity of the investigative agencies as well as the prosecutorial authorities. However, the judiciary needs to play a far more important role in ensuring that a greater degree of rigorousness is applied in cases relating to corruption. Constitutional governance imposes certain obligations on the part of all institutions of government, including the judiciary, to take all steps to ensure that the powers are exercised within the constitutional framework. The courts are given the authority to determine whether these powers have been properly exercised and to determine the appropriate punishment for improper exercise of power in accordance with law. Anti-corruption legislation should be used much more effectively by the courts. Judicial response in developing a jurisprudence of anti-corruption is critical in India, where courts continue to enjoy the utmost institutional credibility, legitimacy, and moral authority to respond to corruption. It is a fact that without a fundamental right to corruption-free services in India, the content of other fundamental rights remains meaningless. Thus, it is imperative for the judiciary to expand Article 21 of the Constitution of India to include such an important right, which it has failed to do so far.

---

[54] If breaking rules get greater gains then that would become the ruling norm, as in India. For discussions in the context of tax evasion see M.G. Allingham and A. Samdmo, 'Income Tax Evasion: A Theoretical Ananlysis', 1 *J. Pub. Econ.* 323 (1972), available at http://darp.lse.ac.uk/papersdb/Allingham-Sandmo_ (JPubE72).pdf (last visited 13 May 2011).

Further, the judicial indifference in dealing with corruption is worth pointing out, as it explains why the otherwise 'activist' judiciary fails to promote transparency in administration and other social institutions. For example, in *A. Wati v. State of Manipur*,[55] the accused, an IAS officer, was charged with misuse of office under Section 5(1)(d) of the Prevention of Corruption Act, 1947. The trial court convicted him and sentenced him to imprisonment *till the rising of the court* and a fine of Rs 10,000. The high court upheld the conviction and the sentence. The Supreme Court, instead of correcting the error committed at the lower levels of the judicial hierarchy, justified the decision on the following grounds:

a. the appellant was a *respectable person*;
b. he had a number of dependents;
c. the certainty of appellant losing his job required him to earn a living for himself and his family members;
d. the present being first offence committed by him; and
e. the spectre of the incident hanging on his head for about half a decade.

Unfortunately, none of these factors actually make out a case for awarding a sentence less than the minimum prescribed by the aforesaid act, that is, imprisonment for one year. It is a fact that corruption continues to be a low-risk, high-profit activity. One of the fundamental responses to corruption is to strengthen law enforcement mechanisms such that engaging in acts of corruption becomes a highly risky endeavour and the sanction of punishment deters potential offenders. While the courts in India and in particular, the Supreme Court of India, have expanded the scope and application of the fundamental rights to achieve justice, corruption is one important problem confronting the legal and political system where the judiciary has remained largely indifferent. This indifference may also demonstrate the inherent weaknesses of the judiciary as an institution to deal with core issues of politics and governance. Recent approaches to tackling corruption in India have moved beyond the notions of perceiving corruption as a law enforcement problem that

[55] AIR (1996) SC 361.

deserves only a criminal law response. Instead, such approaches have recognized corruption as a manifestation of a crisis in 'governance',[56] a crisis can be dealt with, partly through the development of greater transparency in governance,[57] and through greater accountability at all levels of governmental decision-making. As part of the promotion of transparency in governance, the right to freedom of information has been actively promoted in India and has resulted in the passing of a new law.[58] Such a strategy to tackle corruption is based upon the objective of empowering the Indian citizenry to seek transparency and accountability in the government.[59] Corruption in India is an institutionalized phenomenon. The empowering of citizens as a tool to fight corruption is useful when corruption is deeply entrenched in the administrative system as it is in the case of India.[60]

As observed by Philip B. Heymann,

A corrupt, democratic government is likely to look as if it is for the wealthy and the well-connected, not a government by and for the people. If the choice to much of the population appears to be one between elected figures serving the interests of narrow but wealthy constituencies or authoritarian governments serving much broader interests, democracy is very much at risk. ...

[56] For some useful insights on the development of governance discourse, see Thomas G. Weiss, 'Governance, Good Governance and Global Governance: Conceptual and Actual Challenges', 21 *Third World Q.* 795, 795–814 (2000); Philip Alston, 'International Governance in the Normative Areas', in *Background Papers: Human Development Report* 1 (1999); Yash P. Ghai, 'The Rule of Law, Legitimacy and Governance', 14 *Int'l J. Soc. L.* 179, 179–208 (1986).

[57] See Saladin Al-Jurf, 'Good Governance and Transparency: Their Impact on Development, Transnational Law and Contemporary Problems', 9 *Transnat'l L. & Contemp. Probs.* 193 (1999).

[58] For further reading, see Bunker Roy, 'Villages as a Positive Force for Good Governance: The Right to Information and India's Struggle against Grass-Roots Corruption', 37 *UN Chron.* 86 (2000).

[59] Pritha Sen, 'The Right to Information Act: Turning it into an Effective Tool to Combat Corruption in Governance', available at http://www.lawforall.ashoka.org/sites/ase/files/Arvind%20Kejriwal_0.pdf (last visited 17 June 2008).

[60] See Susan Rose-Ackerman, *Corruption and Government: Causes, Consequences, and Reform* (1999) (Cambridge: Cambridge University Press).

High-level corruption is far more dangerous to democracy than low-level corruption. ... Systemic corruption is far more dangerous to democracy than occasional and sporadic corruption.[61]

## CORRUPTION AND ITS RELATIONSHIP WITH HUMAN RIGHTS

Human rights are fundamental rights relating to life, liberty, dignity, and equality. Over the years, human rights law has undergone a dramatic expansion, constantly evolving the legal and institutional mechanisms to enforce the rule of law, ensuring transparency in governance, promoting accountability, and, most of all, fostering a sense of human dignity.[62] Both the domestic and international human rights frameworks are under challenge due to the social expectations generated by the language of human rights documents and their unfulfilled promises, and the gap between the rhetoric of human rights and the reality of their enforcement. It is in this context that there is a need to examine the relationship between corruption and human rights.[63]

Corruption has a pervasive impact on all institutions that are working towards the protection and promotion of human rights. In fact, it can be argued that the elimination of corruption in a number of sectors of governance can significantly strengthen the enforcement of human rights. For example, the police in most countries are known to have powers relating to arrest and other forms of law enforcement power.[64] We also know that the human rights framework places a lot of emphasis on the law enforcement machinery being held accountable and making certain that no human rights violations are committed in the course of enforcing the law. A case in point is the

[61] Philip B. Heymann, 'Corruption and Democracy', 20 *Fordham Int'l L.J.* 323, 325 (1996).

[62] See International Council on Human Rights Policy (ICHRP) and Transparency International (TI), 'Corruption and Human Rights: Making the Connection' (2009).

[63] Ibid.

[64] See Naved Ahmad and Oscar T. Brookins, 'On Corruption and Countervailing Actions in Three South Asian Nations', 7 *Pol'y Reform* 21 (2004).

evolution of freedom from torture and other related rights that have emerged out of the human rights movement to make the police and other law enforcement machinery accountable.[65] Now, if the police department or related departments in a country are corrupt (which is indeed the case in most developing countries), then the basic framework for human rights and law enforcement, including the principle of equality and non-discrimination, is violated.[66] Torture is a tool that is regularly adopted by the police and law enforcement officials in many developing countries—including India—for the purposes of investigation of crimes, and in extreme cases with a view to fulfilling an illegal order by certain powerful interests.[67] The relationship between torture and corruption is interesting. The ability of people to pay bribes and engage in acts of corruption can facilitate the torture of individuals who are accused of crimes. Paying of bribes by the accused may actually prevent them from being tortured by the police and other law enforcement officials. Similarly, if the accused persons are not in a position to pay bribes, then the chances of torture being committed against them is indeed higher.

Moreover, the law enforcement machinery as a pervasive system of corruption among law enforcement officials would make the potential victims of crimes and abuse of power feel threatened. Conversely, the perpetrators of crimes would feel emboldened—they know that since the police are corrupt, they can always escape the clutches of the law and the justice system by paying bribes or other forms of illegal gratification. The victims would feel threatened, as they know that since the system is corrupt, they have little or no recourse to law, and that the justice system will not be able to respond to their

[65] See Sondhi, 'Combating Corruption in India'.

[66] See International Council on Human Rights Policy (ICHRP), 'Integrating Human Rights into the Anti-corruption Agenda: Challenges, Possibilities and Opportunities' (2009).

[67] Shabnam Mallick and Rajarshi Sen, 'The Incidence of Corruption in India: Is the Neglect of Governance Endangering Human Security in South Asia?' Institute of Defence and Strategic Studies Singapore, Working Paper No. 103, January 2006, available at http://www.rsis.edu.sg/publications/WorkingPapers/WP103.pdf (last visited 12, May 2011).

victimization. In fact, the plight of poor victims is much worse as they do not have the capacity to pay bribes.[68] Thus, the cycle of a corrupt system of governance would have little incentive to protect the human rights of the people. The focus of this system would then be to enforce the law in a discriminatory manner where the people who give bribes are given favoured treatment.[69] This linkage between the existence of corruption and the lack of enforcement of human rights can be examined with regard to *all* human rights—civil, political, economic, social, and cultural. Thus, this work is expected to improve the understanding of the problem of corruption from the standpoint of human rights and democratic governance. The following sections provide a brief overview of how corruption affects specific human rights, which will be considered in detail during the course of the work. In particular, the work will examine in detail the relationship of corruption to:

(1) The Right to Access to Justice
(2) The Right to Development

## CORRUPTION AND ITS IMPLICATIONS FOR THE RULE OF LAW

Protecting the rule of law is essential for progress and development in all societies. Most countries, including countries in Asia, have laws against corruption.[70] The problem of corruption has been recognized, and the legal and institutional framework to fight against corruption has been strengthened. However, there is a threshold problem that the countries in Asia face concerning the protection of the rule of law. The laws relating to corruption are violated like many other laws, and the enforcement machinery is too weak to pursue action against the violators. The relationship of the rule of law to corruption can

---

[68] See UN Development Programme, 'The Impact of Corruption on the Human Rights Based Approach to Development' (2004).

[69] Sondhi, 'Combating Corruption in India', p.13.

[70] Kumar, 'Report of the Consultant for the UNDP Project for Strengthening of the Commission to Investigate Allegations of Bribery or Corruption', p. 15.

be understood in three stages. First, there is wide disregard for the law and its instrumentalities, and consequently, a lack of respect for law. This includes a lack of respect for laws relating to corruption. Second, corruption is used as a method to violate laws, break rules and regulations, abuse powers, and also exercise discretion in a wrongful manner. In all these aspects, the regulatory framework of the state apparatus is made dysfunctional due to institutionalized corruption across all departments of the government. Third, laws, legal institutions, and enforcement mechanisms are manipulated by way of corruption in a manner by which corruption becomes a tool for promoting lack of respect for the rule of law. In this context, many violations and violators overcome legal scrutiny or law enforcement by paying bribes and engaging in other forms of corrupt behaviour. This has created a situation where the rule of law is replaced by the rule of powerful people, be it politicians, bureaucrats, business persons, or other powerful interest groups who are able to manipulate the law enforcement machinery through corruption. Even when anti-corruption cases come before the courts, there is a strong element of non-legal and political factors in play that undermines the neutrality of the criminal justice system and all the legal and judicial processes related to fighting corruption.

The rule of law is protected only when there is a fairly predictable legal system that responds to needs and problems in a fair, non-discriminatory, and effective manner, and when there is access to justice.[71] The problem of law enforcement, including anti-corruption law, attacks the very basis of democracy and the time has come to tackle it in a systematic manner in countries in the Asia–Pacific region.[72] While there is no single solution, it is important to recognize

[71] C. Raj Kumar, 'National Human Rights Institutions and Economic, Social and Cultural Rights: Toward the Institutionalization and Developmentalization of Human Rights', 28 *Hum. Rts Q.* 775 (2003).

[72] Press Release, General Assembly, 'Secretary-General Lauds Adoption by General Assembly of United Nations Convention Against Corruption', UN Press Release SG/SM/8977 (3 November 2003), available at http://www.unis.unvienna.org/unis/pressrels/2003/sgsm8977.html (last visited 13 May 2011).

that initiatives should primarily be intended to inculcate a respect for law among the citizenry.[73]

This means that all legal, institutional, judicial, and constitutional measures to ensure the rule of law should be oriented towards imparting a respect for law on the basis of the belief that it will be enforced equally and fairly.[74] In India, corruption has huge implications for the protection of the rule of law. Commenting on the nature of corruption in India, Krishna Tummala has observed:

[B]oth constitutional and legal provisions are being continuously flouted and/or tampered with for personal, political and partisan reasons and have raised further legal and constitutional issues. Not only is the sanctity of the Constitution undermined but the rule of law is also negated.[75]

As corrupt acts are primarily violations of law, they have serious implications for the protection of the rule of law.[76] The rule of law is based upon the belief that a society should be built around people conducting their activities in a lawful and predictable manner, the government acting on the basis of law, and rules and regulations being made and their enforcement being performed in a non-discriminatory, fair, and reasonable manner. Corruption of the kind that prevails in countries in the Asia–Pacific region threatens the rule-of-law fabric prevailing in society. Laws are constantly violated, creating a vicious cycle of bribery and influence-peddling that has resulted in a cynical public attitude towards law enforcement.[77]

[73] C. Raj Kumar, 'Rule of Law and Legal Education', *The Hindu*, 4 July 2006, available at http://www.hindu.com/2006/07/04/stories/2006070403320800.htm (last visited 11 May 2011).

[74] C. Raj Kumar, 'Corruption as a Human Rights Issue in South Asia: Law, Development and Governance', Paper presented at Human Rights 2006: The Year in Review Conference, Monash University (2006), available at http://www.law.monash.edu.au/castancentre/events/2006/conf-06-kumar-paper.html (last visited 11 May 2011).

[75] Krishna K. Tummala, 'Regime Corruption in India', 14 *Asian J. Pol. Sci.* 1 (2006).

[76] For a very interesting reading on the impact of corruption on the rule of law in India, see Jaffrelot, 'Indian Democracy'.

[77] See Sondhi, 'Combating Corruption in India'.

Even when anti-corruption laws are occasionally enforced, they become political ploys on the part of politicians to settle scores against the opposition.[78] This has further accentuated the twin problems of the 'criminalization of politics' and the 'politicization of crime.'[79] For example, in Laos, the absence of a strong judicial system that is able to inspire the confidence of the people by enforcing corruption-free governance measures has affected the efforts to promote good governance.[80] Thus, there has been a major debate as to whether law and legal mechanisms are effective in fighting corruption in Laos. The UNDP study noted that since 1993, Laos has made several attempts to contain further spread of corruption through instructions and regulatory measures (in 1993, 1998, and 1999).[81] Most of these measures were drafted without going through a consultation process.[82] Thus, they did not have the expected effect, resulting in a growing lack of confidence of the citizens in the anti-corruption policies.

In the context of India, the Vohra Committee Report, commenting on this problem, has observed:

A network of mafias is virtually running a parallel Government pushing the state apparatus into irrelevance... There has been a rapid spread and growth of criminal gangs, armed senas, drug mafias, smuggling gangs, and economic lobbies in the country, which have over the years developed an intensive network of contacts with bureaucrats, government functionaries at

---

[78] C. Raj Kumar, 'Democracy and the Rule of Law in India', *The Hindu* (21 September 2007), available at http://www.hindu.com/2007/09/21/stories/2007092150071000.htm (last visited 11 May 2011).

[79] Deepak Sanyal, 'Maintenance of Public Law and Order', in Human Rights Manual for District Magistrate 22 (New Delhi: National Human Rights Commission, 2007), available at *nhrc.nic.in/Publications/MANUAL_DM.pdf* (last visited 11 May 2011).

[80] Patrick Keuleers, UN Development Programme, 'Corruption in the Laos PDR: Underlying Causes and Key Issues for Consideration' (Bangkok: UNDP, 2002), available at http://www.aman-palestine.org/English/documents/Official/Laos.pdf (last visited 13 May 2011).

[81] Ibid., p. 18.

[82] Ibid., p. 17.

local level, politicians, media persons, and strategically located individuals in non-state sector.[83]

It is useful to understand the jurisprudential foundations of the rule of law in order to be able to relate them to the issue of corruption. In its Rule of Law Project, the International Commission of Jurists[84] defines the rule of law as '[t]he principles, institutions and procedures, not always identical but broadly similar, which the experience and traditions of lawyers in different countries of the world, often themselves having varying political structures and economic backgrounds, have shown to be important to protect the individual from arbitrary government and to enable him to enjoy the dignity of man.'[85]

Summarizing the various conceptions of the rule of law given by modern theorists, Hernandez-Truyol has observed that there are three characteristics central to a cogent notion of the rule of law: (1) the absence of arbitrary power on the part of the government, (2) the administration of ordinary law by ordinary tribunals, and (3) the existence of a general rule of constitutional equality resulting from the ordinary law of the land. With these characteristics, the rule of law serves three purposes: (1) it protects against anarchy; (2) it allows persons to rely on laws and plan their lives in a way by which they can predict what consequences will flow from their actions; and (3) it protects against arbitrary and capricious actions of the government.

From the above conceptions of the rule of law, it is particularly useful to see how corruption affects the fulfilment of the rule of law and thereby undermines law and justice. The following are the specific circumstances generated due to bribery and other forms of corruption, thereby negatively impacting the rule of law.

---

[83] R. Upadhyay, 'Political Corruption in India: An Analysis South Asia Analysis Group', Working Paper No. 219 (30 March 2001), http://www.southasiaanalysis.org/papers3/paper219.htm. (last visited June 15, 2009).

[84] Int'l Comm'n of Jurists, 'The Dynamic Aspects of the Rule of Law in the Modern Age' (1965).

[85] Ibid. p. 17.

## Arbitrary Decision-making Violates the Rule of Law

Bribery is inescapable in government decision-making in many countries in the Asia–Pacific region. The state and its instrumentalities, which are entrusted with the responsibility of distributing resources in a fair and non-discriminatory manner, often conduct their activities in an arbitrary manner.[86] This arbitrariness is further promoted by irrelevant criteria infused into the decision-making process on account of corruption. This violates the rule of law and leads to the Indian citizenry losing faith in the administrative system. Thus, arbitrariness on account of corruption has become institutionalized in India.[87] This means that decisions are taken in a fair manner only as an exception. The impact this effect has on the citizenry is profound, as people do not have faith in the criminal justice, or the civil justice systems.

An example of an area of governance where arbitrariness in decision-making leads to corruption is government procurement.[88] A number of countries in Asia have taken steps to address this.[89] In recent years, South Korea has taken on a number of initiatives to reform the government procurement process. It may be noted that

[86] See Harsh Mander and Abha Joshi, 'Movement for Right to Information in India: People's Power for the Control of Corruption', available at http://www.humanrightsinitiative.org/programs/ai/rti/india/articles/The%20Movement%20for%20RTI%20in%20India.pdf (last visited 20 June 2009).

[87] Ibid.

[88] See OECD, 'Fighting Corruption and Promoting Integrity in Public Procurement'.

[89] See OECD Policy Brief, 'Keeping Government Contracts Clean' (2008), http://www.oecd.org/dataoecd/63/21/41550528.pdf, (last visited June 18, 2009); OECD, 'Principles for Integrity in Public Procurement' (2009) available at http://www.oecdbookshop.org/oecd/display.asp?lang=ENSsf1=identifiersSst1=97889264055612; OECD, 'Recommendation on Enhancing Integrity in Public Procurement' (2008), available at http://www.oecd.org/document/32/0,3343,en_2649_33735_41556768_1_1_1_1,00.html (last visited 18 June 2009); OECD, 'Enhancing Integrity in Public Procurement: A Checklist' (2008), http://www.oecd.org/document/46/0,3343,en_2649_33735_41072238_1_1_1_1,00.html, (last visited 18 June 2009).

government procurement in Korea is worth USD 83 billion a year.[90] The regulatory framework includes the Act on Contracts, to which the state is a party, the Enforcement Decree of the Act on Contracts to which the state is a party (this contains the rules for government procurement), and the Government Procurement Act (outlining the role and responsibilities of the Public Procurement Service).[91] It has been noted:

To bolster the integrity of government procurement personnel, Korea has adopted a code of conduct that takes the genuine risks into consideration. Korea also supports high standards of behavior through systematic training that addresses corruption risks. … To prevent the establishment of relationships that could lead to favouritism, Korea rotates its public procurement agents every two years.[92]

## Discrimination in Administration Undermines the Rule of Law

One of the important consequences of corruption is widespread discrimination. Power holders exercise their discretion to discriminate against people, with bribe-givers receiving favourable treatment and the people who do not give bribes being unfairly victimized.[93] Discrimination in administration due to bribery and other forms of corruption promotes a sense of frustration and helplessness among the victimized as there are no effective mechanisms for redress. Inevitably, the victims of this discrimination tend to be the poor, whose capacity to give bribes is far less than that of the middle or upper classes.[94]

---

[90] ADB/OECD Anti-corruption Initiative for Asia and the Pacific, 'Anti-corruption Policies in Asia and the Pacific: Progress in Legal and Institutional Reform in 25 Countries' 69 (2006), available at http://www.adb.org/Documents/Reports/Anticorruption-Policies/anticorruption-policies.pdf (last visited 13 May 2011).

[91] Ibid.

[92] Ibid., p. 70.

[93] Kumar, 'Corruption and Human Rights'.

[94] Ibid.

## Abuse of Discretionary Powers Violates the Rule of Law

Corruption takes place on account of abuse of the discretionary powers vested with the government in decision-making. Notwithstanding the fact that economic reforms have removed some of the traditional rules relating to the exercise of discretion by government officials, there are still a number of areas in which the government remains the sole authority for exercising discretion. While privatization is not the only answer to removing corruption, it is important to infuse enforceable mechanisms of transparency and accountability that will promote fair, non-discriminatory, and reasonable exercise of discretion.[95]

Discretionary power for government officials becomes a fertile ground for abuse and, thus, corruption becomes a norm.[96] In many countries in Asia, where a significant section of the populace is ignorant of its rights and is also impoverished, it is important to ensure that abuses of discretion do not take place. Even if corrective mechanisms in the form of institutions and anti-corruption agencies are in place and are effective (which is anyway not the case), it is important to create accountable structures for the administrators, particularly when they have discretionary power. Further, as far as possible, these discretionary powers should be limited and in due course made on the basis of objective and determinable criteria so that opportunities for bribery and other forms of corruption are reduced, if not altogether eliminated.[97]

[95] See Anne Marie Goetz and Rob Jenkins, 'Hybrid Forms of Accountability: Citizen Engagement in Institutions of Public-Sector Oversight in India', 3 *Pub. Management Rev.* 363 (2001).

[96] See Fidel V. Ramos, 'Good Governance against Corruption', 25 *Fletcher For. World aff.* (2001), available at http://fletcher.tufts.edu/forum/archives/pdfs/25-2pdfs/ramos.pdf (last visited 13 May 2011).

[97] See Yukiko Mike, 'Revealing Corruption through Japan's Information Disclosure Law', in Global Corruption Report 2003 (Transparency Int'l, 2003).

## Unpredictability in Law Enforcement Affects the Rule of Law

Institutionalized corruption in many countries in Asia has created a lot of uncertainty and unpredictability in the enforcement of anti-corruption laws. Further, due to the lack of independence of anticorruption institutions, the level of uncertainty when it comes to cases relating to investigation, prosecution, and conviction of people who are charged on grounds relating to corruption, is high.[98] This has affected the rule of law as the basis for criminal justice, as it has been replaced by other extraneous factors like the political importance of the particular anti-corruption case to the government in power, and the availability of manpower, expertise, and experience of the investigating authority in investigating the particular case. Inefficiency and ineffectiveness of the criminal justice system has infused unpredictability in corruption cases, which ought to be investigated with a sense of professionalism, integrity, and fairness. Much of this has been due to the lack of institutional autonomy and the haphazard manner in which different agencies deal with corruption cases. Jon Quah has observed that the low risk of detection and punishment of acts of corruption in Asia is one of the major causes for rampant corruption.[99] To substantiate this point, he has compared the prosecution rates in Hong Kong and the Philippines. Thus, 'a civil servant committing a corrupt offense in Hong Kong was 35 times more likely to detected and punished than his counterpart in the Philippines.'[100]

Establishing a rule-of-law society becomes essential for ensuring low levels of corruption in governance. The need for a political will in the form of the commitment of the leaders of a particular state or government becomes essential for the eradication of corruption.

---

[98] UNDP/UNODC, 'Report of the Regional Forum on Anti-corruption Institutions', (2005), available at http://europeandcis.undp.org/files/uploads/Lotta/AC%20Forum%20Report.pdf (last visited 13 May 2011).

[99] See Jon S.T. Quah, 'Curbing Asian Corruption: An Impossible Dream?' 105 *Current Hist.* 176 (2006), available at http://iis-db.stanford.edu/pubs/21128/Corruption_article_in_CH.pdf (last visited 11 May 2011).

[100] Ibid., p. 177.

In this regard, Quah notes, 'Success occurs where three conditions are met: comprehensive anticorruption legislation is enacted; an independent anticorruption agency is provided with sufficient personnel and resources; and the independent agency fairly enforces the anti-corruption laws.'[101] The success of Singapore and Hong Kong in substantially eliminating corruption is a useful case in point for many countries in Asia to examine the need for ensuring independent institutions that fight corruption.[102]

[101] Ibid.

[102] See C. Raj Kumar, 'Human Rights Approaches of Corruption Control Mechanisms: Enhancing the Hong Kong Experience of Corruption Prevention Strategies', 5 *San Diego Int'l L. J.* 323 (2004). See also Alan Lai, 'Building Public Confidence in Anti-corruption Efforts: The Approach of the Hong Kong Special Administrative Region of China', 2 *Fed. Crime & Soc'y* 135, 136 (2002). That said, it must be noted that although Hong Kong's ICAC is highly respected, the lack of democratic development in Hong Kong has been a lingering problem that, if not addressed, may have long-term implications for corruption.

# 2

# Corruption and its Impact on Human Rights

## CORRUPTION AND THE HUMAN RIGHTS FRAMEWORK

The global human rights movement has attempted to evolve new meanings and understandings to what constitutes 'human rights' and how they can be promoted and protected. The gamut of civil, political, economic, social, and cultural rights under the Universal Declaration of Human Rights (UDHR), the International Covenant on Civil and Political Rights (ICCPR), and the International Covenant on Economic, Social and Cultural Rights (ICESCR) have only reinforced the international community's desire to provide a normative framework for the protection of the rights of the people. The work of the UN Human Rights Committee (UNHRC) and the Committee on Economic, Social and Cultural Rights (CESCR) under both these covenants has further provided institutional frameworks for the implementation of rights.[1]

That corruption is a crime which attracts criminal law sanctions under domestic statutes is undisputed.[2] Efforts to fight corruption should therefore necessarily include the strengthening of criminal law mechanisms, including the law enforcement machinery and, in

[1] C. Raj Kumar, 'Corruption, Development and Good Governance: Challenges for Promoting Access to Justice in Asia', 16 *Mich. St. J. Int'l* L 475, 518 (2008).
[2] Ibid.

general, the effectiveness of the criminal justice system.[3] But experiences in developing countries in South Asia have demonstrated that corruption, besides being a crime that needs to be punished through principles of criminal law, has other consequences for governance as well. One of the most serious consequences of corruption for governance is its impact on the promotion and protection of human rights.[4]

In countries where corruption is all-pervasive, a uniform pattern of failure of all institutions of governance leads to the lack of law enforcement mechanisms on the one hand, and the exacerbation of development problems on the other. Cambodia is a country in South East Asia that has experienced this in a telling manner.[5] In a report prepared for USAID/Cambodia, it has been noted:

Ordinary Cambodians distrust the legal system, including the formal courts. The police and other enforcement bodies are also seen as corrupt. Impunity is the norm. No one with the patronage of the state is punished, whether for massive pillaging or petty theft. In fact, those most at risk are individuals and organizations that dare to resist corruption. Most Cambodians regard resistance as a futile act. Corruption is structured more or less as a pyramid; with petty exactions meeting the survival needs of policemen, teachers and health workers, but also shared with officials higher in the system. Patronage and mutual obligations are the centre of an all-embracing system. Appointment to public office hinges on political connections or payment of surprisingly large sums, and these payments are recouped through a widely accepted 'right' to collect bribes.[6]

In such a scenario, it takes enormous effort to instill faith among the people that anti-corruption measures that might be initiated by the government are made with the genuine intention of fighting

---

[3] Ibid.

[4] Ibid.

[5] Ibid.

[6] Michael M. Calavan, Sergio Diaz Briquets, and Jerald O'Brien, 'Cambodian Corruption Assessment' 3 (2004), http://www.usaid.gov/kh/democracy_and_governance/documents/Cambodian_Corruption_Assessment.pdf (last visited 20 June 2009).

corruption.[7] The establishment of new institutions or the passing of anti-corruption laws *per se* will not make any tangible difference in fighting corruption. The key factor would require efforts to promote legal and judicial reform, with protecting the rule of law as the central paradigm for fighting corruption.[8]

The first step in developing a theoretical framework for recognizing corruption as a human rights issue is to examine the different types of human rights that are affected through corruption. The right to equality is one of the fundamental human rights that is protected both within domestic and international legal frameworks. Article 26 of the ICCPR states, 'All persons are equal before the law and are entitled without any discrimination to the equal protection of the law.'[9] The constitutions of India,[10] Sri Lanka,[11] Bangladesh,[12] and Pakistan[13] have similar provisions that protect the right to equality of their people. Corruption violates the right to equality as the people who pay bribes are given favoured treatment. Furthermore, people who are unable or unwilling to give bribes are discriminated against. Thus, there is a violation of the right to equality, both substantive and procedural. This basic framework can be further developed by understanding the impact of corruption on the implementation of specific rights that are guaranteed under both domestic and international human rights law. In fact, the problem of corruption is so pervasive in South Asia that it affects both civil and political rights as well as economic, social, and cultural rights in a significant manner. Be it the right to 'freedom

[7] Kumar, 'Corruption, Development and Good Governance', p. 518.

[8] Ibid., p. 519.

[9] International Covenant on Civil and Political Rights, Art. 26, 16 December 1966, 999 UNTS 171. (ICCPR).

[10] India Const., Art. 14 ('The State shall not deny to any person equality before the law or the equal protection of the laws within the territory of India.').

[11] Sri Lanka Const., Art. 12(1) ('All persons are equal before the law and are entitled to the equal protection of the law.').

[12] Bangladesh Const., Art. 27 ('All citizens are equal before law and are entitled to equal protection of law.').

[13] Pakistan Const., Art. 25(1) ('All citizens are equal before law and are entitled to equal protection of law.').

from torture', 'right to a fair trial', 'right to food', or 'right to health', corruption in government departments violates the human rights of people who are entitled to these services.[14]

While it is important to recognize that the mere recognition of corruption as a human rights violation in South Asia will not necessarily immediately reduce the incidents of corruption,[15] using the human rights approach has certain benefits that would lead to the eventual elimination of corruption. Human rights approaches help in exposing violations, and empower victims and others to resist future human rights violations and to seek redress for those that have taken place in the past. This notion of empowerment is deeply embedded in the human rights approach to combating corruption. The form of corruption that is prevalent in countries in South Asia has affected every governance mechanism and institution in place, making a mockery of democracy and the rule of law. In this social and political context, there is an urgent need to examine the problem of corruption from perspectives not strictly limited to the criminal law approach, which pursues corruption as just another serious crime.[16] Corrupt acts by government officials and departments are more than just serious crimes against which the law enforcement machinery is compelled to take action.[17]

There are numerous advantages of recognizing corruption as a human rights violation in countries in South Asia. First, the moment the crime of corruption is recognized as a human rights violation, it creates a type of social, political, and moral response that is not generated by crime, notwithstanding the seriousness of the act.[18] Second, the human rights of people are typically protected under the constitution or other domestic legislations, and would invite serious constitutional scrutiny by courts and other institutions.[19] Third, the

---

[14] Kumar, 'Corruption, Development and Good Governance', p. 519.

[15] Ibid., p. 520.

[16] Ibid.

[17] Ibid.

[18] Ibid.

[19] Ibid.

recognition of corruption as a human rights violation, besides invit-ing international attention, would also possibly bring into focus the violations of provisions of the international human rights treaties that countries in South Asia have ratified.[20] Finally, the response to human rights violations is based upon efforts to empower individu-als and institutions so that there is proper redress for the victims of violations, and that there is resistance to any such future occurrence. It will be useful to specifically outline some of the consequences of the recognition of corruption as a human rights violation in South Asian countries.[21]

## Legal Effects of Recognizing Corruption as a Violation of Human Rights

The legal system of a country is based upon respect for the legal and constitutional rights of citizens. If corruption is recognized as a hu-man rights violation, then the response of the state when dealing with corruption ought to be the same as when it deals with other human rights violations.[22] Certainly, human rights violations that occur in countries in South Asia do receive greater attention, even though the redress for such violations or, for that matter, the response of the state to such violations may not be as effective as it ought to be.[23] Neverthe-less, corruption couched in the language of human rights becomes more serious than an act of crime. Corruption attacks the very foun-dations of democratic governance, which constitutional democracies in South Asia hope to protect. Thus, constitutionalism and the rule of law cannot be promoted in South Asia without eradicating corrup-tion.[24] The human rights approach is one tool that can be effectively used in highlighting the problem of corruption and, in particular,

[20] Ibid.
[21] Ibid.
[22] Ibid.
[23] Ibid.
[24] Ibid., p. 521.

recognizing the violations of civil, political, economic, social, and cultural rights of the people of South Asia due to corruption.[25]

In some countries in South Asia, the judiciary is regarded with great reverence. The constitutional provisions that protect the workings of these judiciaries have provided a framework for ensuring their independence and autonomy. The judiciary is entrusted with the task of interpreting the constitution and the laws of the state and to adjudicate all disputes.[26] The judiciaries of India, Sri Lanka, Bangladesh, and Pakistan have made good progress in interpreting their constitutions and developing liberal human rights jurisprudence with a view to protect and promote the rights of the people. Although there are challenges to the independence of judiciary in all these countries, and their effectiveness, credibility, and legitimacy may vary within each country, they have made commendable efforts to uphold human rights and the rule of law.[27] It is in this context that the recognition of corruption as a human rights violation can empower the judiciary to appropriately interpret a state's constitution and other laws to ensure corruption-free governance.[28]

To understand the growth and development of the international human rights framework in its present form, it is necessary to appreciate the human rights movement as a continuous negotiation among states on universally accepted principles and norms. However, the so-called 'universal' conception of human rights has come under attack by arguments relating to the cultural relativism of human rights, most recently embodied in the 'Asian Values' debate.[29] While the international human rights framework has moved from its modest origins in creating norms to enforcing human rights obligations and institutionalizing human rights, it has also simultaneously expanded the notion of what constitutes human rights. This expansion has taken

[25] Ibid.

[26] Ibid.

[27] Ibid.

[28] Ibid. For a discussion on how the judiciary can help promote corruption-free governance in the Indian context, see Chapter 4.

[29] Ibid.

place prominently through the work of national courts in certain jurisdictions that have assumed the role of human rights arbiters and have expanded constitutional rights to include a variety of economic and social rights in order to promote good governance.[30]

The human rights frameworks in the ICCPR and the ICESCR are very useful for developing corruption prevention strategies, particularly with regard to the protection of the rule of law and the right to equality and non-discrimination. These corruption prevention strategies would rest on the premise that the human rights framework should provide a right to corruption-free service based on the principle of freedom from corruption.[31]

Article 1 of the ICCPR emphatically observes, 'All people have the right of self-determination' and to 'freely pursue their economic, social and cultural development.'[32] Corruption, as argued earlier, clearly interferes in people's efforts to fulfil their economic self-determination. It also stifles the pursuit of economic, social, and cultural development. The fact that corruption interferes in the free progress of people to realize their rights as mentioned in the ICCPR is a good starting point for the integration of the human rights framework in the development of corruption prevention and elimination strategies. Article 26 of the ICCPR guarantees equality before the law and equal protection of laws, thus prohibiting any form of discrimination. The nature of official corruption is such that it clearly discriminates against people and favours bribe-givers over those who do not give bribes. These bribe-givers receive undue favoured status and are able to sue against the resources of the state, which they may not otherwise be entitled to. Corruption also does not allow for the development of equality before the law as it is fundamentally at odds with the principle of equal treatment.[33]

Corruption clearly divides society on the basis of unfair and illegal considerations, culminating in gross disrespect for law and moral

---

[30] Ibid., p. 522.

[31] Ibid.

[32] ICCPR, Art. 1(1).

[33] Kumar, 'Corruption, Development and Good Governance', p. 522.

degradation. In anti-corruption initiatives that have examined the problem from a public policy standpoint, there is very little emphasis on the discriminatory aspects of corruption. But in practical terms, it is a natural outcome of most corrupt transactions. Individual corruption in day-to-day governmental functioning has reached such alarming proportions in developing countries like India that corruption is institutionalized within the governance system.[34]

The ICESCR, like the ICCPR, refers to the principle of equality and non-discrimination in the exercise of economic, social, and cultural rights. The Committee on Economic, Social and Cultural Rights, in one of its General Comments,[35] has referred to the legal obligation undertaken by state parties to the ICESCR. The non-discrimination aspect in Article 2 of the ICESCR requires that States 'undertake to guarantee' that the relevant rights 'will be exercised without discrimination.'[36] It may be argued that states ought to take steps to ensure that there is no discrimination practiced against citizens in their efforts to exercise their rights to work, food, health, education, and the other rights mentioned in the ICESCR. Corruption in exercise of the above-mentioned rights emerges as a clear violation of this obligation. It is apparent that numerous development-oriented activities of states have been affected by corruption.[37]

Economic and social rights are eroded due to the corrupt transfer of public wealth to a few power holders. This creates a situation of further deprivation and impoverishment.[38] Article 2(1) of the ICESCR obligates states parties 'to take steps' for the realization of the rights.[39]

[34] Ibid., p. 523.

[35] Comm. on Econ., Social and Cultural Rights, General Comment 3: The Nature of State Parties Obligations (Art. 2, Para. 1 of the Covenant), UN Doc. E/1991/23 (14 December 1990) ('ICESCR General Comment 3').

[36] International Covenant on Economic, Social and Cultural Rights (ICESCR), Art. 2(2), 16 December 1966, 993 UNTS 3.

[37] Kumar, 'Corruption, Development and Good Governance', p. 523.

[38] I talk of deprivation and the resultant impoverishment, in the sense used by Amartya Sen. See Amartya Sen, *Development as Freedom* (1999) (Oxford: Oxford University Press).

[39] ICESCR, Art. 2(1).

It is but obvious that the steps taken should include also the removal of impediments in the realization of economic and social rights. As corruption is one of the biggest of these obstacles, states have a core obligation to take efforts against it. The ICESCR has also pointed out that 'all appropriate means, including particularly the adoption of legislative measures,' must be taken to fulfil the legal obligations of member states under this covenant.[40] The argument for freedom from corruption rests on the basic premise that other economic and social freedoms are significantly threatened by corruption. In particular, it is obvious that the democratic rights of citizens under Article 25 of the ICCPR are deeply impinged upon by corruption in the electoral process. This may extend to other democratic rights if corruption is deeply imbedded in the political processes of the state.[41]

The need for promoting transparency and accountability has been noted as an important requirement for corruption-free governance. The Indian experience has demonstrated that the recognition of the right to information in India is an important step in ensuring this.[42] Numerous factors played a part in the passage of the Right to Information Act, 2005, that recognized this right, such as the existing sound international human rights framework that provided for the right to information. India is ā party to the ICCPR, and Article 19 of the ICCPR protects the 'freedom to seek, receive and impart information.'[43] It is notable that during the first session of the UN General Assembly in 1946, it adopted Resolution 59(1), which stated that 'freedom of information is a fundamental human right and ... the touchstone of all the freedoms to which the UN is consecrated.'[44] The consequences of corruption on development are immense as the national and international funds that are allocated for development may be siphoned off due to corruption. Developing countries

---

[40] Ibid.

[41] Kumar, 'Corruption, Development and Good Governance', p. 524.

[42] Ibid.

[43] ICCPR, Art. 19(2).

[44] Article 19: Global Campaign for Free Expression, 'What You Don't Know Can Hurt You', *India Together* (January 2001), http://www.indiatogether.org/stories/art19.htm (last visited 13 March 2008).

like India are provided with loans by other nations and multilateral lending institutions for various development-related activities. This has resulted in social expectations generated within the countries for development-related work. Yet this pursuit of development work is constantly disrupted as the funds are misused due to corruption, thereby delaying, and on numerous occasions deterring, the development process.[45]

## CORRUPTION AND ITS RELATIONSHIP WITH SPECIFIC HUMAN RIGHTS

### Right to Access to Justice

Corruption, as stated earlier, creates a major obstacle to access to justice. To understand this relationship, it is necessary to know the determinants of access to justice:

#### Availability of the Legal and Institutional Framework

It is necessary to establish the necessary legal and institutional frameworks for ensuring access to justice. In most countries, the judiciary is one of the most important institutions directly involved in ensuring access to justice.[46] There are also quasi-judicial institutions that may perform certain judicial functions. If these institutions are themselves corrupt or not in a position to adequately respond to corruption, then the fundamental fabric of access to justice

---

[45] For an understanding of the impact of corruption on development, see Cheryl W. Gray and Daniel Kaufmann, 'Corruption and Development', 35 *Fin. & Dev.* 7 (1998), available at http://www.imf.org/external/pubs/ft/fandd/1998/03/pdf/gray.pdf (last visited 11 May 2011).

[46] See Ramaswamy Sudarshan, 'Rule of Law and Access to Justice: Perspectives from UNDP Experience', paper presented to the European Commission Expert Seminal on Rule of Law and the Administration of Justice as part of Good Governance, Brussels (2003), available at http://www.undp.org/oslocentre/docsjuly03/Rule%20of%20Law%20and%20Access%20to%20Justice_Perspectives%20from%20UNDP%20experience1.doc (last visited 11 May 2011).

is undermined.[47] The existence of institutions that are free from corruption is necessary for ensuring access to justice. Governments ought to take steps to create such legal and institutional mechanisms.[48] In fact, the efficiency of the government and its functioning will, to a large extent, depend upon its ability to translate sound policies into well-executed ones.[49] It is also important that the legal and institutional mechanisms that are established work effectively and not result in the duplication of pre-existing enforcement machinery against corruption. The biggest challenge that needs to be addressed is the ability to develop internal mechanisms of oversight and superintendence within the institutions of government so that transparency and accountability are maintained.[50]

## Awareness of Institutions and Processes

The availability of institutions that work to ensure access to justice needs to be supplemented by *awareness* of these institutions and processes.[51] In many developing countries, due to illiteracy, lack of awareness, and poverty, few people know of the existence of

[47] See Petter Langseth and Oliver Stolpe, 'Strengthening Judicial Integrity against Corruption' (UN Global Programme Against Corruption, Centre for International Crime Prevention, 2001), available at http://www.unodc.org/pdf/crime/gpacpublications/cicp10.pdf (last visited 13 May 2011).

[48] C. Raj Kumar, 'Corruption in Japan: Institutionalizing the Right to Information, Transparency and the Right to Corruption-free Governance', 10 *New Eng. J. Int'l & Comp. L.* 29 (2004).

[49] Sunil Sondhi, 'Combating Corruption in India: The Role of Civil Society', Paper for XVIII World Conference of the Int'l Pol. Sc. Assoc. (2000), http://www.sunilsondhi.com/resources/Combating+Corruption.pdf (last visited 11 May 2011).

[50] Deepa Mehta, 'Tackling Corruption: An Indian Perspective', 126th International Senior Seminar Visiting Experts' Papers, Resource Material Series No. 66, www.unafei.or.jp/english/pdf/PDF_rms/no66/C_p85-p90.pdf (last visited 16 June 2009).

[51] ADB/OECD Anti-corruption Initiative for Asia and the Pacific, 'Anti-corruption Policies in Asia and the Pacific: Progress in Legal and Institutional Reform in 25 Countries' 79–81 (2006), available at http://www.adb.org/

institutions and processes designed to ensure access to justice. If corruption prevails in these institutions, there is very little incentive for the officials to reach out to the people who may be in need of access to justice. Furthermore, the people themselves may not have the confidence and the trust that is necessary to approach the institutions, especially if the institutions have acquired notoriety for corruption. Instilling among the people of a country faith and trust in the institutions and processes that work to ensure access to justice is as important as the task of establishing these institutions.[52] Corruption undermines confidence in the integrity and impartiality of the process of gaining access to justice.[53] In countries where corruption is deep and pervasive and people have little faith in the criminal justice system, or, for that matter, in the anti-corruption institutions, a lot of effort needs to be put into empowering the citizenry to fight against corruption. Notwithstanding the best of intentions to fight corruption, it will not be effective if the people of a society do not come forward with the necessary information and are not sufficiently discouraged to pay bribes to get their work done. This is indeed a complex problem and can be addressed only by a multi-pronged response. Civil society empowerment and education of the people are central to this approach to fighting corruption. There is an urgent need for whistleblower laws that can ensure the confidentiality of the information relating to corruption that is shared by the people.[54] The Law Commission of India in 2001, proposed such a Bill for the protection of whistleblowers.[55] The Cabinet cleared the

---

Documents/Reports/Anticorruption-Policies/anticorruption-policies.pdf (last visited 13 May 2011).

[52] See Moshe Maor, 'Feeling the Heat? Anti-corruption Mechanisms in Comparative Perspective', 12 *Governance* 1 (2004).

[53] Kumar, 'Corruption in Japan'.

[54] See, in this context, the Law Commission of India, 179th Report on Public Interest Disclosure and Protection of Informers 86–113 (2001), available at http://lawcommissionofindia.nic.in/reports/179rptp1.pdf (Recommendations relating to the proposed bill for the protection of whistleblowers) (last visited 19 May 2011).

[55] Ibid.

Public Interest Disclosure and the Protection of Persons Making the Disclosure Bill, 2010,[56] in August 2010,[57] and it is now pending before the Parliament.[58] Despite this movement, it needs to be understood that in a system that is hugely corrupt, the information relating to corruption that is received from people as well as its confidentiality tend to get compromised. This leads to threats to the security of those who have blown the whistle, and discourages other enlightened citizens through giving information relating to corruption.

## Access to Institutions and Processes

Awareness of the existence of institutions and processes that ensure access to justice may not be sufficient if the people do not have the ability, financial or otherwise, to seek access to these institutions. It is in this context that the state and its instrumentalities have an important role to play in empowering victims and providing them with mechanisms to seek access to justice through the institutions and processes that have been established for this purpose. However, corruption inhibits this accessibility as well.[59] Special interests and extraneous factors may come into play in a corrupt legal system, rendering the people most deserving of legal aid and other programmes unable to receive their benefits.[60] Even if the institutions and processes for ensuring access

[56] The text of the bill can be found at http://www.prsindia.org/uploads/media/ Public%20Disclosure/Whistleblower%20Bill%202010.pdf.

[57] 'Cabinet Clears Whistleblower Protection Bill', *The Economic Times* (10 August 2010), available at http://articles.economictimes.indiatimes.com/ 2010-08-10/news/27607778_1_hand-down-harsh-penalty-vitthal-gite-whistleblowers (last visited 19 May 2011).

[58] PRS Legislative Research, 'Pending Bills', http://www.prsindia.org/index. php?name=Sections&id=6&parent_category=1&category (last visited 13 May 2011).

[59] See International Council on Human Rights Policy (ICHRP) & Transparency Int'l, 'Integrating Human Rights into the Anti-corruption Agenda: Challenges, Possibilities and Opportunities' (2009), available at http://www. ichrp.org/files/reports/58/131b_report.pdf (last visited 19 May 2011).

[60] 'Corrupt Legal System Blocks Justice for All', *Jakarta Post* (11 July 1999), available at http://www.thejakartapost.com/news/1999/11/07/corrupt-legal-system-blocks-justice-all.html?1.

to justice are established and functioning effectively, corruption undermines the *integrity* of the process. If corruption prevails in the decision-making process, those who will receive legal aid or legal support from the state will be adversely affected, as will the poor, who are not able to pay bribes. Thus, the effectiveness of the institutions and processes for ensuring access to justice should not only be seen from the standpoint of those dispensing justice, but also from the standpoint of the actual *beneficiaries* of these processes.

## Corruption and Its Relationship to Development

### The Right to Development

Human rights and human development are inextricably connected.[61] It may be argued that an integral approach to human rights and human development is essential for all progress. Fighting corruption is indeed central to achieving both human rights and human development.[62] But this integration needs to be supplemented with policy changes at all levels of decision-making in the government in order for it to be effective. The integration of human rights and human development policies rests upon an examination of the similarities and differences between these two conceptions.[63] They are ideologically close enough to derive motivation and concern for each other, thus promoting

[61] 'Human Rights and Development', available at http://nzaidtools.nzaid.govt. nz/mainstreaming-human-rights/human-rights-development (last visited 19 June 2009).

[62] Manabi Majumdar, 'Human Development and Human Rights Through the "Prism of Gender"', *Int'l Dev. Ethics Assoc. Newsletter* 4 (2000).

[63] See UNDP, Chapter 1, 'Human Rights and Human Development', Human Development Report 2000, 19 (2000), available at http://hdr.undp.org/en/media/ hdr_2000_en.pdf (last visited 19 May 2011).
Amartya Sen has also posed two basic diagnostic inquiries, which are:

(1) How compatible are the normative concerns in the analyses of human development and human rights? Are they harmonious enough—to be able to complement rather than undermine each other?

(2) Are the two approaches sufficiently distinct so that each can add something substantial to the other? Are they diverse enough—to enrich each other?

compatibility and mutual understanding.[64] From an enforcement strategy standpoint, they are different enough to be able to supplement each other.[65] Thus, an integrated approach of these two conceptions can result in significant improvements to human society, thereby facilitating in numerous ways the advancement of dignity, well-being, and freedom of individuals in general.[66] The UNDP's *Human Development Report 2000* has correctly observed that any useful conception of human development cannot ignore the importance of political liberties and democratic freedoms.[67]

If development is a human right, all matters that affect the fulfilment of this right constitute inhibiting factors that affect the achievement of development.[68] Corruption is a strong inhibiting factor for development. Countries take steps to achieve human development by making provisions in the form of financial resources to fulfil the rights to education, food, and health; by taking concrete steps to establish schools and other educational institutions; by creating job opportunities and other avenues that will ensure the accessibility of food to the people; and by establishing hospitals and other health care facilities that will provide access to health care to the people. All these steps are intended to contribute to better standards of living and realizing a higher degree of development. But

---

The answers to both of these foundational questions are definitely in the affirmative.

For a better understanding of the relationship between human rights and human development, see Amartya Sen, *Development as Freedom* (1999).

[64] Human Development Report 2000, p. 19.

[65] Ibid.

[66] These principles are very well explained in Patrick Van Weerelt, 'A Human Rights-Based Approach to Development Programming in UNDP: Adding the Missing Link' (2001), available at http://www.undp.org/governance/docs/HR_Pub_Missinglink.pdf (last visited 19 May 2011).

[67] See Human Development Report 2000, pp. 19–26.

[68] C. Raj Kumar, 'The Human Right to Corruption-free Service: Some Constitutional and International Perspectives', *Frontline*, 14 September 2002, available at http://www.hinduonnet.com/fline/fl1919/19190780.htm (last visited 19 May 2011).

corruption undermines these efforts.[69] It is important to recognize that all acts of human rights violations are not necessarily due to corruption, and that corruption is not the consequence of all human rights violations. To understand what acts of corruption constitute human rights violations, there is a need to understand the impact of corruption on development.

It is not possible to understand the relationship between corruption and development without recognizing that access to justice is the central link between policies that promote governance on the one hand and policies that ensure development on the other. It is in this context that we need to develop our understanding of the meaning of corruption and its consequences for access to justice and development.

## The Effects of Impediments to Development

Corruption impedes development significantly in South Asia.[70] South Asian countries are some of the poorest countries in the world, as demonstrated by the UN Development Programme (UNDP) in its Human Development Index (HDI) published in the *Human Development Report 2006*.[71] The latest HDI rankings of countries in South Asia (as of 2010) are: India, 119; Sri Lanka, 91; Bangladesh, 129; and Pakistan, 125, out of 169 countries that have been ranked.[72] The development objectives of countries are inextricably linked to resources, and the efficient and effective use thereof. If the resources that are supposed to be used for fulfilling development objectives are transferred and wasted due to corruption, it will inevitably impede development and delay progress. Empirical studies have also demonstrated the links between corruption and development. It

[69] Sondhi, 'Combating Corruption in India'.

[70] See Kumar, 'Corruption in Japan'.

[71] UN Development Programme, 'Human Development Report 2006: Beyond Scarcity: Power, Poverty and the Global Water Crisis', 284–5 (2006), available at http://hdr.undp.org/en/media/hdr06-complete.pdf (last visited 13 May 2011).

[72] The 2010 HDI rankings may be found at http://hdr.undp.org/en/statistics/ (last visited 13 May 2011).

has been observed, 'The research generally shows that countries can derive a very large "development dividend" from better governance. We estimate that a country that improves its governance from a relatively low level to an average level could almost triple the income per capita of its population in the long term, and similarly reduce infant mortality and illiteracy.'[73]

The eight millennium development goals (MDGs), which include a range of objectives, from halving extreme poverty to halting the spread of HIV/AIDS,[74] to providing universal primary education to all by the target date of 2015, have a direct relationship with the need to ensure minimally corrupt governance. Corruption undermines the state's capacity to achieve the MDGs. The 2006 Corruption Perception Index (CPI)[75] prepared by Transparency International reinforces the strong linkages between prevalence of corruption and the problem of poverty in poor countries. According to Transparency International Chair, Huguette Labelle observes, 'Despite a decade of progress in establishing anti-corruption laws and regulations, today's results indicate that much remains to be done before we see meaningful improvements in the lives of the world's poorest citizens.'[76] It was noted, 'A strong correlation between corruption and poverty is evident in the results of the CPI 2006. Almost three-quarters of the countries in the CPI score below five (including all low-income countries and all but two African states) indicating that most countries in the world face serious perceived levels of domestic corruption.'[77]

[73] Daniel Kaufmann, 'Back to Basics: 10 Myths about Governance and Corruption', 42 *Fin. & Dev.* 41, 41 (2005).

[74] United Nations Millennium Development Goals, available at http://www.un.org/millenniumgoals/bkgd.shtml (last visited 19 May 2011).

[75] As per the current 2010 CPI, India is ranked at 87, with a score of 3.3/10. See Corruption Perceptions Index 2010 Results, http://www.transparency.org/policy_research/surveys_indices/cpi/2010/results (last visited 13 May 2011).

[76] Transparency Int'l, '2006 Corruption Perceptions Index Reinforces Link between Poverty and Corruption', Press Release en_2006-11-06 CPI 2006 (6 November 2006), http://www.transparency.org/news_room/in_focus/2006/cpi_2006 (last visited 20 June 2009).

[77] Ibid.

Corruption has substantial negative consequences for development.[78] The development of countries in South Asia to a large measure depends upon the economic policies and social consequences of these policies. Corruption affects both these aspects in a number of ways.[79] It affects economic growth; discourages foreign investment; diverts resources meant for infrastructure development; health and other public services such as education and anti-poverty programmes. [80] In essence, corruption poses serious challenges for governance and the countries in South Asia cannot achieve the goals of development without taking steps to curb corrupt acts.

The development process ought to be based upon principles of transparency in governance and accountability of the administration.[81] Due to corruption, however, there is inefficiency and inequity in resource allocation. The countries in South Asia are not able to sufficiently fulfil their MDGs, and in that process, are struggling to achieve social and economic development. In this context, there is a need to formulate integrated governance policies based on human rights and human development. This notion of 'developmentalizing rights' is extremely relevant for countries in South Asia and should be understood by evaluating the effectiveness of rights-based approaches to development and how the 'right to development' can be implemented.[82]

## SOVEREIGNTY IN THE CONTEXT OF GLOBALIZATION, HUMAN RIGHTS, AND DEVELOPMENT

Corruption exists in most countries of the developing world, including India. The human rights–based approaches to understanding the problem of corruption recognize that corruption affects national

[78] Kumar, 'Corruption in Japan'.

[79] Ibid.

[80] Ibid.

[81] Ibid.

[82] See C. Raj Kumar, 'Corruption, Human Rights, and Development: Sovereignty and State Capacity to Promote Good Governance', 99 *Am. Soc'y Int'l L. Proc.* 416 (2005).

sovereignty in ways that threaten human security, undermine human development, and impinge on the fundamental rights and freedoms of people.[83] Sovereignty has always been, and will continue to be, one of the most challenging aspects of international law and international relations. Understanding the contemporary notions of sovereignty is useful when examining its impact on globalization, human rights, and development.[84]

Globalization has altered the relations between people and the state, and the state and the international community, in ways that are still not fully understood. Globalization has resulted in states coming to grips with the reality of opening up their countries to trade, investment, and other forms of social, economic, cultural, and political influences. This has resulted in the emergence of powerful global actors in the form of multinational corporations and business enterprises that are at times economically more powerful than the nation-states themselves.[85] Thus the role of the state in assuming a leadership role in economic activities has diminished. If sovereignty is about states exercising power on the institutions of governance, then globalization has altered the parameters of this power. The intrusion of new domestic and international actors into the economic activities of nation states has added a new dimension to governance. Multilateral institutions like the World Bank, the International Monetary Fund, and the World Trade Organization have had their own impacts on sovereignty.[86]

Human rights have always posed a formidable challenge to sovereignty. Contemporary international law recognizes that human rights violations committed by one state cannot be justified, even though the state commits such violations within its own borders.[87] The development of international law and international human rights law has only strengthened the understanding that states cannot hide under

[83] Kumar, 'Corruption, Development and Good Governance', p. 529.
[84] Ibid.
[85] Ibid.
[86] Ibid.
[87] Ibid.

the veil of sovereignty when they commit human rights violations.[88] The jurisprudence developed by the International Criminal Tribunal for the Former Yugoslavia, the International Criminal Tribunal for Rwanda, and the formation of the International Criminal Court have only strengthened this proposition. In fact, the human rights framework has continually and successfully challenged the principle of sovereignty, such as when humanitarian intervention has been justified in a number of cases, even though there is no consensus among the international community regarding the circumstances under which such interventions may be permissible. Even states that commit violations of human rights never argue that it is their sovereign right to commit such violations against their people; rather, they rely on the denial of such violations having taken place at all.[89]

The human rights framework has challenged the traditional understanding of sovereignty in at least three different ways.[90] First, the institutionalization of human rights in international institutions like the European Court of Human Rights and the UN Human Rights Committee (UNHRC) has resulted in an obligation on the part of states to respect the decision of these institutions, which are outside the sovereign jurisdiction of a country. However, it must be noted that this intervention in sovereignty is somewhat limited—a state has to become a party to the optional protocol to the ICCPR for the decisions of the UNHRC to be binding. Second, the increasing role of nongovernmental organizations (NGOs) worldwide has also posed challenges to sovereignty, but more of a political and moral than a legal kind. The development of transnational civil society has ensured the public 'naming and shaming' of states that violate human rights, as NGOs have become active in mobilizing domestic and international public opinion when human rights violations occur. This has resulted in states increasingly becoming more sensitive in responding to violations. Finally, the development of domestic constitutional

---

[88] Ibid.
[89] Ibid., p. 530.
[90] Ibid.

systems and the rule of law have resulted in the development of comparative human rights traditions in which there is a certain degree of interaction between domestic courts and human rights institutions. This has held in the continuing development of comparative law and the facilitation of different types of regional interaction amongst national human rights institutions. Sovereignty is further eroded when the internal governance structures in a society are gradually influenced by laws, policies, and practices of other states, as officials attempt to justify a certain conduct in such comparative terms. This is particularly relevant in the context of domestic anti-corruption measures implemented due to international anti-corruption treaty mechanisms.

The multilateral institutions involved in development work, such as the World Bank, have also had a profound impact on the sovereignty of nations. The World Bank has exerted influence over the economic policies of states in return for the sanction of loans for development work. Such policies (which are heavily influenced by the World Bank) have been met with serious criticism in developing countries, on the ground that such practices not only undermine sovereignty in a political sense, but also violate the basic principles of democratic governance.

In all these issues relating to development, the question that arises is—to what extent has sovereignty been undermined when the host country is dependent upon the aid and possible governance expertise of intergovernmental organizations like the UN Development Program (UNDP)? This also leads to issues of financial aid and debt relief, which are connected to the prioritization of development work by nations. The development process is complex, and the fact that sovereignty gets undermined is often not emphasized, as most countries silently accept this as a legitimate trade-off for achieving their development goals.[91]

As corruption is at the centre of the challenges that undermine the implementation of developmental policies and access to justice, there is a need to understand it from different perspectives. The

[91] Ibid., p. 531.

forthcoming discussion attempts to demonstrate the relationship between corruption, sovereignty, and human rights.[92]

## Corruption, Sovereignty and Human Rights

Corruption in the institutions of the state, including the acts of corruption committed by politicians and bureaucrats, does not allow the state to exercise its sovereign powers properly or responsibly. In fact, corruption in the state and its institutions means that the state is not functioning to capacity and that the law enforcement machinery is weak.[93]

There are five dimensions to how sovereignty is impacted by corruption:[94]

### Security

The goal of every sovereign state is to ensure national security for its people so that peace and stability prevail in society. Corruption has the potential to threaten this achievement of national security. Human security is but another dimension of sovereignty. It seeks to ensure that the people of a state are empowered to face a wide array of threats, including terrorism, weapons of mass destruction, natural disasters, deadly diseases such as AIDS and SARS, and other environmental disasters due to global warming and climate change.[95] It is important to recognize the connections between corruption and sovereignty from both national and human security standpoints so that all issues of public policy and governance a state is engaged in by way of its sovereign functions are pursued on the basis of transparency.[96]

[92] Ibid.

[93] Ibid.

[94] See C. Raj Kumar, 'Corruption Undermining Democratic Governance', Op-Ed., *The Hindu* (23 December 2005), available at http://www.thehindu.com/2005/12/23/stories/2005122302021000.htm (last visited 19 May 2011).

[95] Kumar, 'Corruption, Development and Good Governance', p. 530.

[96] Ibid.

## Law Enforcement

A sovereign state ought to ensure that laws are enforced in a non-discriminatory manner. Corruption does not allow this to happen. Hence, the criminalization of politics and politicization of crimes has become a common practice in South Asian countries. Through such practices, the sovereign state becomes too weak to enforce the law and all institutions of governance suffer from a crisis of legitimacy, as well as of autonomy and independence, which are required to enforce the law, including that against corruption.[97]

## Good Governance

A sovereign state ought to ensure the best practices of good governance. A corrupt state cannot ensure that its legal and political existence is duly supported by the governance process. The National Human Rights Commissions (NHRCs) in South Asian countries can play an important role in ensuring such good governance. Thus, it is imperative that issues relating to corruption become an integral part of the mandates of the NHRCs.[98]

## Development

The goal of any sovereign state is to ensure the social and economic development of its people. Contemporary international initiatives in the form of the MDGs underline this need effectively.[99] The UN Declaration on the Right to Development also emphasizes this point. It is the responsibility of a number of players, the most important being the state itself, to ensure that the MDGs are achieved. The fulfilment of the MDGs is inextricably related to the state exercising its sovereign functions. However, it is seldom recognized that corruption plays a very important role in the state not fulfilling its

[97] Ibid.

[98] Ibid.

[99] The negative impact of corruption on the achievement of the MDGs has already been considered in the first chapter of this book.

functions. Often, the resources allocated from domestic sources and development aids from international sources are diverted in the form of corrupt transfer of wealth to a few persons who are governing the country. Thus, development aid becomes a source of huge internal conflict and improper use of resources, thereby undermining the sovereignty of the state. These actions delay and undercut the development process.[100]

## Human Rights

The recognition of corruption as a serious human rights issue is based on the realization that the corruption of the state and its institutions hinders the full realization of civil, political, economic, and social rights, which are all related to the exercise of the right to development. Sovereignty as a facet of state responsibility demands that the state exercise its powers in a manner that ensures corruption-free governance. This will ensure better protection and promotion of human rights. Further, the recognition of corruption as a factor that undermines the sovereign exercise of power means that our efforts to prevent and fight corruption lead to empowerment of the people.[101]

Empowered people will have a greater commitment to ensuring good governance and development. In a contemporary attempt to acknowledge this reality, the new Right to Information Act in India has the potential to empower the Indian populace, but it remains to be seen how effectively it will be enforced.[102]

[100] Kumar, 'Corruption, Development and Good Governance', p. 533.
[101] Ibid.
[102] Ibid.

# 3

# Corruption and its Consequences for Governance in Asia: A Comparative Perspective

## THE PROLIFERATION OF CORRUPTION IN ASIA: PROBLEMATIZING THE ISSUE

Corruption is an all-pervasive problem that is widely prevalent in many countries in the Asia Pacific region. Corruption, having become deeply institutionalized within the governance structure, results in ground realities within Asia reflecting a high degree of apathy and helplessness in dealing with the problem.

Corruption profoundly affects the implementation of various policies relating to governance.[1] Governance mechanisms are inevitably undermined due to corrupt acts of the people who hold and exercise powers.[2] Another aspect of governance is related to the misallocation of resources due to corruption, as the governance priorities of a

---

[1] C. Raj Kumar, 'Corruption as a Human Rights Issue in South Asia: Law, Development and Governance', Paper presented at Human Rights 2006: The Year in Review Conference, Melbourne, Australia, http://www.law.monash.edu.au/castancentre/events/2006/conf-06-kumar-paper.html (last visited 17 June 2009.)

[2] Ibid.

country become negatively influenced by corruption.[3] There is a need to understand the relevance of the right to good governance in the process of institutionalization of human rights.[4] The discussion on good governance should also focus on the effectiveness of anti-corruption institutions and how these experiences could be usefully drawn upon for institutionalizing transparency in governance. Ultimately, good governance is instrumental in securing sovereignty.[5]

We have already seen how the Asian Development Bank has spearheaded efforts combat corruption in a holistic manner by engaging with both the public and private aspects of corruption.[6] While the extent of corruption is alarming and its impact on the institutions of governance is profound, there have been numerous instances of struggle and resistance by the people against corruption.[7] Unfortunately, many of these struggles have not in any significant way altered the situation. While the legal and institutional structures related to fighting corruption in Eastern and South Asian countries have been strengthened over time, corruption has become too much of a 'way of life' in many these countries,[8] while political will at the highest levels of government, including the Parliaments and Legislative Assemblies, is minimal.

In order to be able to effectively fight corruption in such a scenario, it is important to first understand how a particular behaviour becomes so pervasive within a society that it is deemed to be a way of life. It may be argued that for corruption to become a way of life in a society, it should have a deep and pervasive impact on the public and private lives of people. And this premise itself may be carried further, given the fact that the impact of corruption in the public

---

[3] Ibid.

[4] Ibid.

[5] Ibid.

[6] See Chapter 1.

[7] Cobus de Swardt, 'A Quest for Social Justice: Fighting Corruption around the World', http://www.transparency.org/content/download/43933/703761 (last visited 18 June 2009).

[8] See U. Myint, 'Corruption: Causes, Consequences and Cures', 7(2) *Asia-Pacific Development Journal* 33 (2000).

sphere might not merely affect the private sphere, but also shape the character, values, and actions of individuals in their private sphere. Discussing the alarming proportions that corruption has attained in the Philippines, Amelia P. Varela observed: 'Graft and corruption reached its all time high during the martial law regime under Marcos. … Graft and corruption under Marcos had permeated almost all aspects of bureaucratic life and institutions which saw the start of the systematic plunder of the country.'[9] Recognizing that a problem has become a 'way of life' in society essentially reflects its seriousness and pervasiveness.[10] In the Philippines, the state capacity to initiate development programmes has been affected drastically by large-scale looting of state resources.[11] A World Bank report in 1999 estimated that the government of the Philippines had 'lost US$47 million annually or a total of US$48 billion to corruption between 1977 and 1997.'[12] Jon S.T. Quah referred thus to this situation: 'In short, corruption is a way of life in the Philippines as both grand and petty corruption is rampant at all levels of the government and society.'[13]

[9] Jon S.T. Quah, *Curbing Corruption in Asia: A Comparative Study of Six Countries* 89 (2003) (University of Michigan: Eastern University Press) (quoting Amelia P. Varela, 'Different Faces of Filipino Administrative Culture', in Prosperpina Domingo Tapales and Nestor N. Pilar (eds), Public Administration by the Year 2000: Looking Back into the Future 161, 174 , (1995) (Papers presented during the Fourth National Conference on Public Administration held in Durzon City, Philippines).

[10] Shabnam Mallick and Rajarshi Sen, 'The Incidence of Corruption in India: Is the Neglect of Governance Endangering Human Security in South Asia?' Institute of Defence and Strategic Studies Singapore, Working Paper No. 103 (January 2006), available at http://www.rsis.edu.sg/publications/WorkingPapers/WP103.pdf (last visited 12 May 2011).

[11] ADB/OECD Anti-corruption Initiative for Asia and the Pacific, 'Anti-corruption Policies in Asia and the Pacific: Progress in Legal and Institutional Reform in 25 Countries' 79–81 (2006), available at http://www.adb.org/Documents/Reports/Anticorruption-Policies/anticorruption-policies.pdf (last visited 13 May 2011).

[12] Ibid., p. 91 (quoting Elena R. Torrijos, '$48B Lost to Graft in 20 Years: WB', *Philippine Daily Inquirer* (2 December 1999) A4.

[13] Ibid. (quoting Jon T.Quah).

The linkage between corruption and access to justice is profoundly reflected in the study of judicial corruption, the theme of Transparency International's (TI) 2007 report,[14] which concluded that 'a corrupt judiciary erodes the international community's ability to prosecute transnational crime and inhibits access to justice and redress for human rights violations. It undermines growth by damaging the trust of the investment community, and impedes efforts to reduce poverty.'[15] TI has noted that the perception of judicial corruption varies significantly across the Asia Pacific region. The study has recognized that while Hong Kong and Singapore have low perceived levels of judicial corruption, India and Pakistan fare poorly, with 77 per cent and 55 per cent respectively of poll respondents describing the judicial system as corrupt.[16]

Corruption is a serious issue that affects the people of the Asia–Pacific region. Very often, the legal systems of these countries demonstrate their seeming willingness to address it. This willingness is manifested most often after elections, when there is a change of government. There have been numerous instances, for example, of actions being taken by newly elected powers to prosecute the politicians and bureaucrats who served under the previous government. However, since most of these efforts are ingenuous and largely intended to settle political scores, they do not withstand the legal processes and almost never end in convictions.[17]

[14] Transparency Int'l, 'Judicial Corruption Fuels Impunity, Corrodes Rule of Law, Says New Transparency International Report', Press Release 2007_05_24_gcr2007_launch (24 May 2007), available at http://www.transparency.org/news_room/latest_news/press_releases/2007/2007_05_24_gcr2007_launch (last visited 18 May 2011).

[15] Ibid.

[16] Mary Noel Pepys, 'Corruption within the Judiciary: Causes and Remedies', in Transparency Int'l, Global Corruption Report 2007: Corruption in Judicial Systems 3, 12 (2007).

[17] See Michael Johnston, 'Party Systems, Competition, and Political Checks against Corruption', http://people.colgate.edu/mjohnston/MJ%20papers%2001/Florence%20revision.pdf (last visited 18 June 2009).

Legal and judicial reforms aimed at ensuring access to justice do not recognize that corruption remains the fundamental problem undermining all efforts to reform the functioning of government and institutions.[18] It needs to be noted that the political establishment of a country will have the least incentive to fight corruption if it is the main beneficiary of this practice.[19] Because of this situation, it is unlikely that genuine and sustainable reform initiatives that can fight corruption will ever come from the existing governance structures. Inevitably, such initiatives will have to originate from the people instead.[20] This notion of empowering the people is the link between corruption, human rights, and access to justice, and the central premise of this book.[21] Thus, all efforts to address corruption need to be connected to the basic objective of empowering people. This includes legal, judicial and institutional reforms aimed at improving governance.

## The Need for Political Will

The proliferation of law and legal mechanisms does not necessarily result in the effective enforcement of anti-corruption measures. A case in point is the Philippines, which has 'relied upon at least seven laws and thirteen anti-graft agencies since its fight against corruption began in the 1950s.'[22] Neither the wide range of laws nor the exhaustive institutional machinery was effective. The reasons for this failure were articulated by none other than lawyer Mike Domingo, convenor

[18] See C. Raj Kumar, 'National Human Rights Institutions and Economic, Social and Cultural Rights: Toward the Institutionalization and Developmentalization of Human Rights', 28 *Hum. Rts Q.* 775 (2003).

[19] See Peter Eigen and Christian Eigen-Zucchi, 'Corruption and Global Public Goods', in Providing Global Public Goods 576–646 (2003).

[20] A clear illustration of this is the civil society movement in India for the passing of the Jan Lokpal Bill. This will be discussed in detail in the subsequent chapters dealing specifically with corruption in India.

[21] This has been explained in Chapter 1.

[22] Jon S.T. Quah, 'Globalization and Corruption Control in Asian Countries: The Case for Divergence', 4 *Pub. Mgmt. Rev.* 453, 459 (2002).

of anti-corruption watchdog People for Empowerment and Truth, and the head of the then Presidential Commission against Graft and Corruption (PCAGC), who concluded in 1997 that, 'the system is not working. We are not making it work',[23] because:

We have all the laws, rules and regulations, especially institutions not only to curb, but to eliminate, corruption. The problem is that these laws, rules and regulations are not being faithfully implemented. ... I am afraid that many people are accepting (corruption) as another part of our way of life. Big-time grafters are lionised in society. They are invited to all sorts of social events, elected and re-elected to government offices. It is considered an honor—in fact a social distinction—to have them as guests in family and community affairs.[24]

As far as China is concerned, the question of the absence of democratic governance and accountability of the Communist Party and its members is writ large in the ineffective control of corruption. The main act of the People's Republic of China that defined corruption and its punishment was adopted as early as 1952.[25] As corruption continued during the post–1978 reform period, Deng Xiaoping's regime relied on the Criminal Law of 1979 as the substantive legal measure to fight corruption.[26] This particular legislation was amended in 1982 to impose stronger punishment for corruption. It led to further amendments in 1997 to include a chapter on corruption, which specified the penalty for corruption depending on the amount involved.[27]

The anti-corruption agencies in China are organized along three different sectors. In the judicial sector, the Supreme People's Procuratorate was re-established in 1978 to combat corruption. It

[23] Ibid., p. 461 (quoting Domingo).

[24] Ibid., (quoting C.C.A. Balgos, 'Ombudsman', in Shelia S. Coronel (ed.), *Pork and Other Perks: Corruption and Governance in the Philippines* 245, 267–8 (1998) (Philippines: Philippine Centre for Investigative Journalism).

[25] Ibid.

[26] Ibid.

[27] Ibid. See also K.M. Chan, 'Corruption in China: A Principal Agent Perspective', in H.K. Wong and H.S. Chan (eds), *Handbook of Public Administration in the Asia-Pacific Basin* 299 (1999) (New York: Marcel Dekker Inc.).

formed the Procuratorial Division of Graft and Bribery in 1989.[28] On
the administrative side, the Ministry of Supervision was re-established
in December 1986 with the objective of curbing corruption and mal-
administration in the civil service.[29] With respect to the Chinese
Communist Party, the Central Disciplinary Inspection Commission
(CDIC) was formed in 1978 to check corruption among its members.[30]
The effectiveness of these institutions has often been called into
question, given the lack of transparency and accountability in their
functioning. In this regard, Burns has noted that even though these
institutions received a number of complaints, they failed to reduce
corruption because 'the authorities appear[ed] to lack the political will
to handle corruption cases among more senior party members.'[31]

While it is well-recognized that in order for anti-corruption efforts
to be effective, political will is necessary, there is a need to rigorously
examine the ways by which such political will can be generated and
sustained. The intensity of political will varies with the different
models of government that prevail in a given country. In democratic
countries, it may be argued that the expectations and aspirations of
the people are reflected in the political will of the government, since
people have the democratic right to express their will and aspirations
through the electoral process, which in turn helps to shape the policies and practices of the government that gets elected. However, when
it comes to fighting corruption even in democracies, the success of
a sustained political will on the part of the government to initiate
effective policies has not been inspiring. While democracies are
clearly better suited to fight corruption than non-democratic states,
there is a need to improve democratic governance and the protection
of the rule of law within countries to do so successfully.[32] If political

[28] Quah, 'Globalization and Corruption Control in Asian Countries', p. 461.
[29] Ibid.
[30] Ibid., pp. 461–2.
[31] John P. Burns, 'Civil Service Reform in China', 2 *Asian J. Pol. Sci.* 44, 57–8
(1994).
[32] C. Raj Kumar, 'Corruption, Development and Good Governance: Challenges for Promoting Access to Justice in Asia', 16 *Mich. St. J. Int'l L* 475, 528
(2008).

will is defined as 'the demonstrated credible intent of political actors (elected or appointed leaders, civil society watchdogs, stakeholder groups, etc.) to attack perceived causes or effects of corruption at a systematic level,'[33] Sahr J. Kpundeh contends that it is a 'critical starting point for sustainable and effective programmes'[34] since '[w]ithout it, governments' statements to reform civil service, strengthen transparency and accountability and reinvent the relationship between government and private industry remain mere rhetoric.'[35]

## MODELS FOR COMBATING CORRUPTION IN ASIA

There have been a few cases decided by the courts in South Asia that have sought to bolster the need for corruption-free governance, but they have been largely made with reference to the principles of the right to equality or other anti-corruption legislation.[36] So far, the judiciaries in South Asia have *not* recognized corruption as a human rights violation, even when doing so would help the judiciary tackle the problem in a more legally and constitutionally coherent manner.[37] In this context, it must be mentioned that there have been allegations of corruption and other forms of abuse of power by judges, strongly indicating that there is a need for ensuring greater transparency and accountability within the judiciary. This becomes important given the fact that judiciaries in South Asian Countries are entrusted with the task of interpreting the constitution and upholding it.[38]

Jon Quah has identified three patterns of corruption control in countries in Asia for assessing their effectiveness.[39] These are:[40]

[33] Sahr J. Kpundeh, 'Political Will in Fighting Corruption', in Sahr J. Kpundeh and Irene Hors (eds), *Corruption and Integrity Improvement Initiatives in Developing Countries* 91, 92 (1998) (New York: United Nations).

[34] Ibid.

[35] Ibid.

[36] Kumar, 'Corruption, Development and Good Governance', p. 525.

[37] Ibid.

[38] Ibid.

[39] Quah, 'Globalization and Corruption Control in Asian Countries'.

[40] Ibid., pp. 457–64.

(i) Anti-corruption laws with no independent agency (Mongolia)

(ii) Anti-corruption laws with many agencies (India, the Philippines, China)

(iii) Anti-corruption laws with an independent agency (Hong Kong, Singapore).

Discussing the experience of Mongolia, Quah has noted that the Law on Anti-corruption (LAC) was enacted in April 1946, with three provisions criminalizing bribery introduced in the Criminal Code.[41] However, Mongolia has no independent anti-corruption agency, and the task of corruption control is shared among the police, the General Prosecutor's Office and the courts.[42] The Indian experience is also disappointing, given the fact that a number of agencies are involved in the fight against corruption. This is notwithstanding the fact that the Prevention of Corruption Act is implemented by the Central Bureau of Investigation (CBI), the Central Vigilance Commission, the State Anti-corruption Bureaus, and the State Vigilance Commissions.[43] S.S. Gill has rightly noted: 'Looking to the number of agencies created to tackle corruption, it would appear that the government was in dead earnest to eradicate this malady.'[44] However, 'this elaborate and multilayered apparatus to control administrative corruption has hardly made a dent on the situation.'[45] It should be noted that the ineffectiveness of the CBI is demonstrated by the low conviction rate in terms of cases—'as only 300 of the 1349 cases (22.2 per cent) in 1972 and 164 of the 1231 cases (13.3 per cent) in 1992 resulted in conviction.'[46]

As will be discussed below, Singapore and Hong Kong adhere to the third model of the creation of an independent institutional

[41] Ibid., p. 458.

[42] Ibid., p. 457.

[43] Ibid.

[44] S.S. Gill, *The Pathology of Corruption* 237 (1998) (New Delhi: Haper Collins).

[45] Ibid.

[46] Quah, 'Globalization and Corruption Control in Asian Countries', p. 459.

machinery to fight against corruption. This approach has proven to be most effective in the fight against corruption.[47]

## Hong Kong's Experience of Fighting Corruption

Hong Kong is considered to have largely succeeded in its fight against corruption. Hong Kong's institutional approach, which involved the establishment of the Independent Commission Against Corruption (ICAC) along with its reputation as a rule-of-law society provides useful insights into the transformation of a society.[48] The nature of these problems, including the problem of corruption in different societies, is such that any proposed solutions and reform initiatives need to be tailored to the specific social, economic and political circumstances of that particular society. Thus, the Hong Kong model is valuable not only for its success in significantly reducing corruption in governance in a fairly short period of time, but also for the potential solutions it has to offer to India. A deeper examination of the situation in Hong Kong, as far as anti-corruption efforts and its impact on protecting the rule of law, access to justice and human rights are concerned, is therefore necessary.

### Historical Perspectives

Today's Hong Kong is known for its integrity in governmental functioning.[49] Transparency International has ranked Hong Kong among the least corrupt societies in the world.[50] Corruption in Hong Kong is no longer tolerated at any level of government, but it is

[47] Kumar, 'Corruption, Development and Good Governance', p. 526.

[48] UNDP, 'The Impact of Corruption on the Human Rights Based Approach to Development' 31 (2004).

[49] C. Raj Kumar, 'Corruption, Development and Good Governance: Challenges for Promoting Access to Justice in Asia', 16 *Mich. St. J. Int'l L* 475, 483 (2008).

[50] Transparency International's 2010 Corruption Perceptions Index ranks Hong Kong at 13, with a score of 8.4 out of 10, above all other Asian countries but Singapore. See Corruption Perceptions Index 2010 Results, available at

important to recognize that this was not always the case.[51] Corruption
was clearly 'a way of life in Hong Kong in the 1960s and 1970s.'[52]
Public resources were procured through corrupt transactions and
bribery was the primary mechanism used to differentiate who would
retain scarce resources and how quickly one could attain them. Alan
Lai, Former Commissioner of the ICAC, commenting on the extent
of corruption in Hong Kong during that time, noted: 'The problem
of corruption reached epidemic proportions ... when it permeated
every aspect of the community. Subtle hints turned into outright
solicitation.'[53]

The problem was further aggravated by a significant degree of
police corruption. Corruption in the police force 'was particularly
rampant ... where powerful corruption syndicates were institutionalizing bribe taking.'[54] Indeed, it was only when a high-ranking police
officer fled to the United Kingdom mid-1973, while under investigation for alleged corruption by the Anti-corruption Office of the
Police, that the issue of corruption came to the forefront of political discourse in Hong Kong.[55] The mis-handling of this case and the
enormity of the incident triggered a series of governmental responses, including the formation of a commission of inquiry headed by
senior puisne judge, Sir Alastair Blair-Kerr, to investigate the matter.[56] Lai has observed that this development 'marked the beginning
of a new chapter in the history of anti-corruption efforts in Hong
Kong.'[57]

---

http://www.transparency.org/policy_research/surveys_indices/cpi/2010/results
(last visited 13 May 2011).

[51] Kumar, note 32, p. 483.

[52] Alan Lai, 'Building Public Confidence in Anti-corruption Efforts: The
Approach of the Hong Kong Special Administrative Region of China', 2 *UN
Forum on Crime and Soc'y* 135, 136 (2002).

[53] Ibid.

[54] Ibid.

[55] Ibid., p. 137.

[56] Ibid.

[57] Ibid.

## Legal Framework for Tackling Corruption and the Formation of the ICAC

As far back as 1897, laws existed in Hong Kong forbidding the solicitation or acceptance of bribes by civil servants.[58] The government passed the Prevention of Corruption Ordinance in 1948 and established an Anti-corruption Branch that was attached to the police in 1952. While these legal and institutional efforts were aimed at curbing corruption, there was little positive impact in the form of empirical reductions in corruption or prosecution of charges of corruption against corrupt individuals.[59] In his 1973 commissioned report, Sir Blair-Kerr, summing up the case for the establishment of an independent agency to tackle corruption, said, 'It is widely believed that the Police (including the Anti-corruption Office) are corrupt, that mutual loyalty inhibits investigation of fellow-officers constitutes sufficient reason to take the Office out of Police hands … and that the formation of a new agency would demonstrate Government's determination to fight corruption and thereby enlist public support.'[60]

The Independent Commission Against Corruption (ICAC) was established on 15 February 1974, through the enactment of the Independent Commission Against Corruption Ordinance and was given broad powers in the form of 'powers of arrest, search, obtaining information, and restraint of property.'[61] Two important aspects distinguished the ICAC from the previously unsuccessful efforts of the government. First, the ICAC was not part of the police. It was created as a separate organization and, thus, there was no functional duplicity in the work of the ICAC. Second, the ICAC was independent from the rest of the civil service. This aspect demonstrated the government's commitment to ensuring that bureaucratic interference or other hurdles did not arise in the fight against corruption. It must also be noted that at that time, public expectations were very high,

---

[58] Kumar, 'Corruption, Development and Good Governance', p. 484.

[59] Ibid.

[60] Daniel Li, 'The Road to Probity', J. Pub. Inquiry (Fall/Winter 2001), p. 13.

[61] Ibid., p. 14.

and tackling the problem of corruption in Hong Kong looked like a nearly impossible task. As a result, the ICAC was provided with an 'integrated, three-pronged anticorruption strategy, involving investigation, prevention and community education.'[62]

## Working and Achievements of the ICAC: A Critical Assessment

While the ICAC was born out of the specific social and political circumstances that prevailed in Hong Kong three decades ago, it is useful to examine the work and achievements of the ICAC in order to understand how it managed to develop a culture of integrity in Hong Kong.[63] To begin with, it is important to recognize that the formation of the ICAC was based upon an understanding that the commission would not be able to succeed in fighting corruption only by adopting law enforcement measures in the form of penalizing the corrupt. What was needed instead was a focus on reforming the administrative system in order to enable the government machinery to respond better to public needs, which in turn, required efforts to change public attitudes towards corruption. Adapting to this realization at the nascent stage of its formation enabled the ICAC to develop a three-pronged strategy to tackle corruption based on the components of investigation, prevention, and education.[64] It is generally assumed that the investigation and prosecution of cases relating to corruption is the only way to effectively fight corruption. While this is absolutely essential, since its inception the Hong Kong model of fighting corruption through the ICAC recognized that it is equally important to make efforts to prevent corruption, and to educate the public and build awareness against it. The ICAC took upon itself these two initiatives so that fighting corruption became connected to building an

---

[62] See Lai, 'Building Public Confidence in Anti-corruption Efforts', p. 138.

[63] C. Raj Kumar, 'Human Rights Approaches of Corruption Control Mechanisms: Enhancing the Hong Kong Experience of Corruption Prevention Strategies', 5 *San Diego Int'l L.J.* 331 (2004).

[64] Kumar, 'Corruption, Development and Good Governance', p. 485.

integrity system for Hong Kong. The concept of a 'National Integrity System' examines corruption and the need for fighting it in all sectors from a broader perspective and is subsumed within the larger objective of establishing a society that is based on integrity in all aspects of governance. It is in this context that the ICAC has three departments: the Operations Department, the Corruption Prevention Department, and the Community Relations Department.[65]

There is no doubt that corruption was a deeply entrenched problem in Hong Kong until the late 1970s, and that systemic efforts of legal and institutional reform have produced truly remarkable results since that time.[66] But there were also other factors that helped make the fight a successful one. Assistant Director of Corruption Prevention Jean Au Yeung has observed the following as various factors of this success: governmental determination, strong legislation, public support, a system of checks and balances, and international cooperation.[67] These factors, combined with the success of the ICAC model of corruption control mechanisms, have resulted in attitudinal changes and ensured the development of an efficient and 'cleaner' civil service, as well as a vigilant public sector.[68]

## Singapore's Experience in Combating Corruption

Along with Hong Kong, the model of Singaporean government and its efforts to tackle the problem of corruption also needs to be recognized. Assessing the experience of different Asian countries in tackling corruption can clearly help us to emulate the best practices in appropriate ways.

[65] Andrew H.Y. Wong, 'Anti-corruption Strategy of the Hong Kong Special Administrative Region of the People's Republic of China', presentation at the 4th Regional Anti-corruption Conference in Kuala Lumpur, 3–5 December 2003 (on file with author).

[66] Ibid.

[67] Jean A. Yeung, 'Indep. Comm'n Against Corruption (Hong Kong)', Fighting Corruption: The Hong Kong Experience (17 February 2000) (unpublished manuscript, on file with author).

[68] Kumar, 'Corruption, Development and Good Governance', p. 486.

Singapore attained self-government in 1959 from the British, and, like India, inherited rampant corruption in its public sphere. The corruption in colonial Singapore was due to a variety of reasons, primarily low salaries,[69] ample opportunities for corruption,[70] and low risk of detection and punishment.[71] Today, however, Singapore is the least corrupt country in Asia according to the annual surveys conducted by the Political and Economic Risk Consultancy and TI.[72] It therefore marks itself as one of the most successful stories of the anti-corruption drive.

To tackle the situation of pervasive corruption in Singapore, the newly elected government initiated a comprehensive anti-corruption strategy by enacting the Prevention of Corruption Act (POCA) and strengthening the Corrupt Practices Investigation Bureau (CPIB). Since corruption is caused by both the incentives and opportunities to be corrupt, the government's comprehensive strategy was based on the 'logic of corruption control' as 'attempts to eradicate corruption must be designed to minimise or remove the conditions of both the incentives and opportunities that make individual corrupt behaviour irresistible.'[73] In Singapore, clear and comprehensive regulations for the conduct of public procurement have been seen as the fundamental prerequisite for curbing corruption in public contracting. Government procurement in Singapore—worth SGD 7.5 billion (about USD 4.5 billion) a year—is subject to regulations of the Government

---

[69] L. Palmier, *The Control of Bureaucratic Corruption: Case Studies in Asia* 25 (1985) (University of Michigan: Allied Publishers).

[70] D.J. Gould and J.A. Amaro-Reyes, The Effects of Corruption on Administrative Performance: Illustrations from Developing Countries 61 (1983) (World Bank Staff Paper No. 580, Washington DC, 1985).

[71] Ibid.

[72] Corruption Perceptions Index 2010 Results, available at http://www.transparency.org/policy_research/surveys_indices/cpi/2010/results (last visited 13 May 2011). See also Jon S.T. Quah, 'Combating Corruption in Singapore: What Can Be Learned?' 9 *J. Contingencies and Crisis Management* 29, 35 (2001).

[73] Jon S.T. Quah, 'Singapore's Experience in Curbing Corruption', in A.J. Heidenheimer, et al. (eds), *Political Corruption: A Handbook* 841, 848 (1989) (London: Transaction Publishers).

Procurement Act and three decrees: the Government Procurement Regulations, the Government Procurement (Challenge Proceedings) Regulations, and the Government Procurement (Application) Order,[74] all of which are strictly enforced both in letter and in spirit.

Today, Singapore has a very strong anti-corruption policy, which recognizes that corruption control has strategic significance for national development. Moreover, there is a growing concern that investors are interested in doing business only in a transparent environment, without being encumbered by bribery. Thus, Singapore has taken the following measures to fight the menace of corruption:[75]

a.  Legislative Measures: After Independence, the political leaders amended the laws to give more powers to CPIB officers. To win public trust and confidence, the leaders themselves created a climate of honesty and integrity.[76] Punishments for corruption offences were enhanced. There is a regular review of the law. CPIB officers now, besides having all the powers relating to police investigations, are also given other special powers. Under the law, the Public Prosecutor can also, among other things, order the Comptroller of Income Tax to provide information on the offenders to the CPIB.

b.  Administrative Measures: Some of the important administrative measures taken included the following: (a) Seconded police officers were replaced with permanent civilian investigators, (b) the CPIB was given a free hand to act without fear, (c) cumbersome administrative procedures were streamlines, and (d) public officers' salaries were regularly reviewed to

[74] ADB/OECD Anti-corruption Initiative, 'Anti-corruption Policies in Asia and the Pacific: Progress in Legal and Institutional Reform in 25 Countries', pp. 110–14.

[75] Muhammed Ali, 'Eradicating Corruption: The Singapore Experience', paper presented at the Seminar on International Experiences on Good Governance and Fighting Corruption, Bangkok, 2000, available at http://www.tdri.or.th/reports/unpublished/os_paper/ali.pdf (last visited 19 May 2011).

[76] For instance, they divested themselves from any financial or commercial ties.

ensure that they were paid adequately and comparable to the private sector.

c. Preventive guidelines: Strict guidelines in form of instruction manuals were issued, to prevent public officers from getting involved in corruption or wrongdoings.

d. Action against Corrupt Public Officers: Persons accused of corruption can now be charged either before a court if there is sufficient evidence, else departmentally. Both the giver and receiver of a bribe are considered guilty of corruption and are liable to the same punishment. Any person who is convicted of a corruption offence can be fined up to SGD 1,00,000 or sentenced to imprisonment of up to five years, or to both. If the offence relates to a government contract or involves a Member of Parliament or a member of a public body, the term of imprisonment can be increased to seven years.

There are various lessons to be learned from the Singaporean experience. Although the high economic and political costs that Singapore can afford to bear in its drive against corruption can act as a difficult proposition for many developing nations in the Asia–Pacific region, nonetheless, it is important to recognize that a concerted effort against corruption is by no means a costless exercise.

## LINKAGES BETWEEN VIOLATIONS OF HUMAN RIGHTS AND CORRUPTION IN ASIA

### The Framework

As noted earlier in this book, the empowerment of the citizenry is essential to combat corruption effectively. Further, empowerment is the key to a human rights–based approach to combating corruption, which recognizes the linkages between corruption, access to justice, and development, and also recognizes that corruption is a human rights violation. While efforts have been made in Asian countries apart from Hong Kong and Singapore to combat corruption by promoting transparency in governance and the right to information, corruption continues to be a major obstacle preventing access to justice in Asian countries, as it tends to negatively impact the poor more than those who can afford to pay bribes. For example, in the context of Indonesia, the problem of corruption is inextricably connected to poverty and unemployment.[77] It has been observed: 'Systematised illegal gold mining in Kalimantan primarily uses poor migrants from Java and Madura for its workforce. The migrants get start-up funds from local businessmen, who then receive half. To ensure there are no governmental raids on the illegal mines, the businessmen then must pay off local police, military and government officials.'[78]

The impact of corruption on the poor in Indonesia underscores the link from corruption to development and access to justice. It has been noted:

Poor villagers in West Java were baffled when their government rice supply suddenly dried up. Suppliers complained that their payment was 60 million rupiah ($6300) in arrears. But villagers were adamant that they had paid the bills, the *Jakarta Post* reported. It was discovered that one local official had collected money from 4,000 poor families and used it to build himself a house. Another village chief spent the money he was handling on a car. A third financed a wedding party. A fourth financed a second wife for himself. … 'Oddly, none of these officials has been prosecuted,' the newspaper reported. An article on the same page of the same newspaper reports that a survey revealed 12000 malnourished children in the central area of Java alone.[79]

The consequence of the above is clearly reflected in the people's lack of faith in the legal system of Indonesia. If institutionalized corruption is rampant across all departments of the government, including the police, law enforcement machinery, judiciary and other

[77] Kumar, 'Corruption, Development and Good Governance', pp. 487–8.

[78] Gary Goodpaster, 'Reflections on Corruption in Indonesia', in Tim Lindsey and Howard Dick (eds), *Corruption in Asia: Rethinking the Good Governance Paradigm* 87, 90 (2002) (New South Wales: Federation Press). See also Anzis Kleden, 'Illegal Miners, Transient Merchants Thrive amid Extortion Culture', *Indonesian Observer*, 25 November 2000.

[79] Goodpaster, 'Reflections on Corruption in Indonesia', pp. 93–4. See also Nury Vittachi, 'Travellers' Tales', *Far Eastern Econ. Rev.*, 7 December 2000, A96.

bodies that are supposed to ensure access to justice, there is a crisis in governance.[80] This is aptly summarized by Gary Goodpaster:

Indonesians have a very low level of confidence in the integrity and competence of their judicial system. Corruption is rampant; decisions can be purchased; the courts are subject to political interference; and legal transparency is inadequate ... Such problems are by no means limited to the judicial system: they also extend to the legal profession, the attorney general's office, administrative agencies, and especially, the police force.[81]

The following will outline the linkages among corruption, access to justice, and human development as they in turn affect human rights, particularly in Asia:

## Governance Paradigm

The governance framework of a country is shaped by a number of policy and institutional priorities.[82] Development is about creating and expanding opportunities for people. The development policies of countries are increasingly shaped by an understanding of the impact of these policies on the lives of people. In fact, the very concept of 'human development' brings the people to the centre of discussions relating to development. If the development needs of people are to be met, there is a need for the efficient and effective use of resources. Corruption of any kind undermines and negatively affects the efficient and effective use of resources.[83] It creates bottlenecks for development and misplaces development priorities. Corruption is antithetical to development as it is based on factors that are personally favourable to the beneficiaries of the corrupt transactions, rather than the people who should actually be benefitted by the development policies.[84]

[80] Kumar, 'Corruption, Development and Good Governance', p. 488.
[81] Goodpaster, 'Reflections on Corruption in Indonesia', pp. 96–7; see also 'Transforming the Legal System: From Rulers' Law to Rule-of-Law' 1 Van Zorge Report on Indonesia 4 (2000).
[82] Kumar, 'Reflections on Corruption in Indonesia', p. 515.
[83] Ibid.
[84] Ibid.

Corruption manipulates development goals and distances the gap between the expectations of people from development and the actual consequences of developmental policies. Distressingly, when the effects of this phenomenon can be so broadly felt across the governance spectrum, it is overtly indicative of much larger issues in governance as a whole.[85]

## Institutional Framework

Governance policies of countries are formulated and implemented by various domestic institutions. It is important that these institutions duly recognize the linkages between corruption, human development, and access to justice.[86] Every institution functions on the basis of self-assigned priorities for achieving certain goals and objectives.[87] Unfortunately, the development goals of a society cannot be achieved if the institutions involved in implementing development policies do not sufficiently understand the need for implementing measures aimed at corruption-free governance and access to justice. The existing institutional frameworks prevailing in most Asian countries have created fairly independent structures for dealing with corruption, human development and access to justice.[88] Corruption, for example, is dealt with in a reactionary manner and, essentially, the criminal law and law enforcement model is the most commonly used approach for responding to corruption. Thus, it is primarily the police and law enforcement agencies that are involved in the fight against corruption. Development tasks are handled by various departments and ministries of governments that deal with policy formulation and implementation. Most of the time, there is very little dialogue and coordination between institutions that deal with responding to

[85] Ibid.
[86] Ibid.
[87] Ibid.
[88] Ibid.

corruption on the one hand and those institutions that are involved in implementing development policies on the other.[89]

The third leg of the triangle, access to justice, is unfortunately kept outside this framework. Since the judiciary is the institution entrusted with the task of adjudication and providing justice, the policies relating to access to justice are typically kept outside the institutions dealing with development.[90] The problem gets even more complicated due to the fact that 'access to justice' has been recognized to be a nebulous concept with varying interpretations. Further, it is important to understand the notion of access to justice from the point of view of its direct implications for corruption and development.[91] This understanding is possible only if the existing institutional paradigm is challenged to provide a more inclusive framework that will take into account the linkages between corruption, human development, and access to justice.[92]

It is useful to refer to the situation of corruption in various countries in Asia to determine how it affects the governance framework differently in these countries. South Korea for example (unlike Hong Kong and Singapore) is one country that has made many efforts over the years to fight corruption, yet has not been able to achieve the expected results. In the context of South Korea, it has been observed that:

Two wheels support corruption: incomplete systems and internalized cultural values. ... To disable the cart of corruption, both of the wheels must be ripped off. Reforming systems and strengthening law enforcement must be among the powerful antidotes used, but they are not sufficient remedies for corruption. ... In Korea, it seems that every kind of systematic approach to anticorruption has been tried, except for a streamlined approach to revitalizing internalized cultural values.[93]

[89] Ibid., p. 516.
[90] Ibid.
[91] Ibid.
[92] Ibid.
[93] Yong-Lin Moon and Gary N. McLean, 'The Nature of Corruption Hidden in Culture: The Case of Korea', in John Kidd and Frank-Jürgen Richter (eds),

## Corruption and Cultural Values

In the context of the 'Asian values' debate, it is useful to examine whether the linkages between corruption, human development, and access to justice in the context of Asia have cultural influences. Human rights in Asia have proceeded largely as a domestic discourse informed by international ideas. However, this notion has been struggling to confront the 'Asian values' argument put forward by a few authoritarian East Asian political leaders with a view to challenging the notion of human rights and democracy.[94] Their basic argument is that the human rights approaches of the West are unsuited to the Asian cultural and political conditions.[95] In fact, the linking of corruption in Asia to cultural values needs an effective response that will recognize the importance of achieving access to justice for protecting human rights and ensuring human development.[96] The Bangkok Declaration of 1993, a formal declaration by the Asian Regional Meeting of the World Conference on Human Rights, demonstrated the cultural exception to human rights while implicitly recognizing certain universal aspects of human rights. The declaration observed that, while human rights are universal in nature, they must be considered in the context of a dynamic and evolving process of international norm setting, bearing in mind the significance of national and regional particularities and various historical, cultural, and religious backgrounds.[97]

---

*Fighting Corruption in Asia: Causes, Effects and Remedies* 297, 303 (2003) (Singapore: World Scientific Publishing Company).

[94] See Christina M. Cerrna, 'East Asian Approaches to Human Rights', 2 *Buffalo J. Int'l L.* 201 (1996).

[95] See Bilahari Kausikan, 'Asia's Different Standard', 92 *Foreign Pol'y* 24 (1993). See also Fareed Zakaria, 'Culture is Destiny: A Conversation with Lee Kuan Yew', 73 *Foreign Aff.* 109 (1994). For a critique of the Asian values argument, see Kim Dae Jung, 'A Response to Lee Kuan Yew: Is Culture Destiny? The Myth of Asia's Anti-democratic Values', 73 *Foreign Aff.* 189 (1994).

[96] Kumar, 'Reflections on Corruption in Indonesia', p. 510.

[97] See 'Declaration of the Ministers and Representatives of Asian States, March 29–April 2, 1993', Asian Cultural Forum on Cultural Development (ed.), in Our Voice, Bangkok NGOs' Declaration on Human Rights (1993).

The human rights framework does recognize the importance of national and regional peculiarities. The process of institutionalization of human rights in various countries and regions is expected to develop a local approach that would bear in mind the social, economic, and political factors of the nation. However, it is not acceptable for the human rights movement or the anti-corruption initiatives to condone authoritarianism in Asia on the grounds of culture.[98] Yong-Lin Moon and Gary N. McLean have observed:

Viewed from this standpoint and in this context, corruption can be defined as a phenomenon in which Confucian values override rationality, fairness, and openness in public activities, such as politics, business, and public administration. ... But when Confucian values are influential in business and public affairs, favouritism and partiality prevail. ... It is necessary, therefore, not to mix the two sets of values by drawing a line around the private and public domains. This may be an effective antidote for corruption in Korea.[99]

It is important to recognize that values have become central to the discourse on corruption in Asia. Much of the Asian human rights discussions by scholars have focused on attacking the Asian values argument. While providing a liberal constitutional and human rights critique of Asian values, Michael Davis has rightly observed that 'the Asian values argument, as a challenge to the implementation of constitutional democracy, is exaggerated and fails to account for the richness of the values discourse in the East Asian region—local values do not provide a justification for harsh authoritarian practices.'[100] Further, there is little theoretical foundation for the existence of pan-Asian values. The countries in Asia are themselves so diverse and have such different historical, social, and political backgrounds that it is not possible to identify a set of values that belong to Asia as a whole. Furthermore, if the purpose of identifying certain values associated with Asia is the sociological critique of human rights or

---

[98] Kumar, 'Corruption, Development and Good Governance', p. 510.

[99] Moon and McLean, 'The Nature of Corruption Hidden in Culture', p. 308.

[100] Michael C. Davis, 'Constitutionalism and Political Culture: The Debate Over Human Rights and Asian Values', 11 *Harv. Hum. Rts. J.* 109, 147 (1998).

good governance, the Asian values discourse has not achieved this purpose.[101] Critiquing the Asian values argument, Yash Ghai has persuasively argued that:

There is no particular coherence in the doctrine of Asian values though. Its intellectual roots are weak and it shifts its ground as expediency demands. Although perceived and intended to be an attack on human rights, it is, in fact, concerned with ethics and the organisation of society and does not engage directly with the nature of human rights. Moreover, it sets up false polarities and has a dubious theory of causation with which it seeks to attack the notion of rights.[102]

Thus, the Asian values argument is at best a weak critique of efforts at the international level to develop universal human rights mechanisms that are aimed at ensuring that constitutionalism and the rule of law are strengthened.[103] The lack of human rights mechanisms due to this misguided argument has, on the flip side, resulted in governments in Asia having difficulties in responding to other social problems, including the need for fighting corruption, promoting transparency and accountability and more importantly, fulfilling the aspirations of the people to actively participate in democratic governance. Thus, in order to effectively combat corruption, the discussions relating to human rights and anti-corruption should move beyond the critique of the Asian values discourse. The experiences of successful models of institutionalization of human rights in other countries and regions of the world should dictate greater acceptability of such practices in Asia.[104]

---

[101] Kumar, 'Corruption, Development and Good Governance', p. 510.

[102] Yash P. Ghai, 'Human Rights in the Asian Context: Rights, Duties and Responsibilities', *Hum. Rts. Solidarity* (September 1997), available at http://www.hrsolidarity.net/mainfile.php/1997vol07no04/301/ (last visited 13 March 2008) (provides a critical and analytical perspective of human rights in the context of Asia).

[103] See Michael C. Davis, 'East Asia After the Crisis: Human Rights, Constitutionalism, and State Reform', 26 *Hum. Rts. Q.* 126 (2004).

[104] Kumar, 'Corruption, Development and Good Governance', p. 510.

There is no evidence to suggest that culture has anything to do with the tolerance or intolerance of corruption. While cultural values may help in shaping the ethics of a society, which themselves evolve over many years, it is difficult to argue that culture alters the framework for determining the prevalence of corruption.

The problem of corruption in Thailand has been situated in the context of the practice known as 'quan-xi' in South East Asia.[105] Quan-xi is a form of networking in which relationships determine who may prevail, or be prevailed upon, for favours, and 'involves honor between the parties, but from its Confucian roots, automatically invokes cronyism and nepotism. These two aspects support several forms of corrupt practices.'[106] The cultural practice of quan-xi in Thai society cannot be overemphasized when attempting to understand corruption in Thailand. Maneewan Chatuthai and Gary N. McLean have observed 'the very strong power distance that makes it difficult, if not impossible, for subordinates to speak out against their superiors, allowing for inappropriate behaviour to be overlooked in deference to the hierarchy.'[107] Thus, while culture should not be used as an excuse for not fighting corruption, the cultural underpinnings of corruption in a given society must be considered when attempting to formulate effective measures against such acts.[108]

## Challenges to Promoting Human Rights in Asia

Writing about the difficulties of promoting human rights in East Asia, Thio Liann observes:

At least three potential obstacles to promoting human rights in the region have already been identified: the antipathy of some ASEAN (Association of

[105] Maneewan Chatuthai and Gary N. McLean, 'Combating Corruption in Thailand: A Call to an End of the "White Buffet"', in John Kidd and Frank-Jürgen Richter (eds), *Fighting Corruption in Asia: Causes, Effects and Remedies* 317, 324 (2003).

[106] Ibid.

[107] Ibid.

[108] Kumar, 'Corruption, Development and Good Governance', p. 511.

South East Asian Nations) states towards civil and political rights, which leads to an emphasis on the economic aspects of the right to development; the paramount importance accorded to collective interests, which has been used to justify broad derogation from human rights in the interest of public order; and ASEAN's general treatment of human rights as matters of national competence.[109]

The Asian discourse on human rights should embrace the need for integrating development and governance perspectives so that human rights issues are recognized as essential factors for achieving development.[110] This is particularly true in the context of fighting corruption, as it has a direct relationship with the strengthening of democratic institutions. The contemporary thinking on the relationship of civil and political rights with economic, social, and cultural rights is based on the understanding that these rights are closely related and need to be protected and promoted together if their aims are to be fully achieved.[111] There cannot be any compromise or derogation of any set of rights for achieving another set of rights. Commenting on the global consensus relating to the 'right to development',[112] Arjun Sengupta, the UN Independent Expert on Right to Development has observed that:

As a result of this consensus, there is no more room for promoting one set of rights as against another, or putting forward some rights, such as economic and social to be fulfilled prior to or in violation of civil and political rights, or vice versa. All rights have to be fulfilled together and the violations of one would be as offensive as that of another. The international community,

[109] Thio Li-ann, 'Implementing Human Rights in ASEAN Countries: Promises to Keep and Miles to Go before I Sleep', 2 *Yale Hum. Rts. & Dev. L.J.* 1, 80 (1999).

[110] For an overview of the impact of other domestic human rights institutions on issues of development in East Asia, see Michael C. Davis, 'The Price of Rights: Constitutionalism and East Asian Economic Development', 20 *Hum. Rts. Q.* 303 (1998).

[111] Kumar, note 32, p. 512.

[112] See 'The Declaration of the Right to Development', G.A. Res. 41/128, UN Doc. A/RES/41/128 (4 December 1986).

instead, has moved on to examine the question of implementation of those rights as a part of the right to development.[113]

Human rights activism in Asia also has to take seriously the role of non-state actors whose work will have a significant impact on the institutionalization of human rights.[114] Non-state actors have come to attain an important place in societies all over the world. The functions of these non-state actors have had a profound effect on human rights both positively and negatively.[115] There are a number of non-state actors like the media, national and international non-government organizations (NGOs), multinational corporations (MNCs), multilateral institutions like the World Bank and IMF, and international development institutions like the UNDP.[116] While this list is by no means comprehensive, it provides idea of what we understand by the term non-state actors. It is time that the nation-state recognized this role and began to understand that the developmentalization of human rights cannot take place effectively if non-state actors are not involved.[117]

Simultaneously, countries in Asia will have to recognize the role played by MNCs in the development process.[118] Often, in the name of free trade, countries tend to ignore the accountability of MNCs with regard to human rights.[119] International institutions like the World Bank and IMF should themselves be committed to human rights. The integration of rights and development for good governance needs to be supplemented by actions that provide support to such

[113] Arjun Sengupta, 'On the Theory and Practice of the Right to Development', 24 *Hum. Rts. Q.* 837, 841 (2002).

[114] Kumar, 'Corruption, Development and Good Governance', p. 512.

[115] Ibid.

[116] Ibid.

[117] Ibid.

[118] Ibid., p. 513.

[119] For further reading, see C. Raj Kumar, 'Human Rights Accountability of Transnational Corporations and Business Enterprises: Governance Perspectives', 6 *Corp. Governance Int'l* 15 (2003).

efforts.[120] The institutionalization of human rights can be developed in Asia by promoting the development of National Human Rights Institutions (NHRIs), as will be outlined in detail in the 'Way Forward', *infra*. While this cannot completely supplant the role played by a comprehensive regional human rights institution, it may very well be a good beginning, where national human rights issues could be handled.[121]

## The Role of Good Governance

There is an unfounded misconception that good governance concerns only issues related to anti-corruption. While anti-corruption is a very important component of any strategy to achieve good governance, it is by no means the only one. In order for anti-corruption strategies to truly empower the citizenry, there is a need to formulate human rights–based approaches to anti-corruption initiatives.[122] The UN Economic and Social Commission for Asia and the Pacific (UNESCAP) has observed that 'good governance' has eight major characteristics:[123] participation, rule of law, transparency,[124] responsiveness, consensus

---

[120] See Balakrishnan Rajagopal, 'From Resistance to Renewal: The Third World Social Movements, and the Expansion of International Institutions', 41 *Harv. Int'l L.J.* 529 (2000).

[121] Kumar, 'Corruption, Development and Good Governance', p. 513.

[122] To understand the rights-based approaches to corruption-free governance in India, Hong Kong and Japan, see respectively, Kumar, 'Corruption as a Human Rights Issue in South Asia'; Kumar, 'Human Rights Approaches of Corruption Control Mechanisms'; C. Raj Kumar, 'Corruption in Japan: Institutionalizing the Right to Information, Transparency and the Right to Corruption-free Governance', 10 *New Eng. J. Int'l & Comp. L.* 1 (2004).

[123] UN Econ. and Soc. Comm'n for Asia and the Pacific, 'What Is Good Governance?' available at http://unescap.org/pdd/prs/ProjectActivities/Ongoing/gg/governance.pdf (last visited June 15, 2009).

[124] Al-Jurf Saladin, 'Good Governance and Transparency: Their Impact on Development', 9 Transnat'l L. and Contemp. Probs. 193, 199 (1999).

orientation, equity and inclusiveness, effectiveness and efficiency, and accountability.[125]

Mainstreaming human rights means enhancing the effectiveness of human rights programmes and integrating them with a broad range of activities including development, governance and the administration of states.[126] It is notable that the United Nation's Secretary General designated human rights as a crosscutting issue of his reform programme in 1997.[127] National institutions need to be established and governance policies formulated for the promotion of the right to good governance. Inevitably, the national institutions that already exist in Asia need to be reformed and re-oriented so that the governance imperative is fully appreciated. Courts will inevitably play an important role in this process. There has to be a concerted effort to recognize that the right to good governance is an important component of developmentalizing rights.[128]

The successful experience of Hong Kong and Singapore in Asia in establishing societies where governance is minimally corrupt and acts of corruption are swiftly dealt with is a valuable lesson to learn from.[129] However, for good governance to become an effective strategy for national growth and progress in a broader sense, it is important that anti-corruption efforts do not violate human rights. Moreover, the right to good governance needs to be institutionalized, and for this purpose, effective institutions like NHRIs and anti-corruption institutions have to be created with the necessary checks and balances to provide for institutional accountability and oversight. The basic idea behind the right to good governance and the rights-based approaches to development is to bring what was hitherto the venue of political discussions into the day-to-day development activities. The impact it can have on creating a humane society based

---

[125] Ibid.

[126] See UN Office of the High Commissioner for 'Human Rights, Human Rights in Development', available at http://www.unhchr.ch/development/mainstreaming.html (last visited 13 March 2008).

[127] Ibid.

[128] Kumar, 'Corruption, Development and Good Governance', p. 513.

[129] Ibid.

on the protection and promotion of civil, political, economic, social and cultural rights for all people without discrimination and with due regard to participation of the populace in decision-making that affect their lives is truly profound. The rights-based approaches to development, which integrates human rights and human development to promote good governance, helps forge deep social and economic partnerships between the government and the people based upon a shared sense of trust and public ownership of resources. The right to good governance as a part of the right to development ensures that there is equal opportunity for all people to social progress and welfare.[130]

[130] Ibid.

# 4

# Existing Framework for Combating Corruption in India

## CONSTITUTIONAL FRAMEWORK FOR PROMOTING TRANSPARENCY IN GOVERNANCE

Transparency in governance requires the functions of the state being exercised in an appropriate and simple manner such that corruption of any kind is nipped in the bud. Corruption-free governance is one important aspect of transparency and ensuring accountability. The objective of transparency in governance is to ensure that the information relating to decision-making processes, including the objective and determinable criteria for selection, is made public in advance. Apart from this, lack of transparency also amounts to inefficiency in governance.

The framers of the Constitution of India were mindful of the challenges faced by an infant democracy. Democracy, thus, became the soul of the Constitution and the relationship between the legislature, executive, and judiciary was defined by a delicate separation of powers. However, over the years, these democratic institutions have significantly lost their credibility due to corruption.

The National Commission to Review the Working of the Constitution observed in its consultation paper, *Probity in Governance*:

The paradox of India, however, is that in spite of a vigilant press and public opinion, the level of corruption is exceptionally high. This may be attributed to the utter insensitivity, lack of shame, and the absence of any sense of public morality among the bribe-takers. Indeed they wear their badge of corruption and shamelessness with equal élan and brazenness ... Corruption today poses a danger not only to the quality of governance but is threatening the very foundations of our society and the State.[1]

Coming from a recently established high-powered commission, these observations are truly significant. Corruption has systematically affected every institution of governance in India. Politicians and bureaucrats have figured prominently in various allegations of corruption that have been levelled against the government by the citizenry.[2] Corruption has also undermined the development and growth impact of social and economic policies that India has adopted.[3] It is correctly observed that 'most government offices typically present a picture of a client-public bewildered and harassed by opaque rules and procedures and inordinate delays, constantly vulnerable to exploitation by employees and touts'.[4] While corruption by itself poses a variety of problems relating to abuse of power and arbitrary decision-making, its direct consequences and its impact on the state machinery include issues like 'a determined denial of transparency, accessibility and

[1] Nat'l Comm'n to Review the Working of the Constitution, 'Probity in Governance' 2.1 (2001), available at http://lawmin.nic.in/ncrwc/finalreport/v2b1-12.htm (last visited June 20, 2009).

[2] In the space of the last two years itself, the government has been left reeling due to scams by high-level officials that have been exposed to the public. One such scam that left the Central Government on the back foot is the highly publicised 2G Spectrum Telecom scam, which has implicated the Union Telecommunications Minister A. Raja (now resigned), as well as DMK Chief M. Karunanidhi's daughter.

[3] For a comprehensive reading on the subject of corruption from a historical and contemporary perspective, see S.S. Gill, *The Pathology of Corruption*.

[4] Harsh Mander and Abha Joshi, 'The Movement for Right to Information in India: People's Power for the Control of Corruption', available at http://www.humanrightsinitiative.org/programs/ai/rti/india/articles/The%20Movement%20for%20RTI%20in%20India.pdf. (last visited 20 June 2009).

accountability, cumbersome and confusing procedures, proliferation of mindless controls, and poor commitment at all levels to real results of public welfare.'[5]

Corruption is a ubiquitous scourge in Indian society that undermines fairness in governance.[6] The institutions of governance make decisions not on the basis of what is best suited to fulfil socio-economic objectives, but rather, on the basis of how to maximize the corrupt interests of a few. Power holders work to abuse power in such a manner that they can earn money through illegal means and wield this power in a socially detrimental manner. Good governance requirements are available, and are based upon a number of factors.[7] The UN Development Programme (UNDP) views governance as 'the exercise of economic, political, and administrative authority to manage a country's affairs at all levels. It comprises mechanisms, processes, and institutions through which citizens and groups articulate their interests, exercise their legal rights, meet their obligations, and mediate their differences.'[8]

Reif has observed that indicators of good governance include a number of practices, such as a professional civil service; the elimination of corruption in government; a predictable, transparent, and accountable administration; democratic decision-making; the supremacy of the rule of law; effective protection of human rights; an independent judiciary; a fair economic system; appropriate

[5] Ibid.

[6] See generally Abid Hussain, 'Nat'l Comm'n to Review the Working of the Constitution, Some Ideas on Governance' (n.d.), available at http://lawmin.nic.in/ncrwc/finalreport/v2b3-2.htm. (last visited June 20, 2009).

[7] See C.P. Barthwal (ed.), 'Good Governance in India' 302 (2003) (New Delhi: Deep and Deep Publications).

[8] Sakiko Fakuda-Parr and Richard Ponzio, 'Governance: Past, Present, Future: Setting the Governance Agenda for the Millennium Declaration', UN Development Programme Paper, 18–19 November 2002), available at http://www.undp.org/governance/eventsites/PAR_Bergen_2002/gov-past-present-future.pdf. (last visited 20 June 2009).

devolution and decentralization of government; and appropriate levels of military spending.[9]

There is little disagreement on the extent of corruption in India, as it is a well-known fact that without paying bribes, it is difficult to get anything done in any office or institution. In a study of petty corruption, India prominently figures among the thirty most corrupt nations in the world. Transparency International (TI) conducted a study in which sixteen states were scanned and around 5,000 rural and urban families were sampled. It estimated that every year ordinary Indians pay as much as a total of US$ 6 billion (1.5 per cent of India's GDP) in bribes. Noting this, Rakesh Kalshian has observed that, 'be it birth and death certificates, admission to schools and universities, bank loans, passports, ration cards, driving licences, electric, water or telephone connections, legal or illegal, you name it, and the corruption "yellow pages" have them all.'[10]

In the Global Integrity Report, 2004, prepared by the US-based Centre for Public Integrity after a year-long study of twenty-five nations around the world, India has been rated as a 'weak democracy' on account of corruption and lack of accountability in its public institutions.[11] The report has put India in the 'weak' category on a 'public integrity index', which measures the existence and effectiveness of laws and institutions that promote accountability and limit corruption. The report explains that a major bottleneck in the Indian democratic and legal framework has been lack of transparency about the functioning of the government. It notes that 'this lack of transparency empowered the bureaucracy in significant ways

---

[9] See Linda C. Reif, 'Building Democratic Institutions: The Role of National Human Rights Institutions in Good Governance and Human Rights Protection', 13 *Harv. Hum. Rts. J.* 1 (2000).

[10] Rakesh Kalshian, 'Corruption Notebook', in Ctr. for Public Integrity (ed.), Global Integrity: An Investigative Report Tracking Corruption, Openness and Accountability in 25 Countries: India 7 (2004), available at http://www.global-integrity.org/reports/2004/docs/2004India.pdf (last visited 20 June 2009).

[11] See 'India's a Weak Democracy: Study', *Times of India*, 23 May 2004, http://timesofindia.indiatimes.com/articleshow/692836.cms. (last visited 15 June 2009).

and paved the way for abuse of power'.[12] As is the case with the enforcement of many other laws in India, the report recognizes that while
powerful anti-corruption laws are in place, the challenges are in their
effective implementation. It adds that the system as a whole does not
seem to have effective checks in place to prevent or tackle corruption.
As far as efforts to curb corruption are concerned, the report observes
that there is no comprehensive effort at eliminating corruption from
the governance machinery. As of now, 'the war against corruption is
largely waged by a few isolated individuals, select citizen groups, a
sprinkling of committed officers and the judiciary.'[13]

It is clear that corruption of *any* form, but particularly the type
of institutionalized corruption that prevails in India, will not allow
good governance to prevail. In fact, corruption is an anathema
to good governance and it is important that Indian society moves
toward reforming the governance system with a view to eliminating
corruption. The consequences of ignoring this problem would mean
that all other efforts in social and economic development would be
adversely affected in a serious manner. Moreover, development of
any kind is possible only in a free society. A society cannot be said
to be free when the governance institutions and the individuals who
operate it are corrupt and decisions are made not on the basis of
merit, but on the basis of vested interests, where bribery is the rule
and integrity the exception.

## Public Interest Litigation (PIL)[14] in India

The Constitution of India provides a robust framework for the protection of human rights and fundamental freedoms. The fundamental objective of the framers of the Indian Constitution was to build

---

[12] Ibid.

[13] Ibid.

[14] For further reading, see A.S. Anand, 'Public Interest Litigation as Aid to
Protection of Human Rights', (2001) 7 S.C.C. (J) 1; Parmanand Singh, 'Promises
and Perils of Public Interest Litigation' 52 *Journal of the Indian Law Institute*
(JILI) 2, pp. 172–88 (April–June 2010).

a new social, economic, and political order where there would be social, economic, and political justice. To this effect, the Constitution provides comprehensive chapters on the fundamental rights and the directive principles of state policy. Further, the principle of judicial review is well entrenched in Indian constitutional jurisprudence, as the Supreme Court of India as well as the high courts have been constitutionally empowered to exercise jurisdiction in enforcing fundamental rights. This has resulted in the judiciary taking an active role[15] on matters that affect good governance in India. In fact, the essential task of enforcing fundamental rights has been assigned to the Supreme Court of India and the high courts. Moreover, Article 32 of the Indian Constitution has ensured that the right to move the Supreme Court for the enforcement of fundamental rights is in itself a fundamental right. The judiciary has taken its constitutionally mandated role quite seriously, and the functions of the Indian judiciary have dramatically evolved over time. The liberalization of standing rules by the Supreme Court of India marked the beginning of the recognition of the inherent weakness of the Indian legal system and the lack of access to justice for the needy, the poor, the marginalized, and the weaker sections of the Indian society.[16] Poverty had so completely disempowered the Indian people that their problems needed to be brought to judicial recognition through some alternative mechanism. For the marginalized sections of Indian society, fundamental rights in the Constitution meant nothing, as they did not have the capacity to assert those rights.[17]

The judicial system in India was ineffective in addressing their needs, and existing rules of *locus standi* prevented the judiciary from entertaining litigations concerning fundamental rights violations. The Supreme Court of India moved towards broadening access

---

[15] Upendra Baxi, 'The Avatars of Judicial Activism: Explorations in the Geography of (in)Justice', in S.K. Verma and Kusum (eds), *Fifty Years of the Supreme Court in India: Its Grasp and Reach* 156–209 (2000) (New York: Oxford University Press).

[16] Anand, 'Public Interest Litigation as Aid to Protection of Human Rights'.

[17] Ibid.

to justice by ensuring that where a legal wrong or a legal injury is caused to a person or to a class of persons who by reason of poverty, disability, or socially or economically disadvantaged position cannot approach the court for relief, any member of the public, social action group, interest group, or concerned citizen[18] acting in good faith can maintain an application in the high court or the Supreme Court to seek judicial redress for the legal wrong or injury caused to such person or class of persons.[19] Public interest litigation (PIL) rests on the jurisprudential foundation that law is an instrument for social change and social engineering, that it is important for the principles of justice to ensure that judicial procedure does not come in the way of constitutional empowerment. The PIL movement in India has, by and large, been successful particularly in promoting a certain degree of governmental accountability, as well as in ensuring that the constitutional rights of the Indian citizenry are duly protected, regardless of their social, economic, and political status.[20] However, there have also been cases of misuse of PIL by those with vested interests, and simultaneous efforts have been taken by the courts to ensure that PILs do not become political tools for settling scores. Such misuse will undoubtedly result in abuse of the judicial process, besides creating serious bottlenecks in the justice delivery system in India.[21]

The present approach of courts with regard to PILs has been that before the court accepts the case, it asks the petitioners to disclose in an affidavit the nature of their concern and their purpose in filing

[18] Ibid.

[19] See Upendra Baxi, 'The State and the Human Rights Movements in India', in Manoranjan Mohanty et al. (eds ), *People's Rights: Social Movements and the State in the Third World* 335–52 (1998) (New Delhi: Sage).

[20] For an overview of public interest litigation in India, see Ashok H. Desai and S. Muralidhar, 'Public Interest Litigation: Potential and Problems', in B.N. Kripal (ed.) *Supreme but Not Infallible: Essays in Honour of the Supreme Court of India* 159–92 (2000) (New Delhi: Oxford University Press).

[21] For a critical reading, see 'Taking Suffering Seriously: Social Action Litigation Before the Supreme Court of India', in Upendra Baxi (ed.), *Law and Poverty: Critical Essays* 387 (1989) (Bombay: Tripathi).

the case.[22] The Supreme Court of India adopted this approach when a PIL[23] was filed by two petitioners alleging large-scale corruption in the functioning of the Garhwal Water Institute, established to provide potable drinking water to the hilly towns and villages of the Garhwal region in Uttar Pradesh.[24]As a response to moves by lawmakers to regulate the institution of PIL and its alleged misuse, the then Chief Justice A.S. Anand differentiated 'judicial activism' on the one hand and the role of the courts in entertaining PIL on the other, and observed that

It would be wrong to call it as [sic] an act of judicial activism when the judiciary in discharge of its constitutional powers seeks to protect the human rights of its citizens in case after case where a citizen has been deprived of his life or liberty otherwise than in accordance with the procedure prescribed by law or when the courts insist upon 'transparency and accountability' in respect of the orders made or action taken by public servants. The requirement that every State action must satisfy the test of fairness and non-arbitrariness are judicially evolved principles which now form part of the constitutional law.[25]

Thus, PILs can be used to ensure that the judiciary effectively checks the corruption and bribery levels of public officials. The constitutionalization of the right to corruption-free service in India marked the beginning of the Supreme Court and the high courts playing a far more constructive role in ensuring greater governmental transparency and accountability. Corruption as an abuse of power would be clearly perceived to be an affront to human rights and dignity, and

---

[22] S. Muralidhar, 'India: Public Interest Litigation Survey 1997–1998', 33–4 Annual Survey of Indian Law 525 (1997), available at http://www.ielrc.org/content/a9802.pdf (last visited 16 June 2009).

[23] *Mahesh Chand Bisht* v. *Union of India* (1997) SCALE Supp 22.

[24] Ibid.

[25] Anand, 'Public Interest Litigation as Aid to Protection of Human Rights', p. 11.

the courts would be empowered to intervene in matters that affect governance in India.[26]

Although the Indian judiciary has intervened in corruption matters from time to time, until recently, the issue of corruption was not dealt with effectively by the Indian courts. In *Vineet Narain v. Union of India*,[27] the Supreme Court of India, commenting on the issue of corruption, held:

Of course, the necessity of desirable procedures evolved by court rules to ensure that such a litigation is properly conducted and confined only to matters of public interest is obvious. This is the effort made in these proceedings for the enforcement of fundamental rights guaranteed in the Constitution in exercise of powers conferred on this Court for doing complete justice in a cause.[28]

'It cannot be doubted that there is a *serious human rights aspect* involved in such a proceeding because the prevailing corruption in public life, if permitted to continue unchecked, has ultimately the deleterious effect of eroding the Indian polity.'[29][emphasis added] Thus, the court did indirectly refer to the possible connections

[26] See S.K. Agrawala, *Public Interest Litigation in India: A Critique* (1986) (New Delhi: Indan Law Institute).

[27] (1998) 1 SCC 226.

[28] Ibid. The Supreme Court of India has used Article 142 of the Constitution of India in a number of cases to ensure governmental accountability and enforcement of orders of the court. For further reading, see R. Prakash, *Complete Justice under Article 142*, (2001) 7 S.C.C. 14, available at http://www.ebc-india.com/lawyer/articles/2001v7a3.htm (last visited 22 May 2011). Article 142 of the Constitution of India reads:

Enforcement of decrees and orders of Supreme Court and orders as to discovery, etc.—(1) The Supreme Court in the exercise of its jurisdiction may pass such decree or make such order as is necessary for doing complete justice in any cause or matter pending before it, and any decree so passed or order so made shall be enforceable throughout the territory of India in such manner as may be prescribed by or under any law made by Parliament and, until provision in that behalf is so made, in such manner as the President may by order prescribe.

[29] (1998) 1 SCC 226.

between corruption and human rights. However, there was no reference to the fact that corruption violates human rights and hinders the full exercise of fundamental rights under the Indian Constitution. Interestingly, in a recent judgment against a public servant for receiving bribes, the Supreme Court has once again brought the issue of corruption to the central focus of judicial intervention. In that case against public servant V. Vasudeva Rao, the Court observed, 'the tentacles of corruption are spreading fast in the society corroding the moral fibre and consequentially in most cases the economic structure of the country. It has assumed alarming proportions in recent times.'[30] On the issue of the institutionalized form of corruption prevalent in India, the court further observed that

... corruption is one of the most talked about subjects today in the country since it is believed to have penetrated into every sphere or activity. It is described as wholly widespread and spectacular. Corruption as such has reached dangerous heights and dangerous potentialities. The word corruption has wide connotation and embraces almost all the spheres of our day-to-day life the world over.[31]

## Towards Formulating a Fundamental Right to Corruption-free Service

Corruption, as demonstrated earlier, profoundly affects the exercise of rights in India. Rights are important political tools that are meant to empower people. The Constitution of India has provided for fundamental rights and directive principles of state policy to ensure that the people are given the necessary legal and constitutional protections for the enforcement of rights. However, when corruption undermines the implementation of constitutional rights, it requires a response that is based on the principle of human rights account-

[30] *State of Andhra Pradesh v. Rao*, 2003 SCALE 566. For more information on this judgment, see 'Corrupt Public Servants Must Face Consequences', *The Hindu*, 15 November 2003, available at http://www.hindu.com/2003/11/15/stories/2003111502351100.htm.
[31] Ibid.

ability. This principle provides for not only recognising the violation, but also remedial measures to seek redress for the violation.[32]

The Constituent Assembly debates in India are a rich source from which to understand the hopes and expectations of the political leaders of that time in creating a Constitution that would pave way for a 'social revolution'. It should be noted that the framers of the Indian Constitution were themselves victims of gross human rights violations through the state apparatus of colonial rule, during which the law was used to justify numerous actions in violation of human dignity. The authors of the Indian Constitution[33] provided for a comprehensive set of fundamental rights that could be enforced against the state.[34] There were also certain rights that could be enforced against private individuals.[35] The Constitution provided a robust framework to ensure that fundamental rights were duly protected and that the government could withdraw individual freedoms only under specific circumstances.[36] Even these circumstances were subject to judicial review and needed to be fair, just, and reasonable in order to be upheld.[37]

Rights have evolved in India through the progressive and liberal interpretation given to them to ensure that they provide a meaningful basis for good governance and freedom from exploitation. Experience has demonstrated that the concept of rights has been used by civil and political society to negotiate their claims within the scheme of democratic governance.[38] These struggles and negotiations have not always been successful from the standpoint of a constitutional

---

[32] C. Raj Kumar, 'Corruption and Human Rights: Promoting Transparency in Governance and the Fundamental Right to Corruption-free Service in India', 17 *Colum. J.Asian L.* 31, 65 (2003).

[33] Mahendra P. Singh, in *Constitution of India*, in V.N. Shukla (ed.), (2003) (Lucknow: Eastern Book Company).

[34] Ibid.

[35] Ibid.

[36] Kumar, 'Corruption and Human Rights', p. 65.

[37] Singh, *Constitution of India*.

[38] Kumar, 'Corruption and Human Rights', p. 65.

system that bases itself on liberty, equality, and dignity. Nevertheless, they have survived for more than half a century to ensure that India remains a constitutional democracy.[39]

The question of corruption as a violation of human rights demands a constitutional response. The fact that the constitutional governance system and the processes of administration are tainted by corruption vindicates the contention that it is time that India provided its people with a constitutionally guaranteed fundamental right to a corruption-free service. The Indian experience in recognizing constitutional rights, judicially enforcing those rights, and empowering the citizenry has not been always encouraging.[40] The public interest litigation[41] movement in India has given some favourable signals to upholding rights through the Constitution by means of an independent judiciary that is socially sensitive and activist.[42] But all these developments have their limitations and have fallen short of the social expectations they generated when the process began.[43] The fact that democracy itself is a tireless pursuit to ensure that the rights and freedoms of individuals are duly protected and that individuals are offered legitimate channels to allow the free expression of frustration and disappointments gives hope that the governance system in India will improve. However, these hopes have been shattered numerous times in the recent past due to the widespread prevalence of institutionalized corruption, as political morality and character are becoming pipedreams and watchdogs are ineffective due to lack of operational independence and institutional autonomy.[44]

In this situation, the Indian judiciary has responded more than once to ensure that the independence of investigative agencies is

[39] Ibid.

[40] For further reading, see Baxi, 'The State and the Human Rights Movements in India'.

[41] See Anand, 'Public Interest Litigation as Aid to Protection of Human Rights'.

[42] Baxi, 'The State and the Human Rights Movements in India'.

[43] Ibid.

[44] Kumar, 'Corruption and Human Rights', p. 67.

protected and that they are free from extraneous influences when handling investigations of corruption allegations and other gross abuses of power.[45] These instances of court interference have obviously drawn swift and determined responses from the executive to ensure that the power of supervision and control of the investigative agencies rests with the political executive. Thus, in terms of corruption in governance and integrity in administration, India is in a quagmire.[46] There is no single solution to the problem of corruption in India. The constitutional response in the form of formulating a fundamental right to corruption-free service would be an important starting point in taking the problem of corruption from the realm of public policy and criminal law enforcement to the central level of political discourse in India. An example of the constitutional empowerment of the citizenry in India with the recognition of economic and social rights is with reference to the right to education. The right to education was originally recognized in India as a part of the right to life. Later, the human rights movement and civil society activism helped in creating a distinct constitutionally recognized fundamental right to education.[47]

The envisaged fundamental right to corruption-free service in India would form a part of Chapter III of the Constitution of India. Former Chief Vigilance Commissioner N. Vittal has supported the evolution of such a right. He has observed that, 'corruption totally distorts the machinery of government namely, the executive, and makes a mockery of the human right for good governance.'[48] This right is expected to empower the Indian citizenry to rightfully claim that governmental conduct needs to be free from corruption. If it is not, it is a violation of their constitutionally recognized rights. Constitutional sanctity has acquired legitimacy in the Indian context largely due the fact that India has been functioning as a constitutional

[45] Ibid.
[46] Ibid.
[47] Ibid.
[48] N. Vittal, *Corruption in India: The Roadblock to National Prosperity* (2003) (New Delhi: Academic Foundation).

democracy since its independence. While corruption in all its forms—political, administrative, bureaucratic, and corporate—is rampant in India and has steadily increased in the last fifty years, the political system has by and large been stable. But this cannot be taken for granted. It is conceivable that shattered social expectations, mal-administration, and poor governance policies over a period of time would endanger the rule of law and the social fabric.[49] Corruption in India has affected development policies, and the Indian citizenry has been deprived of their economic and social rights. The right to corruption-free service would demand good governance, integrity, and probity in administration from those in power.[50]

The fundamental right to corruption-free service in India should be recognized for a variety of reasons: First, it would be a landmark development from the standpoint of constitutional governance, as it would be recognized by the lawmakers as an issue of foremost importance for ensuring good governance. Second, it would provide for obligations on the part of the political executive to ensure that they take positive steps for realizing this fundamental right. Third, Indian courts are well positioned to develop progressive jurisprudence relating to corruption-free rights, given the fact that there are numerous cases in the past, particularly with reference to other fundamental rights in the Constitution of India, where courts have interpreted and developed rights. Fourth, the non-enforcement of the fundamental right to a corruption-free service has the potential to invite judicial scrutiny, and the courts may recommend legal, administrative, and institutional measures and reforms to ensure that freedom from corruption, as provided in the Constitution, is meaningfully realized. Last, it gives a powerful tool to national and international civil society movements to ensure that corruption at every level of governance in India is duly addressed and measures are taken to curb this menace.[51]

---

[49] Baxi, 'The State and the Human Rights Movements in India'.
[50] Ibid.
[51] Kumar, 'Corruption and Human Rights', p. 68.

## Legal and Institutional Framework for Fighting Corruption

The recognition of corruption as a major problem of governance needs to be followed by the formulation of legal and institutional mechanisms to combat it. The challenge of enforcing the rule of law continues to be the single most important impediment to the effectiveness of anti-corruption laws, and thus the larger issue of establishing a rule-of-law society in India needs to be addressed immediately. This would require progressive efforts towards revamping the enforcement machinery and empowering the citizenry.

### Existing Laws to Combat Corruption in India

Historically, the legislative framework for ensuring corruption-free governance in India has largely been based upon two approaches: the promulgation of anti-corruption laws, and vesting police and other similar law enforcement institutions with the task of the investigation and prosecution of crimes relating to corruption.

The prevention of corruption in India has traditionally been perceived as the forte of criminal law and the penal statutes prohibiting bribery.[52] The Prevention of Corruption Act, 1988 (PCA), as stated in its Statement of Objects and Reasons, 'is intended to make the existing anti-corruption laws more effective by widening their coverage and by strengthening the provisions.'[53] This act recognizes that there were provisions already existing in Chapter IX of the Indian Penal Code to deal with public servants and those who abet them by way of criminal misconduct.[54] In addition, the 1944 Criminal Law Amendment Ordinance also inserted provisions enabling the confiscation of wealth obtained through corrupt means, including from transferees of

---

[52] For a comprehensive commentary in the anti-corruption law in India, see P.V. Ramakrishna, *A Treatise on Anti-corruption Law in India* 1563 (2003) (Lucknow: Eastern Book Company).

[53] Ibid., p. 2.

[54] Ibid.

such wealth.[55] Thus, the PCA seeks to incorporate all these provisions with modifications so as to make them more effective in combating corruption among public servants.[56] Thus, the legal framework for combating corruption in India has been established by developing a criminal law approach whereby corruption is recognized as a crime to which the criminal justice system must respond with punishment. Sections 7, 8, and 9 of the PCA discuss the nature of the offences covered under the act.[57]

Section 7: Public servant taking gratification other than legal remuneration in respect of an official act: Whoever, being, or expecting to be a public servant, accepts or obtains or agrees to accept or attempts to obtain from any person, for himself or for any other person, any gratification whatever, other than legal remuneration, as a motive or reward for doing or forbearing to show, in the exercise of his official functions, favour or disfavour to any person or for rendering or attempting to render any service or disservice to any person, with the Central Government or any State Government or Parliament or the Legislature of any State or with any local authority, Corporation or Government Company referred to in clause (c) of Sec.2 or with any public servant, whether named or otherwise, shall be punishable with imprisonment which shall be not less than six months but which may extend to five years and shall also be liable to fine.

In explanation (b) to this section it is observed that the word 'gratification' is not restricted to pecuniary gratifications or to gratifications estimable in money. In *S.N. Bose* v. *State of Bihar*,[58] the question raised was whether a particular promise or act amounted to gratification within the meaning of the PCA. The court held that in order for a promise to amount to gratification, two tests have to be satisfied.[59] First, the act must be something that is calculated to satisfy a person's aim, object, or desire. Second, such an act must be of some value, though it need not be something estimable in terms of money.[60]

---

[55] Ibid.

[56] Ibid.

[57] C. Raj Kumar, 'Corruption and Human Rights', p. 45.

[58] (1968) 3 SCR 563.

[59] Ramakrishna, *A Treatise on Anti-corruption Law in India*.

[60] Ibid., p. 570.

Section 8: Taking gratification, in order, by corrupt or illegal means, to influence public servant: Whoever accepts or obtains or agrees to accept, or attempts to obtain, from any person for himself or for any other person, any gratification whatever as a motive or reward for inducing, by corrupt or illegal means, any public servant, whether named or otherwise, to do or to forbear to do any official act, or in the exercise of the official functions of such public servant to show favour or disfavour to any person, or to render or attempt to render any service or disservice to any person with the Central Government or any State Government or Parliament or the Legislature of any State or with any local authority, Corporation or Government Company referred to in clause (c) of Sec. 2 or with any public servant, whether named or otherwise, shall be punishable with imprisonment which shall be not less than six months but which may extend to five years and shall also be liable to fine.

This section is meant to complement Section 7 and is intended to reach the abettors of the offence; hence, it extends to all persons, whether they are public servants or not. Despite the fact that the legal framework for the fight against corruption has been established, the effectiveness of these laws is far from satisfactory. The criminal justice system has not sufficiently responded to ensure that the corrupt actually get punished. One commentator notes that when the government enacted the PCA, it failed to accept two important recommendations of the Santhanam Committee: first, to establish a Directorate of Central Complaints and Redress under the Central Vigilance Commission (CVC) to look into the grievances of citizens against the administration; and second, to centralize all powers and responsibilities regarding disciplinary matters in the Commission.[61]

Further, the work of the Central Bureau of Investigation (CBI), the central nodal agency to control administrative corruption, has not been effective. In 1972 it registered 1349 cases of corruption as against 231 in 1992.[62] Of these, 300 cases ended in conviction in 1972 and only 164 in 1992.[63] H.L. Mansukhani has observed that the

[61] S.S. Gill, *The Pathology of Corruption*, p. 238.
[62] Ibid.
[63] Ibid.

Prevention of Corruption Act has turned out to be a 'puerile piece of legislation',[64] as it merely emphatically recognized several forms of bribes and corruption, but does not prevent their occurrence.[65] He has argued that it only created a new branch of evidentiary law whose objectives were neither moderate nor practical.[66] Experience has demonstrated that despite the fact that the PCA is equipped with legal provisions intended to ensure that corrupt acts are detected and corruption is punished, the inherent weaknesses in the law enforcement machinery in India, coupled with the lackadaisical approach of the criminal justice system, has created a weak enforcement system with respect to corruption.[67]

The law enforcement machinery of the state is generally weak and the accused in corruption cases abuse legal loopholes. This has resulted in a situation where the institutions that are vested with the task of investigating charges relating to corruption are weakly positioned. From the enforcement standpoint, there may be valid justifications for evolving a criminal law approach to address the problem of corruption, as it is essentially an economic offence. However, the systematic looting of the state's resources and massive corruption in the form of abuse of power by government officers, bureaucrats, police officers, and politicians through bribery and corruption, as is the case in India, demands a more serious and affirmative response from Indian society.

The constitutional approach to dealing with the problem of corruption presupposes the fact that corruption threatens the very foundation of Indian democracy and acknowledges that the Indian state is beginning to lose the faith of its people. Moreover, having taken root

[64] H.L. Mansukhani, *Corruption and Public Servants* 78 (1979) (Noida: Vikas Publishing House).

[65] See Krishna K. Tummala, 'Corruption in India: Control Measures and Consequences', 10 *Asian J. Pol. Sci.* 43, 67 (2002).

[66] Mansukhani, *Corruption and Public Servants.* This was referred to in Tummala, 'Corruption in India'.

[67] C. Raj Kumar, 'Corruption, Development and Good Governance: Challenges for Promoting Access to Justice in Asia', 16 *Mich. St. J. Int'l L* 475, 519 (2008).

in every department of the government, corruption creates a vicious environment that undermines the rule of law and the social fabric of Indian society. The problem has become so alarming that Indian democracy stands to lose its defining qualities if this problem is not approached from the perspective of its impact on constitutional governance in India. Critics of this approach may suggest that since numerous laws in India are not enforced and the criminal justice system is weak and suffers from numerous bottlenecks, addressing the problem of corruption from a constitutional standpoint may not provide the necessary solutions to the problem. However, it is important to contemplate how in past sixty-four-odd years of independence, time and again, corruption has undermined the very ethos of India's democracy and, with criminal law weakly positioned to deal with this menace, a constitutional intervention is the best and most suitable effort to curb this evil.

## Judicial Enforcement of Corruption-free Governance

The Constitution of India has provided for the separation of powers in the Indian governance system, with the judiciary being entrusted with the work of ensuring that the actions of the legislature and the executive are in accordance with the constitution. The Preamble to the Constitution underlines the fundamental aims of the constitution-makers—to build a new socio-economic order where there would be social, economic, and political justice and equality of status and opportunity for all. This basic objective of the constitution mandates that every organ of the state—the executive, the legislature, and the judiciary—work harmoniously to realize the objectives concretized in the chapters on the fundamental rights and the directive principles of state policy.[68] However, the institutionalized corruption prevalent in India has shattered these objectives and the various organs of the

[68] See C. Raj Kumar, 'The Development of International Human Rights Law in National Judiciaries: The Indian Experience', 19 *Ann. Rep. Inst. Jurisprudence* 75 (2003).

state have abused power, become corrupt, and acted in self-interest rather than on the basis of public interest.

The governance machinery is tainted with scams and allegations of corruption regularly coming to the forefront.[69] The Indian judiciary needs to understand that fundamental rights cannot have any meaning for a large number of people in India until policies are reformed to ensure corruption-free governance built on the foundation of the directive principles. A Transparency International study has revealed that the greatest sufferers of this petty corruption are not the middle classes, who often have the ability to grease greedy palms (even if grudgingly), but the urban poor—hawkers, rickshaw-pullers and small teashop owners, small-time mechanics, poor migrants labourers, slum-dwellers: in one word, the city's underbelly, bravely trying to eke out a living in the most heartless and trying circumstances. As for rural poor, consider this: the government spends US$ 8.5 billion annually on them but most of it disappears on the way.[70]

Corruption in the implementation of development policies has culminated in the creation of poverty, lack of education, health care, etc. To the majority of the Indian populace, the rights and benefits conferred by the Constitution and enforced by the judiciary mean nothing. Because of their financial handicap, they lack the capacity to assert their rights. The Constitution has indeed shown great concern for the underprivileged, conferred on them many rights and entitlements, and laid obligations on the state to take measures for improving the conditions of their life. Towards that end, laws have been

[69] In the past two years alone, the Government has been left reeling by many corruption scandals making the headlines, most notably the 2G scam, and the Commonwealth Games scam. See Gulzar Natarajan, 'The Mirage of Corruption Quick Fixes', Live Mint (1 May 2011), available at http://www.livemint.com/2011/05/01203821/The-mirage-of-corruption-quick.html?h=B ((last visited 13 May 2011)).

[70] Rakesh Kalshian, 'Corruption Notebook', in Ctr. for Public Integrity (ed.), Global Integrity: An Investigative Report Tracking Corruption, Openness and Accountability in 25 Countries: India 7 (2004), available at http://www.globalintegrity.org/reports/2004/docs/2004India.pdf (last visited 13 May 2011).

enacted and administrative programmes formulated by the state for bringing about social and economic change and ensuring distributive justice to the people. The judiciary has regarded it as its duty to come to the rescue of the underprivileged, to help them reap the benefits of economic and social entitlements. However, the problem of corruption has undermined the various steps that were taken to promote social and economic development.

The Indian judiciary ought to recognize that one of the main drawbacks the justice delivery system in India is the denial of access to justice to the common man because of corruption. Just as the court has liberated itself from traditional methods of judicial process and made creative use of judicial power by developing a variety of techniques such as PILs to make access to justice a reality, it should also take up the corruption issue directly and recognize the human rights consequences of corruption. Thus, through judicial innovation, cases relating to corruption need to be approached from a human rights standpoint. The lack of legislative thinking and executive inaction on issues relating to corruption, coupled with the exploitation of the masses by power holders, requires the judiciary to work towards ensuring corruption-free governance.

While the judiciary has not yet recognized corruption as a human rights issue in India, there are a few instances where it has intervened in corruption matters.[71] It is useful to refer to the decision of the Supreme Court of India in the case of *Vineet Narain* v. *Union of India*,[72] in which the court conferred statutory status on the CVC and decided to insulate the CBI and the Enforcement Directorate (ED) from political control and pressures. Further, the court referred with approval the recommendations of the Lord Nolan Committee on Standards in Public Life in the United Kingdom. The following seven principles of public life stated in the report by Lord Nolan and commended by the court are: selflessness, integrity, objectivity,

[71] See, for example, *Shivsagar Tiwary* v. *Union of India* (1996) 6 SCC 558; *B.L. Wadhera* v. *India*, AIR (2002) SC 1913; *UP State Road Transport Corporation* v. *Suresh Chand Sharma* 2010 (6) SCALE 87.

[72] AIR (1998) SC 889.

accountability, openness, honesty, and leadership.[73] The Supreme Court observed further:

These principles of public life are of general application in every democracy and one is expected to bear them in mind while scrutinizing the conduct of every holder of a public office. ... Any deviation from the path of rectitude by any of them amounts to a breach of trust and must be severely dealt with instead of being pushed under the carpet. If the conduct amounts to an offence, it must be promptly investigated and the offender against whom a prima facie case is made out should be prosecuted expeditiously so that the majesty of law is upheld and the rule of law vindicated.[74]

Further, in *Common Cause* v. *Union of India*,[75] the Supreme Court observed that:

It is high time that the public servants should be held personally responsible for their malafide acts in the discharge of their functions as public servants. ... We take it to be perfectly clear, that if a public servant abuses his office either by an act of omission or commission, and the consequence of that is injury to an individual or loss of public property, an action may be maintained against such public servant. ... No public servant can arrogate to himself the power to act in a manner which is arbitrary.[76]

The Court has elaborated on this principle as recently as 2011 in *V.S. Achuthanandan* v. *R. Balakrishna Pillai*,[77] where it lamented the fact that cases involving corruption charges against public officials inevitably take a much longer time to reach finality than other cases, and therefore it directed the high courts to give priority of hearing to corruption cases and conclude such cases within a reasonable time.[78]

---

[73] See the Summary of the Nolan Committee's First Report on Standards in Public Life (1995), available at http://www.archive.official-documents.co.uk/document/parlment/nolan/nolan.htm (last visited 22 May 2011).

[74] Narain, note 73, p. 917.

[75] AIR (1996) SC 3539.

[76] Ibid., p. 3551.

[77] (2011) (2) SCALE 346.

[78] Ibid.

Although the question of delays in the trial process is a larger issue that has affected the ability of the criminal justice process to effectively respond to corruption, it has also undermined public confidence in relation to the judicial process.[79]

The link between transparency, the right to information of public affairs, and human rights and good governance has been emphasized earlier. The Supreme Court in *Dinesh Trivedi* v. *Union of India*[80] was confronted with the issue of whether to make public the background documents and investigatory reports of the Vohra Committee, which had disclosed alarming links between politicians and criminal syndicates, such that they seem to be running a parallel system of government. This case recognized the right of the people to be made aware of what is happening in the public domain, with a view to promoting democratic governance. The Supreme Court, while upholding the sanctity of the right to information, also stated that the right was not absolute, and thus in cases of 'transactions that have serious repercussions, secrecy can legitimately be maintained because it would then be in the public interest that such matters are not publicly disclosed or disseminated.'[81] While the court in this case did not grant the relief sought by the petitioners, one of its final suggestions has helped crystallize the current movement against corruption for seeking transparency and ensuring accountability in the functioning of government institutions. In the words of the Supreme Court:

We are of the view that the grave nature of the issue demands deft handling by an all-powerful body which will have the means and the power to fully secure its foundational ends ... In view of the seriousness of the charges involved and the clout wielded by those who are likely to become the focus of investigation, it is necessary that the body which is entrusted with the task of following the investigation through to the stage of prosecution, be such that it is capable of enjoying the complete trust and confidence of the

[79] Jayanth Krishnan and C. Raj Kumar, 'Delay in Process, Denial of Justice: The Jurisprudence and Empirics of Speedy Trials in Comparative Perspective', 42 *Georgetown J. Int'l L.* (forthcoming, 2011).

[80] (1997) 4 SCC 306.

[81] Ibid.

people. ... The Nodal Agency, in its present form, may not command the confidence of the people in this regard; this is a serious handicap for, in such matters, people's confidence is of the essence. An institution like the Ombudsman or a Lokpal, properly set-up, could command such confidence and respect.[82]

This statement can be seen as the forerunner of the present movement in the country to set up the Lokpal to act against corruption. Most recently, in 2011, when the legality of the appointment of Mr P.J. Thomas as the Central Vigilance Commissioner was challenged in *Centre for PIL v. Union of India*,[83] the Supreme Court explained in detail the role and responsibilities of the CVC. It described it as an 'integrity institution' that has been given statutory status under the 2003 CVC Act.[84] It observed that when selecting the Commissioner:

The [High Powered Committee] must also take into consideration the question of institutional competency into account. If the selection adversely affects institutional competency and functioning then it shall be the duty of the HPC not to recommend such a candidate. Thus, the institutional integrity is the primary consideration which the HPC is required to consider while making recommendation under Section 4 for appointment of Central Vigilance Commissioner.[85]

The jurisprudence developed by the Supreme Court of India in relation to cases against corruption has focused on four important aspects: First, it has attempted to use the existing legal framework for fighting corruption and dealt with individual cases of corruption under the Prevention of Corruption Act. Second, the court has used basic principles of administrative law and constitutional jurisprudence to recognize that any form of arbitrariness in the governmental decision-making process is unacceptable under the framework of constitutional governance. Acts of corruption and other forms of extraneous considerations in the decision-making processes

---

[82] Ibid.
[83] (2011) (3) SCALE 148.
[84] Ibid.
[85] Ibid.

have been challenged by the court and specific remedies have been provided. Third, the court has in a few important cases empowered anti-corruption institutions and their ability to fight corruption to ensure that the independence and impartiality of these institutions are protected. This is one area where the Supreme Court has been most effective. However, it may be noted that the Indian judiciary, including the Supreme Court, has not recognized that corruption as it affects the Indian democracy is a larger issue of the violation of the human rights of the Indian citizenry and clearly violates the constitutional principles of equality and non-discrimination. Given the importance of corruption as an issue that has significantly undermined all efforts to improve the quality of governance and to guarantee the public good to the Indian citizenry, there is a need for the judiciary to step up its focus on relating corruption to the violation of fundamental rights recognized by the Constitution of India.

The fact that the judiciary in India has taken a proactive role in ensuring good governance by intervening in issues that have traditionally been the province of the executive has received considerable attention. This kind of judicial intervention has arisen due to the fact that the legislature and the executive have failed in certain key areas, and the governance machinery needs to be made aware of the fact that the rule of law needs to be protected. It is important for the judiciary to take a strong position when it comes to corruption, and to recognize that widespread bribery and other forms of corruption promote a culture of disrespect for law and the institutions that are established for protecting law and order and promoting justice. Until this is recognized, the work of the judiciary, like other institutions, will be crippled by the challenge of enforcement of human rights that arise due to corruption in government functioning.

While corruption at the higher level of the judiciary may not be rampant, lower levels of the judiciary in India are notorious for their own acts of corruption.[86] Recently, however, even the higher judiciary,

---

[86] For further reading see 'Civil Society to Assist Probe Against Justice Dinakaran', Rediff.com (18 May 2011), available at http://www.rediff.com/news/report/civil-society-to-assist-in-probe-against-justice-dinakaran/20110518.

high court judges in particular, have come under the corruption scanner with the exposure of the 'Uncle Judges' syndrome, provident fund scams in the high courts and other allegations of corruption.[87] This is indeed a dangerous trend and poses a serious threat to the rule of law, social stability, and democracy in India. The judiciary has a difficult task cut out for itself as it should not only ensure that other wings of the government are not corrupt, but should also develop mechanisms of accountability for itself so that corruption within the judiciary does not get institutionalized.

The existing procedure for inquiries into the misbehaviour or incapacities of Supreme Court and high court judges is provided in the Judges Inquiry Act of 1968. Currently there are two cases under investigation under this act—those of Justice Soumitra Sen[88] of the

---

htm (last visited 21 May 2011); 'Corruption Charges Slapped on Justice Dinakaran', *Times of India* (19 March 2011), available at http://articles.timesofindia. indiatimes.com/2011-03-19/india/29145433_1_justice-dinakaran-dishonest-judicial-decisions-dishonest-administrative-actions (last visited 21 May 2011). Rajeev Dhavan, 'Judicial Corruption', *The Hindu* (22 February 2002), available at http://www.hinduonnet.com/2002/02/22/stories/2002022200031000. htm (last visited 22 May 2011); P.P. Rao, 'The Judiciary', *The Hindu* (15 May 2003), available at http://www.hinduonnet.com/thehindu/2003/05/15/ stories/2003051500361000.htm (last visited 22 May 2011); Rajeev Dhavan, 'Judicial Propriety and Tehelka', *The Hindu* (29 November 2002), available at http://www.hinduonnet.com/thehindu/2002/11/29/stories/2002112901181000. htm (last visited 22 May 2011).

[87] V. Eshwar Anand, 'Op-ed Law, Corruption in Judiciary: Time for Action', *The Tribune* (3 December 2010), available at http://www.tribuneindia. com/2010/20101203/edit.htm#6 (last visited 24 May 2011); S. Balan, 'Corruption in Judiciary', *New Age Weekly* (14 May 2011), available at http://www. newageweekly.com/2011/05/corruption-in-judiciary.html (last visited 24 May 2011).

[88] Justice Sen has been found to have misappropriated sales proceeds to the tune of Rs 24 lakhs in the 1990s. See Dhananjay Mahapatra, 'Panel Chargesheets Justice Soumitra Sen', *Times of India* (18 April 2010), available at http://articles. timesofindia.indiatimes.com/2010-04-18/india/28148068_1_impeachment-motion-justice-sen-cji (last visited 22 May 2011).

Calcutta High Court, and Justice Dinakaran[89] of the Sikkim High Court. Before this, the only case of impeachment under this act was that of Justice Ramaswamy in 1993, but the Parliament did not pass the motion to remove him from office. The Proposed Judicial Standards and Accountability Bill, 2010,[90] replaces the Judges Inquiry Act and seeks to:[91]

(1) create enforceable standards for the conduct of high court and Supreme Court judges;
(2) change the existing mechanism for investigation into allegations of misbehaviour and incapacity of judges;
(3) change the process of removal of judges;
(4) enable minor disciplinary measures to be taken against judges; and
(5) require that judges declare their assets.

The bill seeks to set standards and promote accountability among judges through a two-pronged approach—the first, to lay down certain standards of prohibited conduct, and the second, to put forth a proper effective procedure for taking actions against any allegations of misconduct on the part of judges.[92] The bill seeks to do this by establishing the National Judicial Oversight Committee, the Complaints Security Panel, and an Investigation Committee.[93]

---

[89] Justice Dinakaran has been charged with corruption, land-grabbing, and abuse of Judicial Office. See 'Justice Dinakaran Faces 16 Charges Including Corruption, Land Grab', NDTV (19 March 2011), available at http://www.ndtv.com/article/india/justice-dinakaran-faces-16-charges-including-corruption-land-grab-92721 (last visited 19 May 2011).

[90] For a comprehensive analysis of this Bill, see Anirudh Burman and Vivake Prasad, 'The Judicial Standards and Accountability Bill 2010', PRS Legislative Research, available at http://prsindia.org/index.php?name=Sections&action=bill_details&id=6&bill_id=1399&category=46&parent_category=1 (last visited 19 May 2011).

[91] Ibid.

[92] Ibid.

[93] Ibid.

Anyone can make a complaint to the Oversight Committee regarding the misbehaviour of any judge. Further, a motion for the removal of a judge on grounds of misbehaviour can also be made in Parliament. It is then to be referred to the Oversight Committee, which can issue advisories and warnings to judges, as well as recommend their removal to the President.[94] However, complaints and inquiries are to be kept confidential, with frivolous and vexatious complaints penalized. The bill is currently pending before the Lok Sabha.[95]

The judiciary as an institution still commands immense respect from the people of India, and there are legitimate social expectations generated due to judicial interventions in cases of mal-administration. The judiciary has also created a sense of accountability in government institutions through its interventions. This accountability of the government to the people needs to be established by developing jurisprudence relating to corruption-free governance as a part of human rights commitments and constitutional governance.

## International Legal Framework for Fighting Corruption

Official corruption has become a universal phenomenon and hence efforts have been taken at the international level to curb this activity. On 31 October 2003, the UN General Assembly approved the first internationally negotiated treaty against corruption, which included a clause under which governments will be obligated to repatriate any stolen assets bought under their jurisdiction.[96] The anti-corruption treaty, which was presented for signatures in December 2003 in Merida, Mexico, entered into force ninety days following the deposit of the instrument of ratification by the thirtieth state.[97] This treaty,

[94] Ibid.

[95] V. Venkatesan, 'Judicial Accountability Bill introduced in Lok Sabha', *The Hindu*, 2 December 2010, available at http://www.hindu.com/2010/12/02/stories/2010120265661500.htm (last visited 24 May 2011).

[96] See 'General Assembly Approves International Treaty Against Corruption' (31 October 2003), http://www.globalpolicy.org/images/pdfs/1031convention.pdf (last visited 18 June 2009).

[97] Ibid.

the UN Convention Against Corruption,[98] which took the 130 UN member delegations two years to draft, is made up of 71 articles covering topics that include public procurement, bribery, illicit enrichment, embezzlement, misappropriation, money laundering, protection of whistle-blowers, freezing of assets, and cooperation between states. India has recently ratified the Convention.[99]

The importance of the treaty is demonstrated by the statement of UN Secretary General Kofi Annan on the adoption of the UN Convention Against Corruption by the General Assembly: 'Corruption is an insidious plague that has a wide range of corrosive effects on societies. It undermines democracy and the rule of law, leads to violations of human rights, distorts markets, erodes the quality of life, and allows organized crime, terrorism and other threats to human security to flourish.'[100] Prior to this recent remarkable development, the United Nations had taken efforts in 1996 to ensure that formulating the Declaration against Corruption and Bribery in International Commercial Transactions eliminates governmental and institutional corruption.[101] This declaration called upon the member states to criminalize corrupt acts in transnational settings.[102]

In addition to this declaration, there are a number of other international anti-corruption instruments that have been signed

[98] United Nations Convention Against Corruption, Art. 2, 31 October 2003, 2349 UNTS 41.

[99] See 'India Ratifies UN Convention Against Corruption', *The Hindu* (12 May 2011), available at http://www.thehindu.com/news/national/article2012804.ece (last visited 24 May 2011).

[100] See 'UN Secretary-General Kofi Annan, 'Statement on the Adoption by the General Assembly of the United Nations Convention Against Corruption' (31October 2003), available at http://www.unodc.org/unodc/en/treaties/CAC/background/secretary-general-speech.html (last visited 18 June 2009).

[101] UN Declaration Against Corruption and Bribery in International Commercial Transactions, GA Res. 51/191, UN Doc. A/RES/51/191 (16 December 1996).

[102] See Luz Estalla Nagle, 'The Challenges of Fighting Global Organized Crime in Latin America', 26 *Fordham Int'l L. J.* 1649 (2003).

by international bodies over the last several years.[103] The following represents a partial list:[104]

(i)   International Code of Conduct for Public Officials;[105]

(ii)  General Assembly Resolution 54/128, in which the Assembly subscribed to the conclusions and recommendations of the Expert Group Meeting on Corruption and its Financial Channels, held in Paris from 30 March to 1 April 1999;[106]

(iii) Report of the Tenth UN Congress on the Prevention of Crime and the Treatment of Offenders;[107]

(iv)  Recommendation 32 of the Senior Experts Group on Transnational Organized Crime endorsed by the Political Group of Eight in Lyon, France, on 29 June 1996;[108]

(v)   Twenty Guiding Principles for the Fight against Corruption adopted by the Committee of Ministers of the Council of Europe on 6 November 1997;[109]

(vi)  Convention on Combating Bribery of Foreign Public Officials in International Business Transactions adopted by the Organization for Economic Cooperation and Development

---

[103] Ibid.

[104] Ibid., see also 'An Effective International Legal Instrument Against Corruption', GA Res. 55/61, UN Doc A/RES/55/61 (2001).

[105] International Code of Conduct for Public Officials, GA Res. 51/59, UN Doc. A/RES/51/59 (1996).

[106] GA Res. 54/128, UN Doc. A/RES/54/128 (2000).

[107] Tenth UN Congress on the Prevention of Crime and the Treatment of Offenders, 10–17 April 2000, Vienna Declaration on Crime and Justice: Meeting the Challenges of the Twenty-first Century, UN Doc. A/CONF.187/4/Rev.3.

[108] Follow-up to the Naples Political Declaration and Global Action Plan Against Organized Transnational Organized Crime, ESC Res.1997/22 (21 July 1997).

[109] Committee of Ministers of the Council of Europe, Resolution (97) 24 (6 November 1997), available at https://wcd.coe.int/ViewDoc.jsp?id=593789&BackColorInternet=9999CC&BackColorIntranet=FFBB55&BackColorLogged=FFAC75 (last visited 15 June 2009).

(OECD Anti-Bribery Convention), opened for signature 18 December 1997;[110]

(vii) Agreement Establishing the Group of States against Corruption (GRECO), adopted by the Committee of Ministers of the Council of Europe in May 1999;[111]

(viii) Criminal Law Convention on Corruption adopted by the Committee of Ministers of the Council of Europe on 4 November 1998;[112]

(ix) Joint Action on Corruption in the Private Sector adopted by the Council of the European Union on 22 December 1998;[113]

(x) Declarations made by the first Global Forum on Fighting Corruption, held in Washington, DC, during 24–26 February 1999, and the second Global Forum held in the Hague in 2001;[114]

---

[110] OECD Convention on Combating Bribery of Foreign Public Officials in International Business Transactions, 21 November 1997, available at http://www. oecd.org/document/21/0,3343,en_2649_34859_2017813_1_1_1_1,00.html (last visited 15 June 2009).

[111] See Committee of Ministers of the Council of Europe, Resolution (98) 21 (5 May 1998), available at http://conventions.coe.int/Treaty/EN/PartialAgr/ Html/Greco9807.htm (last visited 15 June 2009).

[112] Criminal Law Convention on Corruption, available at http://conventions. coe.int/Treaty/EN/Treaties/Html/173.htm (last visited 15 June 2009).

[113] See EUROPA: Summaries of Legislation, 'Corruption in the Private Sector', available at http://europa.eu/scadplus/leg/en/lvb/l33074.htm (last visited 15 June 2009) (describing the adoption of Joint Action 98/742/JHA of 22 December 1998).

[114] For the Declaration of the First Global Forum on Fighting Corruption: Safeguarding Integrity Among Justice and Security Officials, see http://www. state.gov/www/global/narcotics_law/global_forum/appendix2.html (last visited 15 June 2009). For the Final Declaration of the Global Forum on Fighting Corruption and Safeguarding Integrity II, see http://bvc.cgu.gov. br/bitstream/123456789/1694/1/Final+Declaration.pdf (last visited 15 June 2009).

(xi)  Civil Law Convention on Corruption, adopted by the Committee of Ministers of the Council of Europe on 9 September 1999;[115]

(xii)  Model Code of Conduct for Public Officials, adopted by the Committee of Ministers of the Council of Europe on 11 May 2000;[116] and

(xiii)  Principles to Combat Corruption in African Countries of the Global Coalition for Africa.[117]

The states parties to the Criminal Law Convention, acknowledged that 'corruption threatens the rule of law, democracy and human rights, undermines governance, fairness and social justice, distorts competition, hinders economic growth and endangers the stability of democratic institutions and moral foundations of society.'[118] In the Summit of the Americas Declaration of Principles and Plan of Action in 1994, the heads of state of thirty-four nations of the southern hemisphere established a clear link between the survival of democracy and the eradication of corruption.[119] 'Effective democracy,' they declared, 'requires a comprehensive attack on corruption as a factor of social disintegration and distortion of the economic system that undermines the legitimacy of political institutions.'[120] The UN Declaration against Corruption and Bribery in International

[115] Civil Law Convention on Corruption, available at http://conventions.coe.int/Treaty/en/Treaties/Html/174.htm (last visited 15 June 2009).

[116] See Committee of Ministers of the Council of Europe, Explanatory Memorandum to Recommendation (2000) 10 on Codes of Conduct for Public Officials (10 May 2000), available at https://wcd.coe.int/ViewDoc.jsp?Ref=ExpRec(00)10&Sector=CM&Lang=en (last visited 15 June 2009).

[117] See Principles to Combat Corruption in African Countries (23 February 1999), available at http://www.gca-cma.org/ecorrup.htm#prin. (last visited 15 June 2009).

[118] Criminal Law Convention on Corruption, Preamble.

[119] Ndiva Kofele-Kale, 'The Right to a Corruption-free Society as an Individual and Collective Human Right: Elevating Official Corruption to a Crime Under International Law', 34 *Int'l L.* 149, 155 (2000).

[120] Ibid.

Commercial Transactions describes the economic costs of corruption and bribery, and points out that a stable and transparent environment for international commercial transactions in all countries is a *sine qua non* for the attraction of investment, finance, technology, skills, and other resources across national borders.[121] Member states pledged in the declaration to criminalize bribery of foreign public officials in an effective and coordinated manner and to deny the tax deductibility of bribes paid by any private or public corporation or individual of a member state to any public official or elected representative of another country.[122] Further, corruption was also the subject of a 1997 UN General Assembly Resolution entitled 'Action against Corruption'. The resolution underscored the General Assembly's concern about the serious problems posed by corrupt practices to the stability and security of societies, the values of democracy and morality, and to social, economic, and political development.

Kale has argued that an emerging customary law norm that treats corruption as a crime under international law draws strong support from

(i)   consistent, wide-spread, and representative state practice proscribing and criminalizing the practice of corruption;

(ii)  the widespread condemnation of acts of corruption reflected in the preambles of these multilateral anti-corruption treaties and in declarations and resolutions of international organizations;

(iii) pronouncements by states in recent years that evidence a universal condemnation of corrupt practices by public officials;

[121] See C. Raj Kumar, 'Corruption and Human Rights', *Frontline* (14–27 September 2002), available at http://www.flonnet.com/fl1919/19190780.htm (last visited 22 May 2011); see also C. Raj Kumar, 'Corruption and Human Rights II', *Frontline* (28 September–11 October 2002), available at http://www.frontlineonnet.com/fl1920/stories/20021011008607500.htm (last visited 22 May 2011).

[122] See Kumar, 'Corruption and Human Rights'; and Kumar, 'Corruption and Human Rights II'.

(iv)  a general interest in cooperating to suppress acts of corruption; and

(v)   the writings of noted publicists recognizing corruption as a component of international economic crimes.

In consideration of these factors, he has argued that there is a strong argument for treating corruption as a crime under international law, for which individual responsibility and punishment must be attached.[123]

---

[123] Kofele-Kale, 'The Right to a Corruption-free Society as an Individual and Collective Human Right'.

# 5

# New Legislative and Institutional Reforms for Eliminating Corruption in India

## LEGISLATIVE MEASURES REQUIRED

The problem of corruption needs to be addressed urgently if the efforts to improve governance and seek development are to be successful. As a number of past efforts in this regard have not achieved their intended results, there is a need to seek new legislative and institutional reforms for eliminating corruption.[1] The cornerstone of these new reforms is the empowerment of the citizenry for the fight against corruption.[2] Past legislative efforts have dealt with corruption as a crime,[3] but not necessarily as a problem that undermines the enforcement of human rights. Human rights violations of the nature created by corruption require radical reforms of the state apparatus and galvanized civil society activism that are different from those required in regard to criminal violations. Undoubtedly, certain reforms in the Criminal

---

[1] See Alan Doig and Stephanie Mclvor, 'Corruption and its Control in the Developmental Context: An Analysis and Selective Review of the Literature', 20 *Third World Q.* 657 (1999).

[2] Ibid.

[3] On this see Upendra Baxi, *Liberty and Corruption* (1989) (Lucknow: Eastern Book Company).

Procedure Code (CrPC), 1973, are long-awaited as well. For instance, under Section 197 of the CrPC, no court can take cognizance of any offence alleged to have been committed by a public servant without prior sanction of the government in whose affairs he is employed.[4] Thus, Professor Baxi laments the fact that 'the protection given by the colonial law-makers to the public servants in the Code of 1898, still continues.'[5] This recognition will pave way for developing strategies to fight corruption that was hitherto not considered.

## Rights-based Approaches to Anti-corruption Measures[6]

Having recognized that corruption affects human rights and the rule of law, it is important to develop the right to corruption-free governance through a number of rights-based strategies in India. Rights-based approaches to governance are those strategies that rest on the conceptual foundation that social and economic goals do not remain policy objectives, but get transformed into rights that are vested with the citizenry, increasing incentives for public vigilance.[7] In this conception there are 'right-bearers' and 'duty-holders'. Evolving rights-based approaches to governance will also help India achieve the Millennium Development Goals (MDGs). The people of the subcontinent would then actually be able to enjoy rights relating to various social and economic goals that were hitherto described as policy objectives.[8] Government representatives will be vested with the duty of ensuring the protection and promotion of particular rights. It is not that the rights-based approaches to anti-corruption measures will automatically ensure corruption-free governance, nor is it that this approach is itself free from problems relating to

[4] See also Prevention of Corruption Act, 1947, §6.

[5] Baxi, *Liberty and Corruption*, p. 53.

[6] This section is drawn from a previous work, C. Raj Kumar, 'Corruption, Development and Good Governance: Challenges for Promoting Access to Justice in Asia', 16 *Mich. St. J. Int'l L* 475 (2008).

[7] Doig and Mclvor, 'Corruption and its Control in the Developmental Context'.

[8] Kumar, 'Corruption, Development and Good Governance', p. 550.

enforcement. Rights by their very nature are claims on the government or its representatives to act in a particular manner.[9] There are numerous legal, jurisprudential, and philosophical bases for rights to be enshrined in the constitution, or for that matter, to be used effectively for promoting democratic governance. By the same token, there are criticisms of rights-based approaches to constitutional governance, particularly in the area of economic, social, and cultural rights.[10] Even while recognizing the inherent limitations of rights-based approaches, it needs to be noted that the empowering dimensions of such an approach far outweigh its weaknesses.

The real bone of contention is whether rights ought to be expanded so as to include economic, social, and cultural rights. Some commentators have observed that it is important to limit rights so that expanding the notion of rights and their attendant non-enforceability does not result in the dilution of traditional rights.[11] But in the context of India, the judiciary has significantly developed the notion of rights without diluting these traditional rights. Where the judiciary is concerned, there is little scepticism or doubt on continuing its interventions when these rights are violated either in a constitutional sense or by legislation. In fact, the development of the 'right to life' jurisprudence is one such example in which the courts have not hesitated to include new rights as a part of the evolving nature of human rights and human dignity.[12]

In another example, the fundamental right to education was initially recognized by the Supreme Court of India and later followed by a constitutional amendment that specifically incorporated this right into the constitution.[13] While the notion of rights-based approaches

[9] Ibid.

[10] Ibid.

[11] See Terry Collingsworth, 'Key Human Rights Challenge: Developing Enforcement Mechanisms', 15 *Harv. Hum. Rts. J.* 183 (2002).

[12] The Supreme Court has developed a robust jurisprudence in regard to the expansion of the right to life. See, for example, *Olga Tellis* v. *Bombay Municipal Council* (1985) 3 SCC 545 (holding that the right to life under Article 21 includes the right to livelihood).

[13] See A.S. Anand, 'Public Interest Litigation as Aid to Protection of Human Rights', (2001) 7 SCC (J) 1.

to development and governance is not without controversy or criticism, the conceptual basis for such an approach is useful for formulating various effective anti-corruption measures. In this regard, it is useful to propose that there is a case for developing a fundamental right to corruption-free service in India. The formulation of such a right, along with the development of other rights-based approaches to development, will help in eliminating corruption and promoting integrity and good governance.[14]

## India's Domestic Anti-corruption Legal Framework

The institutional approach to tackling the problem of corruption has been quite successful in Hong Kong[15] due to the work of the Independent Commission Against Corruption (ICAC).[16] There have been human rights concerns[17] raised regarding the activities of the ICAC in its law enforcement measures. However, these concerns have, by and large, been duly addressed through appropriate checks and balances.[18] In India, various attempts have been made to tackle the problem of corruption. Institutional measures have been taken by adopting legal and administrative regulations to ensure that corrupt individuals are punished under the law.[19] Before India's independence, the British established the Delhi Special Police Establishment

---

[14] Kumar, 'Corruption, Development and Good Governance', p. 551.

[15] Alan Lai, 'Building Public Confidence in Anti-corruption Efforts: The Approach of the Hong Kong Special Administrative Region of China', 2 *Fed. Crime & Soc'y* 135, 136 (2002).

[16] See Thomas Chan, 'Corruption Prevention: The Hong Kong Experience', UNAFEI Resource Material Series No. 56, p. 365 (2000), available at http://www.unafei.or.jp/english/pdf/PDF_rms/no56/56-26.pdf (last visited 17 June 2009).

[17] Daniel R. Fung, 'Anti-corruption and Human Rights Protection: Hong Kong's Jurisprudential Experience', 8th International Anti-corruption Conference (1997), available at http://8iacc.org/papers/fung.html (last visited 2 June 2009).

[18] Ibid.

[19] For some insightful critical analysis on this see Baxi, *Liberty and Corruption*, p. 3.

(DSPE) to control corruption, which was rampant during the Second World War.[20] The Prevention of Corruption Act was passed in 1947 and an Administrative Vigilance Division (AVD) was formed in the Ministry of Home Affairs in 1955.[21] This led the appointment of vigilance officers in each ministry to inquire into charges of corruption against employees in various organizations.[22] Interestingly, the First Five Year Plan in 1952 dealt with the issue of integrity in public life, and observed that corruption 'not only inflicts wrongs which are difficult to redress, but it undermines the structure of administration as well as in public life.'[23]

The fact that corruption potentially affects development was perceived by the early planners of India,[24] but the legal and institutional measures that were attempted at that time to address the issue were half-hearted, ineffective, and lacked enforcement mechanisms.[25] In one of the earliest methodical approaches to tackling corruption in India, the Santhanam Committee Report[26] recommended the establishment of the Central Vigilance Commission (CVC), which would be independent of ministerial control. The CVC was formed in 1964.[27] Amendments to the Prevention of Corruption Act were initiated to broaden the definition of criminal misconduct, which would now include those in possession of assets beyond known means of income for which no satisfactory information was available. The creation of the Central Bureau of Investigation (CBI) in 1963, which incorporated the DSPE as its investigation and anti-corruption division, was also one of the outcomes of the Santhanam

[20] Gill, *The Pathology of Corruption*, p. 237.

[21] Ibid.

[22] Ibid.

[23] Krishna K. Tummala, 'Corruption in India: Control Measures and Consequences', 10 *Asian J. Pol. Sci.* 43, 51 (2002).

[24] Doig and Mclvor, 'Corruption and its Control in the Developmental Context'.

[25] Ibid.

[26] Christophe Jaffrelot, 'Indian Democracy: The Rule of Law on Trial', 1 *Indian Rev.* 17, 22 (2002).

[27] Gill, *The Pathology of Corruption*, p. 237.

Committee Report.[28] Since there is very little political consensus on issues relating to processes of combating corruption, the institutional approaches that were attempted largely failed to ensure corruption-free governance.[29]

Commenting on the efforts in investigating corruption, A.G. Noorani has observed that 'the initiation of an investigation into crime or an inquiry into charges of corruption or maladministration must not depend on the wishes of the men in power. If it does, it ceases to be government according to the rule of law.'[30] The legal and institutional approaches to the issue of corruption have vested the power to initiate investigation into allegations of corruption with the very people who are in power and who may themselves be involved in the corrupt governance system.[31] The independence of the investigating authority is thus very important in ensuring that all allegations of corruption against government representatives are handled in an impartial, fair, and unbiased manner.[32]

In India, the conferral of statutory status to the CVC in the wake of the Supreme Court judgment in *Vineet Narain* v. *Union of India*[33] is a step in the right direction to ensure that investigative agencies like the CVC are not directly subjected to pressures from the political class while dealing with cases of corruption. This judgment also endowed the CVC with wider powers, including supervision over the CBI and Enforcement Directorate (ED). This will definitely help reduce, to a certain extent, the unpredictability surrounding the investigation of corruption cases and their effects on the rule of law.[34] The realization

[28] Ibid.

[29] Baxi, *Liberty and Corruption*, p. 3.

[30] A.G. Noorani, 'Lok Pal and Lok Ayukta: Commissions of Inquiry', in S. Guhan and Samuel Paul (eds), *Corruption in India: Agenda for Action* 221, 226 (1997) (New Delhi: Vision Books).

[31] Baxi, *Liberty and Corruption*, p. 3.

[32] C. Raj Kumar, 'Corruption and Human Rights: Promoting Transparency in Governance and the Fundamental Right to Corruption-free Service in India' 17 Colum. *J. Asian L.* 31, 65 (2003).

[33] (1997) 7 SCALE 656; A.I.R. 1998 S.C. 889.

[34] Noorani, et al., 'Commissions of Inquiry'.

of rule of law requires a certain level of predictability that violations of law will be met with certain consequences.[35] This predictability has not been supported in cases relating to corruption in India; hence, it is important to take steps to reform the criminal and civil justice systems to correct this and to remove uncertainty from the protection of the rule of law.[36] Although the recent passing of a Right to Information Act has helped to ensure transparency in governance,[37] India does not yet have the necessary legal and institutional frameworks for whistleblower protection. The Government of India did examine a proposed piece of legislation in 2002 called The Public Interest Disclosure and Protection of Informers Bill, which was drafted by the Law Commission of India.[38] In light of the recommendations, the Ministry of Personnel, Public Grievances and Pensions (Department of Personnel and Training) passed a resolution (Government of India Resolution No. 89, *Gazette of India* Part I Section I) to give protection to whistleblowers.[39]

While the protection that is granted under this resolution is not similar to statutory protection, it may be useful to provide a minimal degree of confidence to whistleblowers. The resolution authorized the CVC as the designated agency to receive written complaints or disclosures on any allegation of corruption or misuse of office by any employee of the Central Government or of any corporation established by or under any Central Act, government companies, societies, or local authorities owned or controlled by the Central Government.[40] The limitation of 'owned or controlled by the Central Government' has clearly excluded private companies, corporations and private institutions from the ambit of whistleblower protection,

[35] Ibid.

[36] Baxi, *Liberty and Corruption*, p. 3.

[37] S.P. Sathe, *Right to Information* (2007) (Lucknow: Eastern Book Company).

[38] Ibid.

[39] Government of India Res. No. 89, *Gazette of India*, Part I, Section I, Ministry of Personnel, Public Grievances and Pensions (Dept of Personnel and Training), 21 April 2004 (as amended 29 April 2004).

[40] Ibid.

thereby adopting a narrow approach of protection, unlike the similar Japanese legislation. Section 6 of the resolution states that if a person is aggrieved by any action on the ground that he is being victimized due to the fact that he had filed a complaint or disclosure, he may file an application before the designated agency seeking redress.[41] Section 7 provides for witness protection.[42] However, this is based on the opinion of the designated agency that the witness needs protection. Overall, the protection that is granted to whistleblowers by way of policy regulations is very minimal and grossly underestimates the need for protection for whistleblowers.[43]

The Indian Government, as noted earlier,[44] has now approved a Whistleblower Protection Bill, which is pending before Parliament. Nevertheless, it is important to consider the arguments for the passing of this law:

## Recognition

The recognition of corruption as a serious issue that violates human rights, undermines the rule of law, and distorts the development process is the starting point for the discussion relating to the possible responses for fighting corruption.[45] The role of the CVC, Central Information Commission (CIC) and the CBI and non-governmental organizations like Transparency International in India may be helpful in the fight against corruption.[46] But all these institutions, when dealing with corruption, are to a large extent crippled without a vibrant and active civil society that is fully empowered to fight against corruption.[47]

---

[41] Ibid.
[42] Ibid.
[43] Kumar, 'Corruption, Development and Good Governance', p. 546.
[44] See Chapter 2.
[45] Doig and McIvor, 'Corruption and its Control in the Developmental Context'.
[46] Ibid.
[47] Kumar, 'Corruption, Development and Good Governance', p. 547.

## Response

The case for the passing of a whistleblower protection law in India is based on underlining the need for a protective system for people who are willing to take the risk of exposing acts of corruption.[48] The notion of a whistleblower involves a number of different aspects. It has been observed that there are three pre-requisites for whistle-blowing:[49]

(i)  Whistleblowers must be confident that they will be protected if they do so, and that the decision to blow the whistle would not result in any adverse effects either on their employment or legal liability. This is very important not only to generate confidence among persons working in an organization, but also to create an environment of mutual trust and a culture of integrity. Further, given the nature of corrupt acts committed by powerful and 'well-connected' individuals, there is a good chance that persons who have information relating to these acts of corruption may be hesitant for fear of reprisal or action against them for blowing the whistle. There should be a system in place to ensure that there is physical and legal protection against such threats that the act of reporting might pose to whistleblowers. The fundamental rationale for supporting the notion of whistleblowers' protection is that they can be useful for bringing information relating to acts of corruption to the knowledge of the investigation officials or to the concerned institutions.[50]

(ii)  Whistleblowers must believe that their exposure of corruption will serve some good purpose and that appropriate action

[48] Ibid.

[49] Chris Wheeler, 'Drafting and Implementing Whistleblower Protection Laws', in *Controlling Corruption in Asia and the Pacific* 127 (2004) (Asian Development Bank), available at http://www.adb.org/Documents/Books/Controlling-Corruption/chapter5.pdf (last visited 22 May 2011).

[50] Moshe Maor, 'Feeling the Heat? Anticorruption Mechanisms in Comparative Perspective', 12 *Governance* 1 (2004).

will be taken by the agency. This is a question of institutional credibility. The legitimacy of any anti-corruption institution is dependent upon the trust and confidence it can generate from the people who are the real stake holders. Whistleblowers will expose wrongdoing if and when they know that their act will result in appropriate action that the agency may take. This is dependent upon the reputation of the agency and factors like the impartiality, objectivity, functional independence, operational efficiency, and financial autonomy of the institution. There is a need to ensure that these factors are in place so that the whistleblower is encouraged to come forward with the relevant information that may be useful for fighting corruption.

(iii) Whistleblowers must be aware that they can make disclosures, and of how they should go about doing so, including to whom, how, and what information can be released as a part of their act. This is a crucial factor for whistle blowing to be successful. Most of the time, there is no proper guidance available regarding which type of information is not confidential or which information is appropriate to be released. Further, there is a tendency among governments to use secrecy and confidentiality as a tool to ensure that little information is available in the public domain regarding how the government functions. This approach has begun to change in India with the passing of the right to information law and the establishment of the central and state information commissions.

## Empowerment

One of the important problems encountered in fighting corruption, particularly at the lower end of government services, is that the victims of corruption are disempowered in the sense that they are helpless and are forced to pay bribes. The bribe receivers, or those who are the perpetrators of corruption, wield enormous power and are able to abuse it with little control on the exercise of their powers.[51] Further,

---

[51] Baxi, *Liberty and Corruption*, p. 3.

there exist only a few oversight or supervisory mechanisms for the exercise of these powers, and even if such bodies exist, corruption seems to have entered into these bodies as well. In this context, any approach to fight corruption ought to bear in mind that the trust and confidence deposed on individuals and institutions should be minimal. There is a need, to the greatest possible extent, for a broad-based anti-corruption mechanism, with many institutions acting as a check on the exercise of powers. It is in this context that the system of whistleblower protection is extremely valuable. However, whistleblowers need to be truly empowered so that their zeal and enthusiasm to support corruption-free governance is legally and institutionally protected.[52]

The whistleblower could be anybody, including, but not limited to, somebody who is a victim of corruption or a person who has some knowledge or information relating to a corrupt transaction; someone within the government who has received information relating to acts of corruption, but it is not within his or her mandate to take any action on the particular complaint; a press reporter; an anti-corruption activist; or an NGO representative working in the field of corruption. The objective is to expand the base of persons who could be whistleblowers. In a truly democratic society, there is a need for every concerned citizen to act as a whistleblower, and it ought to become a central duty and responsibility of citizenship.[53] But the state cannot expect its citizens to discharge these types of duties of responsible citizenship until and unless there is a proper legal and institutional mechanism that provides protection to the whistle-blower.[54] Therefore, the Parliament should pass a Whistleblower Protection Act at the very earliest that conforms to the above-stated requirements.

[52] Sathe, *Right to Information*.

[53] Jon S.T. Quah, 'Corruption in Asian Countries: Can It Be Minimized?' 59 *Pub. Admin. Rev.* 483 (1999).

[54] Kumar, 'Corruption, Development and Good Governance', p. 549.

## INSTITUTIONAL MEASURES: NATIONAL HUMAN RIGHTS COMMISSION

While the UN has toyed with the idea of establishing national institutions to protect human rights for a long time, the actual formation of National Human Rights Institutions (NHRIs) is a recent phenomenon.[55] NHRIs, however, can only make meaningful contribution to the protection of human rights if their establishment meets certain standards and principles governing their existence and performance.[56]

### Institutional Priorities and Norms Enforcement

NHRIs are domestic institutions established through a provision in the constitution, legislation, or by way of a presidential decree or executive order.[57] To some extent, the manner of formation of

[55] See Linda C. Reif, 'Building Democratic Institutions: The Role of National Human Rights Institutions in Good Governance and Human Rights Protection', 2 *Harv. Hum. Rts. J.* 1 (2000) (stating that as of the year 2000, most human rights institutions had been created in the past two or three decades).

[56] See UN Secretary-General, 'National Institutions for the Promotion and Protection of Human Rights: Rep. of the Secretary-General', 2, UN Doc. E/CN.4/1197/41 (1997) (explaining the importance of national institutions in the promotion and protection of human rights).

[57] For NHRIs that have a constitutional foundation, see, for example, the South African Human Rights Commission, http://www.sahrc.org.za/sahrc_cms/publish/cat_index_26.shtml (last visited 17 June 2009); The Commission on Human Rights and Administrative Justice, Ghana, http://www.chrajghana.org/index?articleId=0001. (last visited 18 June 2009). For NHRIs created on the basis of legislation passed by the national Parliament, see, for example, the National Human Rights Commission, India, http://nhrc.nic.in/ (last visited 20 June 2009); the Human Rights Commission of Malaysia, http://www.suhakam.org.my/en/index.asp. (last visited 19 June 2009). For an example of a NHRI created on the basis of a presidential decree, see the Human Rights Commission of the Maldives, http://www.hrcm.org.mv/ (last visited 18 June 2009) For a detailed analysis of the powers and functions of NHRIs, see C. Raj

NHRIs also determines their power and functions, as well as their institutional legitimacy, functional independence, and financial autonomy. The protection and promotion of human rights are clearly important functions of the state. While fundamental rights are generally couched in the language of negative rights against the state, the state apparatus ought to function in an active manner that protects the rights and freedoms of its people. In fact, the important wings of the government—the legislature, executive, and judiciary— function with the aim of ensuring the rights and freedoms of people. But there is something fundamental and basic about NHRIs that is different from the state and its aforementioned instrumentalities. Unlike other institutions, which are vested with the task of governing a country (legislature and executive) and the administration of justice (judiciary), the exclusive mandate of NHRIs is to protect and promote human rights. While various functions of other institutions can ensure the protection and promotion of human rights, this is the core mission and fundamental purpose of NHRIs. However, performance assessments of NHRIs indicate that they tend to become another arm of the state apparatus, producing less accessible bureaucratic styles of responding to human rights violations.[58] To distinguish themselves from the state, NHRIs must embrace their founding mission to ensure that human rights become the focal point of governance and development agendas of a country; that all institutions of the government conduct their affairs in conformity to domestic and international human rights norms and constitutional obligations; and that human rights are inculcated in the civic and political culture of a society.

---

Kumar, 'National Human Rights Institutions: Good Governance Perspectives on Institutionalization of Human Rights', 19 *Am. U. Int'l L. Rev.* 259 (2003).

[58] See International Council on Human Rights Policy (ICHRP), Performance & Legitimacy: National Human Rights Institutions (2004), available at http://www.ichrp.org/paper_files/102_p_01.pdf; see also ICHRP, Assessing the Effectiveness of National Human Rights Institutions (2005), available at http://www.ichrp.org/paper_files/125_p_01.pdf (last visited 22 May 2011).

## India's National Human Rights Commission

The National Human Rights Commission (NHRC) in India was established by the 1993 Protection of Human Rights Act with an exclusive mandate for the protection and promotion of human rights.[59] The NHRC was established in order to provide an institutional framework for protecting human rights so as to create an independent body whose task is legislatively mandated to protect and promote human rights.[60] During the last fifteen years, the NHRC has developed an international reputation and domestic credibility for raising human rights issues in India and advocating the protection of the rights of the people. But when it comes to enforcement of human rights, there are still huge institutional challenges that the NHRC needs to confront. In the eighteen years since the establishment of the NHRC, more than fifteen states in India have established their own State Human Rights Commissions (SHRCs).[61] Now is a good time not only to examine the functioning and effectiveness of NHRC and SHRCs in India, but also to identify and work towards confronting the central human rights challenges of India's future. Human rights is a powerful discourse that immediately creates unparalleled social expectations and invites equally powerful civil society scrutiny from national and international actors. It is important that Human Rights Commissions (HRCs) succeed in their efforts to promote and protect human rights. The legitimacy and credibility of human rights commissions rest on their ability to address the human rights problems in a society.

[59] Charles Norchi, 'The National Human Rights Commission of India as a Value-Creating Institution', in John D. Montgomery (ed.), *Human Rights: Positive Policies in Asia and the Pacific Rim* 113, 127 (1998) (Hollis, NH: Hollis Publishing) (detailing the positive aspects of India's NHRC and its effectiveness in community decisions).

[60] See South Asia Human Rights Documentation Centre, Judgment Reserved: The Case of the National Human Rights Commission of India (2001) (providing a working assessment of the Indian NHRC).

[61] M.K. Sinha, 'Role of the National Human Rights Commission of India in Protection of Human Rights', available at http://www.rwi.lu.se/pdf/seminar/manoj05.pdf (last visited 19 June 2009).

## Securing Human Rights Accountability

HRCs[62] are relatively new and innovative institutions born out of initiatives by the United Nations[63] to ensure domestic protection of human rights. The fact that international human rights law has moved towards national constitutionalization of human rights has strongly shaped the development of HRCs in numerous jurisdictions. HRCs perform a variety of functions, including investigating alleged human rights violations; conducting public inquiries; exercising advisory jurisdiction; enforcing human rights in prisons and other custodial institutions; providing advice and assistance to governments; promoting human rights education and awareness; promoting interaction, exchange, and better coordination among other NHRIs[64] in the region and worldwide; promoting interaction and exchange with NGOs; and publishing annual reports.[65] While there is a high degree of consensus on what ought to be the functions of HRCs, the actual performance of the commissions and their institutional effectiveness vary significantly from country to country.[66]

[62] See Office of the High Commissioner for Human Rights, Fact Sheet No. 19: National Institution for the Protection and Promotion of Human Rights, available at http://www.unhchr.ch/html/menu6/2/fs19.htm (last visited 22 May 2011) (indicating the need to create national institutions for promoting human rights to assist the United Nations in effectively implementing its goals in this area).

[63] UN Sec-Gen Report on National Institutions, note 56, p. 2 (noting the importance of national institutions in the promotion and protection of human rights).

[64] See Reif, 'Building Democratic Institutions'.

[65] For a critical appraisal of human rights commissions, see Kumar, 'Corruption, Development and Good Governance', pp. 283–4. See also C. Raj Kumar, 'Role and Contribution of National Human Rights Commissions in Protecting National and International Human Rights Norms in the National Context', 47 *Indian J. Pub. Admin.* 222, 225 (2001) (outlining the functions and role of NHRIs).

[66] See Brian Burdekin, 'Human Rights Commissions', in Kamal Hossain et al. (eds), *Human Rights Commissions and Ombudsman Offices: National Experiences Throughout the World* 801, 807–8 (2000) (London: Klumer Law International)

Some HRCs have acquired national legitimacy and an international reputation for having worked towards the protection and promotion of human rights in an impartial and independent manner, while some others, in the method of their creation and the exercise of regular functions, demonstrate the state apparatus' aim to legitimize numerous actions that are not in harmony with human rights. In this regard, the subject of human rights commissions has also invited much academic attention in recent years in addition to assessments by UN bodies, and civil society scrutiny by virtue of numerous international NGOs conducting independent assessments of the work of HRCs.[67]

One of the important aspects to be noted in connection with HRCs and their attempts to secure human rights accountability is that they are not the panacea for all human rights problems that affect a society.[68] HRCs tend to be effective only under a given set of circumstances, but most importantly, much will depend upon the level of funding, functional independence and institutional autonomy that is guaranteed to the HRC.[69] Further, the composition of the HRC will matter to a large extent in determining the kind of focus and activism that it will promote. Given these constraints, HRCs are important institutional approaches that can ensure the protection and promotion of human rights.[70]

The effectiveness of HRCs does not directly depend upon the pre-existing human rights structure in any society. What is important to understand is how a particular human rights commission situates itself in a society and is able to confront the human rights issues that come before it. There are various ways by which states ensure human rights accountability. Traditional approaches to human rights

(mentioning the advantages of developing national institutions based on human rights instruments).

[67] See C. Raj Kumar, 'Developing a Human Rights Culture in Hong Kong: Creating a Framework for Establishing an Independent Human Rights Commission', 11 *Tulsa J. Comp. & Int'l L.* 407, 426 (2004).

[68] Ibid.

[69] Ibid.

[70] Ibid.

protection and promotion have tended to focus on constitutional judicial review, human rights provisions in the constitution or other legislations, and the interpretation of these laws by the courts of the particular jurisdiction. Such mechanisms directly ensure the enforceability of human rights through the directions of courts.[71] However, this method of ensuring human rights accountability is not without its weaknesses. Since the courts in most jurisdictions are inundated with civil, criminal, constitutional, commercial, corporate, and other types of cases that come before them, direct focus on human rights issues and cases tends to be weak.[72] This creates a situation where human rights cases also have to be clubbed under administrative law or some other public law issue for them to receive the right kind of attention from the courts. Moreover, the elaborate legal processes and the procedures involved in court cases tend to complicate human rights issues in a court environment. Human rights issues need to be directly and seriously confronted by a body that is exclusively mandated to perform such a task. It was this realization that resulted in international opinion moving towards the formation of HRCs. It must, however, be clarified that HRCs are most effective when their tasks are adequately supported and supplemented by other legal, judicial, and institutional mechanisms that ensure the accountability of the government. They cannot work in isolation from courts due to their quasi-judicial nature and soft power. And so it is important that their functioning is supplemented by an efficient system of government institutions.

## Imparting Human Rights Education

A culture of human rights[73] ought to be promoted through human rights education, which is especially important in India, given that

[71] See Harold Hongju Koh, 'How is International Human Rights Law Enforced?' 74 *Ind. L.J.* 1397, 1408–16 (1999) (discussing how states, non-governmental organizations, and individuals all play a role in enforcing international human rights).

[72] Kumar, 'Developing a Human Rights Culture in Hong Kong', p. 426.

[73] See Jose Ayala Lasso, 'A Culture of Human Rights', 34(4) UN Chronicle (1997), available at http://findarticles.com/p/articles/mi_m1309/is_n4_v34/ai_20518046/ (last visited 22 May 2011).

the society is witness to numerous human rights violations and abuse of powers, and that the ability of the people to fight these injustices is limited. Awareness relating to rights is very important for empowering the Indian people to seek good governance policies from the government. The strategy for inculcating a human rights culture among the people of India needs to be based upon a number of factors: social, legal, political, judicial, and institutional.

Human rights education has been a focal point of UN activities in creating the UN Decade for Human Rights Education (1995–2004) in December 1994. In this process, the UN General Assembly (UNGA) defined human rights education as 'a life-long process by which people at all levels of development and in all strata of society learn respect for the dignity of others and the means and methods of ensuring that respect in all societies.'[74] The international significance of this is demonstrated by the fact that the UNGA sought the support of the international community and civil society between 1995 and 2004 in its efforts to promote a culture of human rights worldwide through human rights education and training. The NHRC has taken several significant steps in promoting this in India. Recently, it has proposed to include lessons on human rights in the curriculum for schools and colleges. The objective of this is to make common citizens understand what human rights are, right from the school level.

## Role of Academia

Human rights education in India needs to go beyond the frontiers of academic learning or, for that matter, professional pursuit. Human rights education should aim to forge social transformation and promote a worldview based on the respect for the rights and freedoms of humanity.[75] Thus, the need for empowering the people of India

[74] See Office of the High Commissioner for Human Rights (OHCHR), 'Human Rights Education: Lessons for Life' (November 1998), available at http://www2. ohchr.org/english/about/publications/docs/50kit4.htm (last visited 22 May 2011).

[75] C. Raj Kumar, 'Corruption, Development and Good Governance: Challenges for Promoting Access to Justice in Asia', 16 *Mich. St. J. Int'l L* 475, 556 (2008).

cannot be better achieved than by developing varied components of human rights education. A sustained development of human rights education in India can result in the promotion of a culture of human rights.[76] Understanding the impact of corruption on promoting and protecting human rights is part of the responsibility of academia. How human rights education can be promoted and to what extent the promotion of human rights education can actually facilitate the development of a human rights culture needs to be seriously examined.[77]

The starting point can be to develop knowledge and capacity building in imparting greater awareness of the Constitution of India and the working of HRCs. In the process of promoting a culture of human rights, human rights education can also ignite human rights activism. In recent years, in the context of formulating a legal and institutional framework for implementing the right to information, India has witnessed a unique type of civil society activism that seeks to promote transparency and accountability of the government. Human rights activism is, thus, another facet of accountability-seeking endeavours.[78]

## Role of Business Houses

The impact of globalization on the Indian economy and politics is profound. In this scenario, multinational corporations and business enterprises need to assume human rights obligations that were hitherto not recognized by them.[79] Business houses need to recognize that corporate social responsibility demands that their working and functions are in accordance with both domestic and international human rights frameworks. Business houses thus have a duty to share responsibilities in promoting human rights education. They should support the activities of educational institutions, NGOs,

---

[76] Ibid., p. 557.
[77] Ibid.
[78] Ibid.
[79] Ibid.

and civil society organizations with a view to promoting human rights education.[80]

The culture of human rights that we seek to achieve in India necessitates a rights education that critically examines the policies that affect human rights, and aims to shape the responses of human rights commissions and civil society, with the goal of enforcing accountability and good governance.[81]

## Expanding the Mandate of the NHRC

The challenge of protecting a number of human rights in India is connected to ensuring corruption-free governance. It is in this context that it is proposed that the NHRC should play a definitive and limited role in fighting corruption, particularly when acts of corruption are either responsible for human rights violations or for further exacerbating the degree of such violations. It is useful to refer to the legal framework outlined in the Protection of Human Rights Act, 1993, for determining the extent to which the NHRC can be involved in the fight against corruption so as to protect human rights. Section 12 of the Protection of Human Rights Act enumerates the functions of the Commission. The following provisions need to be examined:

The Commission shall perform all or any of the following functions, namely (a) inquire, *suo motu* or on a petition presented to it by a victim or any person on his behalf, into complaint of (i) violation of human rights or abetment thereof or (ii) negligence in the prevention of such violation, by a public servant...

(b) review the safeguards provided by or under the Constitution or any law for the time being in force for the protection of human rights and recommend measures for their effective implementation...

Section 12 of the act, thus, gives enough flexibility for the NHRC to determine what steps it ought to take for the protection and promotion

[80] Ibid.
[81] Ibid.

of human rights. Section 2(1)(d) of the act defines human rights: "'human rights" means the rights relating to life, liberty, equality and dignity of the individual guaranteed by the Constitution or embodied in the International Covenants and enforceable by courts in India.' Section 12 of the act has provided for the NHRC to take cognizance of a complaint relating to human rights if it is satisfied that there was negligence in the prevention of a human rights violation by a public servant. This negligence could have been due to corruption or other forms of illegal actions by public servants. Thus, we see that examining issues of corruption can legally come within the jurisdiction of the NHRC as it exists.

In May 2006, the NHRC organized a conference on 'Effects of Corruption on Good Governance and Human Rights' in New Delhi.[82] This was the first time the Indian NHRC examined the issue of corruption from a human rights standpoint.[83] The gravity of human rights violations resulting from corrupt practices is no less than that of custodial violence or any other form of violations of civil, political, economic, social, and cultural rights. The most fundamental question the conference posed that still needs to be addressed is: How can the NHRC operationalize the right to corruption-free governance with a view to protecting and promoting human rights in general?[84]

Human rights have traditionally been understood to be rights relating to life, liberty, equality, and dignity, which have been recognized in the definition of human rights in the Protection of Human Rights Act.[85] The preamble to The Right to Information Act, 2005, notes the specific issue of corruption: '...democracy requires an informed citizen and transparency of information which are vital to its functioning and also to contain corruption and to hold governments

---

[82] See C. Raj Kumar, 'Corruption as Human Rights Violation', *The Hindu*, 30 May 2006, available at http://www.hindu.com/2006/05/30/stories/2006053005351000.htm (last visited June 18, 2009)

[83] Ibid.

[84] Ibid.

[85] Protection of Human Rights Act 1993, §2(d).

and their instrumentalities accountable to the governed...'[86] Further, human rights in India have also been given a strong constitutional foundation and have developed through innovative judicial interventions over more than six decades.

The good governance agenda includes protection and promotion of human rights and rule of law. Neither function will be fully accomplished if corruption is rampant in government.[87] It is important that institutions like the NHRC provide a framework to take up cases of corrupt acts of individuals and institutions that result in human rights violations.[88] The NHRC should attempt to understand the implications of corruption for human rights not only from a theoretical perspective but also from a practical standpoint.[89] It is useful to examine how many of the various cases that come before the NHRC are due to some act of bribery or other forms of corruption.[90] Further, the NHRC's research division may consider supporting studies on the human rights consequences of corruption as well as how far the human rights approach can help in ensuring corruption-free governance.[91]

One of the important developments due to the institutionalization of human rights in India—through the setting up of the NHRC and the SHRCs—is that they have come to occupy a certain democratic space within the domestic political spectrum and discourse. However, the existence of democratic institutions does not necessarily mean that human rights violations do not occur or that their incidence is reduced.[92] What it means is that there are institutional mechanisms available for victims to seek justice. The effectiveness of these institutions in India is still a matter of opinion but, by and large, the NHRC has come to acquire a certain reputation because of its impartiality

[86] Preamble, The Right to Information Act 2005, available at http://www.cgg.gov.in/images/RTIAct2005CGGManual.doc.
[87] Kumar, 'Corruption as Human Rights Violation'.
[88] Ibid.
[89] Ibid.
[90] Ibid.
[91] Ibid.
[92] Ibid.

and independence. Of course, its powers are limited and its opinions on human rights issues are only recommendations, though they carry a lot of legitimacy and persuasiveness because of the composition of the Commission.[93]

The law enforcement agencies that are engaged in the task of anti-corruption work (such as the Central Vigilance Commission [CVC], the Central Bureau of Investigation [CBI], and the Enforcement Directorate [ED], etc.) would be truly empowered if institutions like the NHRC take cognizance of cases relating to corruption when it involves a human rights issue.[94] This will bring the corruption problem to the centre of the governance paradigm in India as it will be considered a human rights violation and the consequences of such actions will be significant. As discussed earlier, the recognition of corruption as a human rights issue does not warrant any amendment to the Protection of Human Rights Act, 1993. The definition of 'human rights' given in Section 2 and the functions of the NHRC given in Section 12 are wide enough to include corruption as a violation of human rights.[95]

## Rights-based Approach

In this regard, it is encouraging to note that the NHRC has been developing rights-based approaches to development in the areas of population stabilization and combating HIV. The NHRC can also engage with the leading anti-corruption agencies, which, most of the time, are on the 'other side' when it comes to its work relating to human rights. However, this institutional engagement must be a facet of good governance. For, if the NHRC has to take a proactive role in promoting good governance policies, it has to understand the problem of corruption from a criminal law enforcement perspective as well.

[93] Ibid.
[94] Ibid.
[95] Ibid.

Having recognized that corruption affects human rights and the rule of law, it is important for the NHRC to develop the right to corruption-free governance through a number of rights-based strategies in India. As noted earlier, rights-based approaches to governance are those strategies that rest on the conceptual foundation that social and economic goals do not remain mere policy objectives, but get transformed into rights that are vested with the citizenry, thereby increasing incentives for public vigilance.

While making a case for the NHRC in India to deal with issues relating to corruption, it is useful to note that there are other national human rights institutions which have embarked successfully upon the responsibility of dealing with corruption. The Fiji Human Rights Commission has recognized good governance to be an integral part of human rights protection.[96] It has defined good governance to be the process through which public institutions conduct public affairs, manage public resources, and guarantee the realization of human rights.[97]

To demonstrate the linkages between human rights and corruption, the Kenya National Commission on Human Rights has developed a framework by which its citizens are able to appreciate the impact of corruption on the ordinary lives of people.[98] It has also published a two-volume report on the topic titled 'Living Large: Counting the Cost of Official Extravagance in Kenya.'[99] The commission's website states: 'The publications chronicle wasteful use of public resources by public officers and the aim is to stir reform in the public sector by

[96] Maina Kiai, 'The Role of National Human Rights Institutions in Combating Corruption', 2, Int'l Council on Human Rights Policy Review Meeting, Geneva (28–9, July 2007), available at http://www.ichrp.org/files/papers/133/131_-_Maina_Kiai_-_2007.pdf (last visited 22 June 2011).

[97] Ibid.

[98] Ibid.

[99] Kenya Nat'l Comm'n on Human Rights, 'Living Large: Counting the Cost of Official Extravagance in Kenya' (2006), available at http://www.knchr.org/dmdocuments/LivingLarge.pdf (last visited 20 May 2011).

discouraging such waste and to empower citizens to demand value for their money.'[100]

Although the legislation that established the NHRC in India may not have an express mandate for fighting corruption, given the extent of human rights violations that occur due to it, there is a need for the NHRC to interpret its role and functions with regard to the effect of corruption on upholding human rights.

The Commission on Human Rights and Administrative Justice (CHRAJ) of Ghana was established in October 1993, combining three institutions under one umbrella, a human rights institution, the Ombudsman and an Anti-corruption Agency.[101] Under Act 456, the CHRAJ, along with other powers and functions, is empowered to investigate complaints of violations of fundamental rights and freedoms, injustice, corruption, abuse of power, and unfair treatment of any person by a public officer in the exercise of his official duties; to investigate all instances of alleged or suspected corruption and the misappropriation of moneys by officials; and to take appropriate steps, including reports resulting from such investigations to the Attorney-General and the Auditor General.[102] These powers empower the CHRAJ to deal with corruption in Ghana as it is widely recognized as a major cause for many human rights violations.[103]

---

[100] Kenya National Commission on Human Rights, KNCHR Publications, available at http://www.knchr.org/index.php?option=com_contentandtask=viewandid=73andItemid=85 (last visited 15 June 2009).

[101] See Anna Bossman, 'Promoting and Protecting Human Rights, Ensuring Administrative Justice and Fighting Corruption in Ghana' (2007), available at http://www.thecommonwealth.org/Shared_ASP_Files/UploadedFiles/783FC49E-D904-4AC4-BD55-785E4EF00E0C_GHANA.pdf (last visited 30 May 2009).

[102] Ibid.

[103] Anna Bossman, 'The Anti-corruption Mandate of Ghana's Commission on Human Rights and Administrative Justice', UN Conference on Anti-corruption Measures, Good Governance and Human Rights, Warsaw (8–9 November 2006), available at http://www2.ohchr.org/english/issues/development/governance/docs/Bossman.pdf (last visited 20 May 2011).

It is useful to refer to developments in the international human rights arena that can provide a framework for responding to human rights violations that take place due to corruption. In December 1998, the Committee on Economic, Social and Cultural Rights (CESCR) adopted General Comment 10,[104] which deals with the role of NHRIs in the protection of ESCRs.[105] The CESCR, addressing the issue of the progressive and full realization of the International Covenant on Economic, Social and Cultural Rights (ICESCR), recognized that one of the ways this can be achieved is by galvanizing the work of NHRIs. General Comment 10 states that it is essential that full attention is given to Economic, Social and Cultural Rights (ESCRs) in all of the relevant activities of NHRIs.[106] Such activities were identified as including:

(a) the promotion of educational and informational programmes designed to enhance awareness and understanding of economic, social and cultural rights both within the population at large and among particular groups such as the public service, the judiciary, the private sector and the labour movement;

(b) the scrutinizing of existing laws and administrative acts, as well as draft bills and other proposals, to ensure that they are consistent with the requirements of the ICESCR;

(c) the provision of technical advice, or by undertaking surveys in relation to economic, social and cultural rights, including when requested by public authorities or other appropriate agencies;

(d) the identification of benchmarks at the national level against which the realization of ICESCR obligations can be measured;

(e) conducting research and inquiries designed to ascertain the extent to which particular economic, social and cultural rights are being realized,

[104] Committee on Economic Social and Cultural Rights (CESCR), General Comment No. 10, 'The Role of National Human Rights Institutions in the Protection of Economic, Social and Cultural Rights', UN Doc. E/C.12/1998/25 (14 December 1998), available at http://www.escr-net.org/resources_more/resources_more_show.htm?doc_id=425231 (last visited 22 May 2011).

[105] Ibid.

[106] Ibid.

either within the country as a whole or in areas in relation to communities that are particularly vulnerable;

(f) monitoring compliance with specific rights and providing reports to the public authorities and civil society; and

(g) examining complaints alleging violations of applicable economic, social and cultural rights standards within the state.[107]

Significantly, the CESCR also called upon states parties to the ICESCR to ensure that the mandates accorded to all NHRIs are expanded, if necessary, so that appropriate attention is given to ESCRs.[108] It is in this context that NHRIs are in a position to take cognizance of corruption as a major impediment to the implementation of ESCRs. The problem of corruption with regard to the enforcement of ESCRs needs to be addressed by NHRIs not only as a part of their domestic human rights agenda, but also in response to the international human rights movement. The NHRIs themselves have started to take initiatives to recognize the importance of ESCRs in their work.

A number of important issues relating to the implementation of ESCRs by NHRIs were discussed in an International Round Table on National Institutions Implementing Economic, Social and Cultural Rights that was held in New Delhi in December 2005.[109] While the focus of the New Delhi Round Table was on the implementation of

---

[107] Ibid. p. 3.

[108] Ibid. p. 4. For a comprehensive article on the incorporation of international human rights in a few selected constitutions, see Yash P. Ghai, 'Universalism and Relativism: Human Rights as a Framework for Negotiating Interethnic Claims', 21 *Cardozo L. Rev.* 1095 (2000).

[109] The Round Table was a collaborative venture of the National Human Rights Commission of India and the Office of the United Nations High Commissioner for Human Rights (OHCHR). The Round Table was attended by representatives of twenty-four NHRIs from Afghanistan, Albania, Argentina, Burkina Faso, Costa Rica, the Democratic Republic of the Congo, Fiji, Ghana, India, Ireland, Jordan, Kenya, Kyrgyzstan, Mexico, Mongolia, Morocco, Nepal, New Zealand, the Republic of Korea, Senegal, South Africa, Sri Lanka, Thailand, and Uganda. For more information, see The New Delhi Concluding Statement (29 November–1 December 2005), available at http://www.nhri.net/pdf/RT_ New_Delhi_Conclusions_011205.pdf (last visited 22 May 2011).

ESCRs in the domestic context, a plan of action was formulated that would help the NHRIs to deal with ESCRs.[110]

The fundamental problem with the NHRIs is with respect to the enforcement of human rights, which is directly related to their institutional status and powers that are granted under the law or policy that establishes these institutions. This institutional limitation affects the NHRIs in ensuring the protection and promotion of CPRs, and is likely to have more effects in relation to ESCRs. One of the ways by which the NHRIs can attempt to address this issue is to emphasize the indivisibility and interdependence of CPRs and ESCRs, and the fact that CPRs cannot be meaningfully realized without due regard to the protection and promotion of ESCRs. Corruption affects the enforcement of both CPRs and ESCRs, and becomes an important factor that undermines the effectiveness of NHRCs in fulfilling their mandate to promote and protect human rights.[111]

The human rights discourse has come to accept that ESCRs are as important as CPRs—that human rights are universal, indivisible, and interdependent. However, the recognition of ESCRs as the equal of CPRs does not ensure that the enforcement mechanism is in place for the protection, promotion, and fulfillment of all these human rights. Article 2 of the ICESCR describes both, the type of legal obligations that arises under the Covenant, and the necessary implementation mechanisms for states parties.[112] States are required to take steps to make the greatest use possible of their available resources to ensure that the rights identified in the ICESCR are progressively realized.[113]

If corruption is identified as an obstacle to the promotion and protection of any of the rights in the ICESCR, it becomes necessary

[110] Ibid. p. 5.

[111] See generally C. Raj Kumar, 'National Human Rights Institutions: Good Governance Perspectives on Institutionalization of Human Rights', 19 *A.m. U. Int'l L. Rev.* 259 (2003).

[112] For a comprehensive analysis of this relationship in the context of Canada, see Ontario Human Rights Commission, 'Human Rights Commissions and Economic and Social Rights', available at http://www.ohrc.on.ca/en/resources/discussion_consultation/EconomicSocialRights/pdf (last visited 29 June 2009).

[113] Ibid.

for the NHRC to take the necessary steps to address it. As noted by the Limburg Principles on the Implementation of the International Covenant on Economic, Social and Cultural Rights, 'States parties shall use all appropriate means, including legislative, administrative, judicial, economic, social and educational measures, consistent with the nature of the rights in order to fulfill their obligations under the Covenant.'[114] Similarly, the Maastricht Guidelines on Violations of Economic, Social and Cultural Rights note:

Like civil and political rights, economic, social and cultural rights impose three different types of obligations on States: the obligations to respect, protect and fulfill. Failure to perform any one of these three obligations constitutes a violation of such rights. The obligation to respect requires States to refrain from interfering with the enjoyment of economic, social and cultural rights. ... The obligation to protect requires States to prevent violations of such rights by third parties. ... The obligation to fulfill requires States to take appropriate legislative, administrative, budgetary, judicial and other measures towards the full realization of such rights.[115]

A conceptual basis is essential for the NHRC in India to formulate various effective anti-corruption measures. Its role in protecting human rights by evolving rights-based approaches to development will help in eliminating corruption and promoting integrity and good governance in the following specific ways:

## Corruption-free Constitutional Governance

The recognition of the right to corruption-free governance by the NHRC has the potential to bring the problem of corruption to the forefront of the political discourse. This will ensure that the state

[114] See 'The Limburg Principles on the Implementation of the International Covenant on Economic, Social and Cultural Rights', UN Doc. E/CN.4/1987/17/Annex (8 January 1987), reprinted in 'The Limburg Principles on the Implementation of the International Covenant on Economic, Social and Cultural Rights', 9 *Hum. Rts. Q.* 122 (1987).

[115] See 'The Maastricht Guidelines on Violations of Economic, Social and Cultural Rights', 20 *Hum. Rts. Q.* 691, 693–4 (1998).

and all its instrumentalities act in accordance with the Constitution and do not engage in any form of corrupt actions that will violate the fundamental rights of the Indian citizenry.[116] This would require governance to be based upon the underlying ideals, goals, objectives, aspirations, and values of the Constitution, which have been undermined by corruption. All individuals and institutions within the government would be expected to take the necessary steps to fulfil this fundamental right.[117]

## Empowering the Judiciary and other Institutions

The recognition of the right to corruption-free governance will quickly empower the judiciary to bring forward the integration of the anti-corruption initiatives and the human rights approach. Both these approaches are essentially about increasing the legitimacy of the state and ensuring accountability of the administration.[118] The judiciary is best suited to maintain this role as it has attempted in the past to create greater transparency and infuse institutional autonomy and independence in investigative agencies engaged in anti-corruption work. With the development of such a human right by the NHRC, the judiciary is in a far better position to develop jurisprudence relating to good governance.[119]

## Galvanizing Social Consciousness

The development of the human right to corruption-free governance will help in galvanizing social consciousness.[120] It is necessary for the NHRC to garner the support of the citizens, as it is their apathy and indifference to abuse of power that has resulted in corruption becoming institutionalized in India.[121] Political morality cannot be brought

[116] Kumar, 'Corruption, Development and Good Governance', p. 551.
[117] Ibid.
[118] Ibid., p. 552.
[119] Ibid.
[120] Ibid.
[121] Ibid.

about without the development of individual morality. This particular right can help in creating greater support for corruption-free governance and also result in the citizens valuing integrity and rectitude as important criteria for electing their representatives. At the same time, citizens will feel a greater sense of obligation to report corrupt activity.[122] This requires a participatory and bottom–up approach.

## Revamping the Mandate of the NHRC

There is a need for the NHRC to revamp its mandate in light of the massive institutionalized corruption that has not left any institution in India untouched.[123] The fact of the matter is that all human rights are violated due to corruption. The Protection of Human Rights Act, 1993, in the first paragraph notes that it is '[a]n Act to provide for the constitution of a National Human Rights Commission... for better protection of Human Rights and for matters connected therewith or incidental thereto.'

The NHRC must ensure that its investigations make due note of the fact that corruption is the root cause of potential violations of human rights. In this regard, the NHRC may have to work in cooperation with anti-corruption agencies like the Central Vigilance Commission. The purpose of the NHRC's new initiatives should be to ensure the protection of human rights and promotion of corruption-free administration as a *sine qua non* for good governance.

The need for promoting transparency and accountability has been noted as an important requirement for corruption-free governance. The Indian experience has demonstrated that the recognition of the right to information in India is an important step in ensuring corruption-free service.

[122] Ibid.

[123] See Norchi, 'The National Human Rights Commission of India as a Value-creating Institution', p. 127 (detailing the positive aspects of India's NHRC and its effectiveness in community decisions). See also South Asia Human Rights Documentation Centre, 'Judgment Reserved: The Case of the National Human Rights Commission of India' (2001) (providing a working assessment of the Indian NHRC).

# The Way Forward

The NHRC ought to be engaged in efforts to fight corruption with a view to strengthening the legal and institutional framework for protecting human rights. The following are some specific aspects of institutional initiatives that need to be taken by the NHRC for anti-corruption efforts to become part of its human rights agenda.

## Anti-corruption Efforts as Part of Human Rights Protection

The NHRC has to recognize internally that there are a number of human rights violations that take place in India due to institutionalized corruption across various law enforcement agencies, especially recognizing the ineffectiveness of the criminal justice system in dealing with corruption. There are a number of provisions in the Protection of Human Rights Act, 1993, that sufficiently empower the NHRC to recognize the problem of corruption as a violation of human rights. This recognition by the NHRC will go a long way in providing a policy framework for all bodies working within the NHRC, including the research, law and investigative divisions that are engaged in the promotion and protection of human rights.

## Investigation of Human Rights Violations

The investigative division of the NHRC, which examines allegations of human rights violations committed by police and other law enforcement machinery, ought to examine the issue of corruption as the cause of such violations. Such an investigation ought to take place independent of any complaint that has been lodged or otherwise of a possible act of corruption committed by the police or other law enforcement machinery. The nature of corruption, like human rights violations, is such that the victims face threats and feel too insecure to disclose the names of the perpetrators for fear of reprisal. The investigation of human rights violations should include, in a substantial manner, investigation into acts of corruption that have taken place, if any. The investigation should also examine the role of corruption in obstructing the investigation of human rights violations.

## Cases Decided by NHRC on Human Rights Violations

The NHRC ought to bear in mind the inextricable connection between human rights violations and corruption leading to abuse of power in the Indian context. Given this nexus, it will become essential for NHRC to seek the help and assistance of anti-corruption bodies and other investigative agencies such as the Central Vigilance Commission (CVC) and the CBI in investigating matters relating to corruption and its impact on human rights. Given the lack of independence of some of these institutions, in these joint investigative efforts among the CVC, CBI, and the Investigative Division of the NHRC, it is essential for NHRC to closely monitor the investigative process.

## Research on Corruption and its Impact on Human Rights

The NHRC should also sponsor and conduct a number of theoretical and empirical studies relating to corruption and its impact on the promotion and protection of human rights. The research division of the NHRC has a major responsibility to assume a leadership role in identifying researchers and practitioners in commissioning working papers for evolving policy documents on the question of corruption and human rights.

There is also a need to develop a comparative understanding of these issues and in particular to examine the practices of other national human rights institutions in dealing with acts of corruption. All this could provide useful guidance to the NHRC in formulating and evolving its own policies. The role of the research division of the NHRC becomes critical in this regard. It needs to examine the history of a number of human rights violations through empirical evidence that can provide a clearer understanding of the linkages between corruption and human rights.

Corruption is deeply pervasive in all aspects of governmental exercise of power. The NHRC is concerned with the promotion and protection of human rights. This role and function of the NHRC can be performed effectively only if corruption is reduced, if not eliminated. Thus, it becomes the duty and responsibility of the NHRC to take steps to fight corruption as a part of its core responsibility of promoting and protecting human rights. NHRCs are useful institutions and can make an immense contribution to the promotion and protection of human rights.[124]

However, at present, NHRCs suffer from not only structural problems and functional deficiencies, but also from a lack of adequate mechanisms for enforcement of human rights.[125] Mere institutionalization of human rights is not sufficient, unless it helps transform the governance agenda. In India, this transformation cannot happen without addressing corruption as the single most important factor that undermines governance and violates human rights. One should not confuse NHRCs with courts and other quasi-judicial institutions and other government bodies. The idea underlying the establishment of NHRCs is to ensure that they remain vigilant over those who hold and exercise powers so that their conduct conforms to national and international human rights norms. The work of NHRCs, therefore, must constantly evolve and focus on all those activities that result in the violation of human rights, whether in a direct or indirect manner. If NHRCs understand their proper role and are able to function freely, bearing in mind the objectives for which they were established, they will be able to fulfil social expectations of victims of human rights violations and society on account of corruption. At the same time, NHRCs should not compete for the democratic space that has

---

[124] See Audrey R. Chapman, 'A "Violations Approach" for Monitoring the International Covenant on Economic, Social and Cultural Rights', 18 *Hum. Rts. Q.* 23, 30 (1996) (concluding that the absence of national institutions committed to the protection of ESC rights presents challenges to protecting those rights).

[125] See Philip Eldridge, 'Emerging Roles of National Human Rights Institutions in Southeast Asia', 14 *Pacifica Rev.* 209, 215–21 (2002) (analysing the workings of NHRIs in the Philippines, Indonesia, Thailand, and Malaysia). See also Hum. Rts Watch, 'Government Human Rights Commissions in Africa, Protectors or Pretenders? Governing Human Rights Commission in Africa' (2001), available at http://www.hrw.org/reports/2001/africa/overview/summary.html (finding that the number of countries with NHRIs has increased is significantly between 1980 and 2000) (last visited 22 May 2011).

been hitherto within the province of the legislature, executive, and judiciary.

Since the human rights discourse is not only a public policy discourse, but also a social and political empowerment discourse, the NHRC's democratic space should maintain its independent functions in fulfilling the mandate to promote and protect human rights. The rationale for this space is to elevate the discussion of human rights, the right against corruption, and rights relating to development from policy guidelines to central political principles of any democratic society. NHRCs must become independent democratic institutions with the institutional capacity to link issues relating to human rights, corruption, development, and good governance.

## INSTITUTIONAL MEASURES: CENTRAL INFORMATION COMMISSION AND THE RIGHT TO INFORMATION

The recognition of the right to information and the establishment of the CIC are important milestones in India's efforts to promoting transparency and accountability in governance. The CIC provides for an institutional framework that will ensure transparency and is wholly engaged in the implementation of the right to information.

### Transparency in Governance through the Right to Information

The good governance approach of administering states should ideally focus on the principles of transparency and accountability.[126] It is important for decisions to be taken in a transparent manner and for decision-makers to be held accountable. This good governance form of accountability is broader than that of mere electoral accountability. While electing the ruled to office, democratic governance involves some form of accountability for ensuring respect for the rules,

---

[126] C. Raj Kumar, 'Corruption and Human Rights: Promoting Transparency in Governance and the Fundamental Right to Corruption-free Service in India', 17 Colum. *J. Asian L.* 31 (2003).

accountability of governance seeks to ensure that the people who are making decisions are involving the public in the process of making these decisions.[127] This is possible only when decisions are made in a transparent manner. Governmental decisions acquire legitimacy if the people's right to information is duly protected and they are in a position to enforce this right. In order to ensure a corruption-free society, it is necessary to empower the people so that they can resist the practices of official corruption. From the perspective of civil society activism, such resistance to corruption needs to start with the empowerment of the citizenry, and this is possible through the full development of the right to information. For democratic governance to be meaningful, it is necessary that 'citizens must have access to information about what their government is doing and how decisions have been reached.'[128]

The recent struggles to curb corruption in India at all levels of governmental decision-making have taken the form of efforts to promote transparency and enforce accountability by promoting the right to information at the state and central levels. It needs to be noted that the right to information is a powerful tool for formulating the right to corruption-free governance. The right to information is the first step in checking governmental corruption, as the people of India ought to be empowered by the availability of information on the decisions taken by the government that affect their lives. Commenting upon the relevance of the right to information for the control of corruption, Harsh Mander and Abha Joshi have observed that

... the right to information is expected to improve the quality of decision making by public authorities, in both policy and administrative matters, by removing unnecessary secrecy surrounding the decision-making process. ... The cumulative impact on control of corruption and the arbitrary exercise

---

[127] Ibid.

[128] Lotte E. Feinberg, 'Open Government and Freedom of Information: Fishbowl Accountability?' in Philip J. Cooper and Chester A. Newland (eds), *Handbook of Public Law and Administration* 376 (1997) (San Francisco: Jossey-Bass).

of power, of the availability of such information to the citizen, would be momentous.[129]

The constitutional foundation of the right to information rests on Part III of the Constitution of India, which deals with fundamental rights. Even though there is no specific right to information or, for that matter, right to freedom of the press as such in the Constitution, the right to information has been creatively interpreted and read into it by the judiciary.[130] The Constitution has a sound framework for protecting human rights in the form of the right to equal protection of laws and the right to equality before the law (Article 14), the right to freedom of speech and expression (Article 19[1][a]), and the right to life and liberty (Article 21). This is further supported by the right to constitutional remedies provided in Article 32, which is the right to approach the high courts and the Supreme Court through their writ jurisdiction for remedies in cases of violation of these rights.

The Right to Information movement initially started with the work of a grassroots mass-based organization known as the Mazdoor Kisan Shakti Sangathan ('Labour Farmer Strength Organization'; MKSS), in the state of Rajasthan. The origin of MKSS was so nondescript that it did not invite much attention. Members of the MKSS walked from village to village asking simple questions: Did the people know the amount of funds that were coming to their village for development? How was the money that came from different

---

[129] See generally Harsh Mander and Abha Joshi, 'The Movement for Right to Information in India: People's Power for the Control of Corruption', available at http://www.humanrightsinitiative.org/programs/ai/rti/india/articles/The%20Movement%20for%20RTI%20in%20India.pdf. (last visited 20 June 2009).

[130] See Granville Austin, *The Indian Constitution: Cornerstone of a Nation* (1966) (New Delhi: Oxford University Press); see also Granville Austin, *Working a Democratic Constitution: The Indian Experience* (1999) (New Delhi: Oxford University Press).

sources actually spent? Although these questions were simple, the poor and impoverished of India had never dared to ask.[131]

When this information was collected, the MKSS went to the Government Block Office, which is the authority that administers development funding in about a hundred villages, with a request to provide detailed information on development expenditure.[132] In response, they were told that there was no government rule that would allow villagers to demand such information and receive it.[133] This culminated in the MKSS launching a people's campaign in the state of Rajasthan. The aim of the campaign was to conduct numerous public hearings in which cases of corruption and misappropriation of public funds were shared with a lot of people.[134]

Aruna Roy of the MKSS has observed that the right to information in Rajasthan was aimed at ending the arbitrary use of power.[135] The MKSS campaign had focused on demanding transparency of official records, a social audit of government spending and a redressal machinery for people who had not been given their due.[136] The result of this powerful, mass-based, grass-roots civil society activism in the form of social struggle resulted in the state of Rajasthan passing a law on the right to information, as well as creating an environment in which corruption was tolerated less and accountability of the government officials was enforced.[137]

The MKSS movement to seek the right to information came about due to large-scale, rampant embezzlement of public funds. The

---

[131] Bunker Roy, 'The Power of Information: A Grassroots Organization in India Defeats Corruption', 2 D+C Development and Cooperation 28 (2002), available at http://www.inwent.org/E+Z/zeitschr/de202-11.htm (last visited 22 May 2011).

[132] Ibid.

[133] Ibid.

[134] Ibid.

[135] Kalpana Sharma, 'Right to Information Will Check Corruption', The Hindu (24 February 2002), available at http://www.hinduonnet.com/2002/02/24/stories/2002022400251200.htm. (last visited 18 June 2009).

[136] Ibid.

[137] Ibid.

consequences of these corrupt actions were 'non-employment of, or under-payment to, the local workforce, and non-existent or bad quality assets on the ground, which were meant for education, housing, or health facilities for the rural poor.'[138] The linkage between the human rights violations on account of institutionalized corruption and the lack of transparency and accountability[139] in governance led the MKSS to establish a 'connection between the manipulation of official records and denial of life opportunities to the rural poor.'[140]

This resulted in the movement to seek the right to access to official records as a part of the right to life and livelihood.[141] This civil society activism was followed by a nationwide movement to seek national legislation on freedom of information, inspired by the work of the MKSS in Rajasthan. The important links among lack of transparency, absence of accountability, and institutionalized corruption gave the social and political impetus to seek the formulation of the right to information.[142]

The relevance of the right to information[143] in India is much more than merely allowing the free flow of information from the

[138] Ibid.

[139] For further reading, see 'Improving Accountability in Panchayati Raj', *India Together*, January 2003, available at www.indiatogether.org/2003/jan/gov-karpri02.htm (last visited 18 June 2009) (adapting the Karnataka Working Group's 2002 Report on Decentralization). See also Prashant Bhushan, 'India: Approves Freedom of Information Law Approved: The Freedom of Information Bill 2002', FreedomInfo.org (December 2002), available at http://www.freedominfo.org/news/20021200.htm (last visited 18 June 2009); Neelabh Mishra, 'A Battle Half Won', Combat Law (February 2003), available at http://www.indiatogether.org/combatlaw/issue6/halfwon.htm (last visited 22 May 2011).

[140] Mishra, 'A Battle Half Won'.

[141] See sources cited in note 141.

[142] For further reading, see 'Improving Accountability in Panchayati Raj', *India Together*; and 'Reinventing Rural Governance', *India Together* (January 2003), available at http://www.indiatogether.org/2003/jan/gov-karpri01.htm (last visited 20 June 2009) (adapting the Karnataka Working Group's 2002 Report on Decentralization).

[143] Bela Bhatia and Jean Dreze, 'Freedom of Information is Key to Anti-corruption Campaign in Rural India', *Transparency Int'l Newsl.*, 1 September

government to the public. It is about people exercising their right to seek necessary information from the government so that it and its representatives are held accountable to the public. The right to information ensures that governmental decisions are made in a transparent manner and that the people are informed of decisions that affect them. Interestingly, the right to know, 'receive, and impart information has been recognized within the right to freedom of speech and expression'[144] has been read under Article 19 (1)(a) of the Constitution.[145] The right to information law has now been enacted in a few states in India, including Rajasthan, Madhya Pradesh, Maharashtra, Goa, Tamil Nadu, Karnataka, Delhi, and Andhra Pradesh.[146] The Freedom of Information Bill was passed by the Lok Sabha (the lower house of the Indian Parliament) on 3 December 2002 and by the Rajya Sabha (the upper house) on 16 December 2002.[147] Furthermore, seeking to ensure greater and more effective access to information, the Government of India resolved that the Freedom of Information Act of 2002 be made more progressive, participatory, and meaningful.[148] This was done after the proposals by the National Advisory Council suggested a number of changes. To facilitate these changes, the government decided to repeal the Freedom of Information Act, 2002, and adopted a new legislation, namely, The Right to Information Act, 2005 (Act No. 22 of 2005).[149] This was published in the Gazette of India (Extraordinary) Part II—Section I, on 21 June 2005, and the Act received the assent of the President on 15 June 2005.[150]

---

1998, available at http://www.transparency.org/content/download/8849/58609/file/tiq-september_1998.pdf (last visited 20 June 2009).

[144] *S.P. Gupta* v. *Union of India* AIR (1982) SC 149, 234. See also Secretary, Ministry of I&B, *Government of India* v. *Cricket Association of Bengal* (1995) 2 SCC 161.

[145] Mahendra P. Singh, *Constitution of India.*

[146] Bhushan, 'India: Approves Freedom of Information Law Approved'.

[147] Mishra, 'A Battle Half Won'.

[148] Shalu Nigam, *Right to Information Law and Practice* 155 (2006).

[149] Ibid.

[150] Ibid., p. 156.

The preamble to The Right to Information Act, 2005, notes:

An Act to provide for setting out the practical regime of right to information for citizens to secure access to information under the control of public authorities, in order to promote transparency and accountability in the working of every public authority, the constitution of a Central Information Commission and State Information Commissions and for matters connected herewith or incidental thereto.[151]

Noting the specific issue of corruption, the preamble to the Act states that 'democracy requires an informed citizen and transparency of information which are vital to its functioning and also to contain corruption and to hold governments and their instrumentalities accountable to the governed.'[152]

The Central Information Commission is constituted so as to ensure that its independence as an institutional mechanism to enforce the right to information is maintained. This Information Commission is created with powers similar to that of the Election Commission of India.

The CIC is an institutional mechanism that is designed to implement the right to information.[153] The relationship between the right to information and its ability to reduce corruption needs to be understood. Information Commissioner M.M. Ansari has noted:

Lack of transparency and accountability encourage the government officials to indulge in corrupt practices, which result in lower investments due to misuse or diversion of funds for private purposes. As a result, the government's social spending yields no worthwhile benefits, because for instance the teachers do not teach, doctors and nurses do not attend health centres,

---

[151] Preamble, Right to Information Act 2005. See also Nigam, *Right to Information Law and Practice.*

[152] Ibid.

[153] For a discussion on historical evolution of the Right to Information Act, see S.P. Sathe, *The Right to Information.*

ration card holders do not receive subsidized food grains and the promised jobs are not provided to the people.[154]

Such a situation obviously leads to a crisis in governance where the most fundamental institutions of governmental interaction with the people become ineffective and do not deliver the goods and services. What the Central Information Commission does is seek accountability and transparency in the functioning of the government so that the people are empowered to obtain answers, if not benefits, from the power holders. The enormous impact of such non-delivery of services to the citizens of India, particularly the poor and vulnerable, exacerbates impoverishment. As noted by M.M. Ansari, 'it perpetuates poverty and harms the poor. It creates an environment of distrust between the people and the government, which impinges on the development and jeopardize democratic'governance.'[155]

The right to information has been used successfully in a variety of areas.[156] The Commission has played an important role in the empowerment of the citizenry. Fighting corruption is one area where a lot of work needs to be done. The nature of corrupt transactions is such that the information concerning them may not be easily available. The CIC thus needs to assume a leadership role so that, with a view to promoting transparency, whatever information is available with government bodies, is obtained and made public. While the legal response to corruption needs to be strengthened, the information relating to transactions becomes vital for both the investigation and prosecution of cases relating to corruption. Abhijeet Singh has observed:

[154] M.M. Ansari, Information Comm'r (India), 'Impact of Right to Information on Development: A Perspective on India's Recent Experiences', 15, lecture delivered at UNESCO Headquarters, Paris (15 May 2008), available at http:// portal.unesco.org/ci/en/files/26828/12113837623A_perspective_on_India_ Recent_Experiences.pdf/A%2Bperspective%2Bon%2BIndia%2BRecent%2BEx periences.pdf. (last visited 20 June 2009).

[155] Ibid., p. 18.

[156] For an excellent analysis of the same, see Sathe, *The Right to Information*.

In the gathering of information relating to development works and detection of corruption therein, a powerful weapon is social audit. Social audit refers to collection of official data and comparing it with actual progress of work ... For instance a social auditor may take the progress report or measurement book for a development work and compare it with the on 'ground construction'[157], thus highlighting discrepancies, if any, between the official version and the actual fact.[158]

The issue of corruption ought to become one of the important focal elements of the working of the CIC. The Commission has been developing jurisprudence on a range of issues, including determining the scope of the Act as well as its powers and jurisdiction.[159] While these are important, the Commission has to develop broader expertise in dealing with corruption and in particular without seeking information related to the functioning of the government and the proper use of its resources.

---

[157] This is referring to ways to ensure that there is no disparity between accounts/numbers on paper, and actually on the ground, so to speak, which is how corruption usually occurs—requirements, numbers etc., are inflated on paper to get more money, yet this money does not find itself actually pumped into the actual work for which it is required. Here, the author is suggesting a way to overcome this problem.

[158] Abhijeet Singh, 'Corruption and Economic Development: Right to Information as a Remedy' (February 2006), available at http://ssrn.com/abstract=1011462 (last visited 22 May 2011).

[159] The decision of CIC in *Shri Subhash Chandra Agarwal v. Supreme Court of India*, Appeal No. CIC/WB/A/2008/00426, is particularly noteworthy in this regard. The CIC observed that 'The Supreme Court of India is an institution created by the Constitution and is, therefore, a Public Authority within the meaning of Section 2(h) of the Right to Information Act' and held in favour of disclosure of judges' assets. A single bench of Delhi High Court in the matter of *the Central Public Information Officer, Supreme Court of India v. Subhash Chandra Agarwal*, WP (C) 288/2009 upheld the decision of CIC. This was further confirmed by the full bench of Delhi High Court in *Secretary General, Supreme Court of India v. Subhash Chandra Agarwal* 166 (2010) DLT 305,

# 6

# The Way Forward: Establishing an Independent Commission against Corruption

## CREATING THE RIGHT POLITICAL ENVIRONMENT FOR COMBATING CORRUPTION

Fighting corruption has inevitably become the most urgent need for addressing all major challenges to governance in India. While a number of approaches have been attempted to fight corruption in India, none of them has been very effective so far. Given the complexities of the multi-layered police and other law enforcement agencies that are working in India, it is important to develop a more focused approach to combating corruption.[1] The proposal to establish an Independent Commission Against Corruption (ICAC) in India recognizes the inherent challenges of any institutional approach to seeking reforms in India, given the bottlenecks and obstacles for enforcement of the rule of law. A number of institutions entrusted with the responsibility of fighting corruption and ensuring probity in governance have not been successful.[2] Establishing an

[1] Moshe Maor, 'Feeling the Heat? Anti-corruption Mechanisms in Comparative Perspective', 12 *Governance* 1 (2004).
[2] Ibid.

ICAC in India will not be the panacea for all ills relating to corruption. There has to be a multi-pronged strategy to fight corruption, which will involve the legal framework, the institutional mechanism, the investigation and prosecution machinery, the public awareness and education strategies, and civil society empowerment approaches.[3] The fight against corruption will work only if all the above strategies are formulated bearing in mind that corruption is a serious problem of governance that violates human rights and undermines development.[4]

Transparency International in its *TI Source Book 2000* describes the necessary framework for a successful anti-corruption agency:

- Committed political backing at the highest levels of government;
- Adequate resources to undertake its mission;
- Political and operational independence to investigate even at the highest levels of government;
- Adequate powers of access to documentation and for the questioning of witnesses;
- 'User-friendly' laws (including the criminalization of 'illicit enrichment'); and
- Leadership which is seen as being of the highest integrity.[5]

The proposal to establish an ICAC in India needs to address each of the above institutional challenges so that the ICAC is duly empowered to fight corruption. It is useful to briefly discuss these challenges here.

---

[3] Ibid.

[4] See Alan Doig and Stephanie McIvor, 'Corruption and Its Control in the Developmental Context: An Analysis and Selective Review of the Literature', 20 *Third World Q.* 657 (1999).

[5] Transparency Int'l, 'Confronting Corruption: The Elements of a National Integrity System', 96 (2000), available at http://www.transparency.org/publications/sourcebook (last visited 17 June 2009).

## Committed Political Backing at the Highest Levels of Government

There is an urgent need for political backing at the highest levels of government in India. While civil society activism and a citizenry that seeks accountability of the government can help in creating the circumstances for developing a political consensus to fight corruption, the much needed political backing is important so that the top political brass in India is both convinced of the seriousness of the problem of corruption and its huge impact on development and governance, and gives its fullest commitment to find ways to fight corruption.[6] This is exactly how it happened in Singapore, when the political leaders made extraordinary efforts to wage a war-footage exercise against corruption. The political consensus that needs to be developed should not be limited to the ruling party, but also should cut across other political parties, including the political opposition. The need for highlighting the negative effects of corruption on the Indian economy and development of various states cannot be underestimated.[7] This will not only raise awareness of the ill effects of corruption among the parliamentarians and legislators, but will also give an opportunity to exert pressure on the citizens belonging to different constituencies to persuade their elected representatives to support this initiative. The biggest challenge in developing political consensus among the politicians in India to support the establishment of an ICAC is their own sense of insecurity that such a move will create tougher legal and institutional frameworks which will impose higher standards of transparency and accountability on their conduct and actions. The proposal thus needs to come from the highest echelons of government, backed by a detailed policy framework and implementation agenda, including a projection of possible results in the form of economic benefit, development dividend, and governance

[6] Doig and Mclvor, 'Corruption and Its Control in the Developmental Context'.
[7] Ibid.

reforms that could be the possible outcome of an independent and effective ICAC.

## Adequate Resources to Undertake Its Mission

The establishment of an ICAC will need allocated resources so that it can function effectively. Resources are critical for the effectiveness of institutions.[8] The proposed ICAC in India should have its resources allocated in a manner that does not in any way compromise and undermine its autonomy. The ICAC needs massive resources to put together a comprehensive framework for the investigation and prosecution of crimes relating to corruption.[9] As discussed earlier, the nature of crimes relating to corruption is such that a range of experts needs to be hired from different disciplines, including, but not limited to, finance, criminology, forensic sciences, and money laundering, in addition to police and law enforcement officials with proven experience in dealing with financial crimes. There is also a need for developing a robust infrastructure for the ICAC as it should be fully empowered to be able to take all steps that are needed to fight corruption.[10] The resources that are needed for the ICAC are not only confined to the infrastructure and people, but are also needed to develop a powerful campaign that will galvanize support to the ICAC and to its ideals among the Indian citizenry. Gathering the support of civil society in India is central to the success of ICAC.[11] This is also one of the reasons for keeping the policing and law enforcement functions of the police separate from the anti-corruption initiatives of ICAC. The staff of ICAC should be fully dedicated to fighting corruption at all levels of government.

[8] Maor, 'Feeling the Heat?'
[9] Ibid.
[10] Ibid.
[11] Sunil Sondhi, 'Combating Corruption in India: The Role of Civil Society' 18–26, Paper for XVIII World Conference of the Int'l Pol. Sc. Assoc. (2000), available at http://www.sunilsondhi.com/resources/Combating+Corruption.pdf (last visited 11 May 2011).

## Political and Operational Independence to Investigate Even at the Highest Levels of Government

There is an inextricable link between each of these requirements for the success of an anti-corruption agency. Political and operational independence to investigate cases relating to corruption, however high up the political ladder a person is, becomes essential for maintaining the legitimacy of the ICAC. It is in this context that there is a need for general political reforms so that other forms of accountability are infused into the political process. In India, most of our institutions have become politicized and are therefore suffering from a credibility crisis.[12] There is, at the same time a need to ensure that the independence of the ICAC does not develop into an institution that is not accountable to any other institution, and may itself assume an agenda without proper checks and balances to control the abuse of power. The *TI Source Book 2000* has recognized this problem and has noted:

...just as an Anti-corruption Agency can be susceptible to those at the highest levels of government; it can also be used as a weapon with which to prosecute political opponents. Even where the independence of the office is respected and an Agency is able to operate freely, it occupies extremely difficult terrain. Imaginative thought has to be given as to how a powerful and independent anti-corruption body can itself be made accountable, and corruption within the organisation minimised.[13]

The power to investigate at the highest levels of government ought to be given to the ICAC so that it can function in an independent manner. Any exception to this principle will weaken the institution in the first place and in due course provide opportunities for undermining the investigative process.

[12] See Upendra Baxi, *The Crisis of the Indian Legal System* (1980) (Noida: Vikas Publishers).

[13] Transparency Int'l, 'Confronting Corruption', p. 104.

## Adequate Powers of Access to Documentation and for Interrogating Witnesses

The powers of the ICAC should be clearly outlined in the legislation constituting it and should include all powers that are necessary for securing access to documentation for the purposes of investigation relating to corruption. The ICAC should be empowered such that it can discharge all functions that are available to police and law enforcement institutions. In this regard, the proposed ICAC should be an institutional mechanism different from the National Human Rights Commission in India. The NHRC's powers, as mentioned in the Protection of Human Rights Act, 1993, result in its effectiveness resting upon its moral authority as opposed to legal sanctions. It is empowered to issue directions that are in the form of 'recommendations', that are not enforceable, although they do have a very powerful persuasive value attached to them, given the NHRC's legitimacy and credibility as an institution. In addition, it is also empowered to take certain matters to the court with a view to seeking the latter's direction to implement its orders. The difference between the NHRC and the proposed ICAC should be clearly understood so that parallels between them are carefully drawn. The ICAC could be comparable to the Election Commission of India (ECI) with the powers and functions that are needed to be exercised as investigating and prosecuting cases relating to corruption constitutes one of the most important responsibilities for governance.

## 'User-friendly' Laws

The legal framework that establishes the ICAC should include all aspects of dealing with corruption. In addition to the criminalization of 'illicit enrichment', the law should have provisions that outline the framework for enforcement of the rule of law.[14] The proposed ICAC should be able to access other legal and judicial institutions so

---

[14] Doig and Mclvor, 'Corruption and Its Control in the Developmental Context'.

that the enforcement regime for fighting against corruption favours its efforts.

## Leadership that is Seen as Being of the Highest Integrity

The leadership of the ICAC and the officers who constitute it should be of the highest integrity. It is important that they be able to function in an independent and professional manner. Time and again, it has been noted in India that the law enforcement agencies are not allowed to function in an impartial and independent manner, a problem that must be rectified. Their work is constantly interfered with by political and other vested interests, leading to the guilty going scot-free.

Brian C. Harms observed:

No matter how effective the machinery one builds, without the proper foundation and support it will most certainly collapse. ... The legal and policy initiatives create disincentives to be corrupt, and incentives to combat corruption. International financial institutions and Transparency International helps to educate the people to develop their own country's internal reform and stop accepting corrupt behaviour. Such internal reforms will establish a foundation upon which further anti-corruption efforts can be built...[15]

Further, it is important to recognize that the police and other law enforcement agencies in India are themselves perceived to be hugely corrupt and face a crisis of credibility. Credible institutions are not only important for all stakeholders in society to have confidence in the independence and impartiality of the institution, but are also necessary for their effective functioning. Credibility of the anti-corruption mechanism is thus critical for its success.

Moshe Maor has observed that '[a] credible judgment by either a public official or an agency requires a wide range of resources which revolves around three ongoing government commitments, namely, a commitment for independence, a commitment for guaranteed

[15] Brian C. Harms, 'Holding Public Officials Accountable in the International Realm: A New Multi-layered Strategy To Combat Corruption', 33 *Cornell Int'l L.J.* 159 (2000).

operational capacity, and a commitment for wide jurisdiction.'[16] The proposed ICAC in India has to be established on the basis of these three fundamental institutional requirements. In fact, these prerequisites are the *sine qua non* for the establishment of the ICAC, and their public legitimacy will depend upon how the government is able to deliver on them.

The commitment of the institution is necessary not only to ensure fairness in the process, but also to protect it from both internal and external threats that may question its integrity. Anti-corruption institutions like human rights institutions cannot be friendly with the government as it is part of their responsibility to keep a check on governmental abuse of power. To maintain a certain degree of autonomy and independence, these institutions have to take tough decisions, which may be adverse to both individuals and in some cases departments of the government. It is in this context that the credibility of an institution like that of the proposed ICAC is critical for its effectiveness in the fight against corruption.

Further, Moshe Maor has noted:

'Credibility' in the context of integrity management presumes these commitments, thus increasing public faith in decisions by public officials or agencies. Once one or more of these commitments is undermined, the result may be a creeping shadow of doubt in the public mind regarding decisions by public officials or agencies. The absence of this doubt is the essence of credibility…[17]

In the fight against corruption in any society, the trust and confidence of the people is critical. The citizenry ought to feel that the fight against corruption through any approach adopted by the government, including the effort of a specialized institution such as the proposed ICAC, is inherently legitimate and is genuinely aimed at improving governance and creating a rule-of-law society. Thus, the investigation, prosecution, and judicial proceedings relating to corruption ought to be fair and transparent.

[16] Maor, 'Feeling the Heat?'.
[17] Ibid.

One of the major challenges in India in its past efforts to fight corruption has been the lack of legitimacy of anti-corruption initiatives due to the problem of politicization of crime in all its dimensions.[18] Serious anti-corruption efforts have been undermined due to the lack of an impartial and unbiased approach to the investigation and prosecution of cases relating to corruption.[19] Unfortunately, anti-corruption cases have become a tool for politicians and political parties to use against opposition parties and politicians belonging to other parties, to score political mileage rather than out of any genuine sense of seeking the truth, punishing the guilty, and upholding justice.[20]

There have been a number of instances when anti-corruption commissions have been established with a view to fighting corruption. But their effectiveness or otherwise will depend upon a number of factors. There is no doubt that the independence and autonomy of the anti-corruption commission is a significant factor that will determine the effectiveness of the commission. John Heilbrunn has observed:

Evidence of dysfunctional anti-corruption commissions is manifest in the numerous agencies that lack independence from the executive, receive no budgetary support from the legislature to investigate venal officials, and have no procedures for forwarding cases of corruption for prosecution by the relevant judicial authorities. Herein lays the dilemma for policymakers who want to reduce corruption and improve governance: whereas it may be desirable to enact policies to reduce corruption, a hollow commission leads to a reputation for token reforms, which undermines the political leadership's credibility. Indeed, it is easy to explain why anti-corruption commissions fail in so many places; it is far more difficult to explain why any succeed.[21]

[18] See Baxi, *Liberty and Corruption*.
[19] Ibid.
[20] Ibid.
[21] John R. Heilbrunn, 'Anti-corruption Commissions: Panacea or Real Medicine to Fight Corruption?' (2004), available at http://siteresources.worldbank.org/WBI/Resources/wbi37234Heilbrunn.pdf. (last visited 19 June 2009).

The effort to establish an ICAC in India is the culmination of the Indian society's desire to eliminate corruption. The citizens of India are indeed desirous of reducing, if not totally eliminating, corruption as it directly affects their lives. The recent Anna Hazare campaign and the resulting social movement to institute a Lokpal is but one reflection of the citizenry in India waking up and demanding a cure to the democratic deficit created by corruption.[22] However, there is neither a political consensus that corruption is the most important governance issue, nor a reference to the approaches that need to be adopted to fight corruption.[23] Under these circumstances, for any institutional approach to fight corruption to emerge is unlikely. However, it is important to develop a framework so that when the issue of corruption comes to the centre stage of politics and governance in India, there is greater understanding of the viable approaches to fight corruption. Heilbrunn has commented that there are four types of anti-corruption commissions. In his view,

...first is the *universal model* with its investigative, preventative, and communicative functions. The universal model is typified by Hong Kong's Independent Commission Against Corruption (ICAC). Second, the *investigative model* is characterized by a small and centralized investigative commission as operates in Singapore's Corrupt Practices Investigation Bureau (CPIB). Both the universal and investigative models are organizationally accountable to the executive.[24]

---

[22] For a good analysis of this issue, see Shamnad Basheer, 'Hazare and the Potential Curing of a Democratic Deficit?' *Law & Other Things* (19 April 2011), available at http://lawandotherthings.blogspot.com/2011/04/hazare-and-potential-curing-of.html (last visited 20 May 2011). For a critique of government's Lokpal Bill, see Iftikhar Gilani, 'The Fatal Flaws in the Government's Lokpal Bill', *Tehelka* (25 May 2011), http://www.tehelka.com/story_main49.asp?file name=Ws050411ACTIVISM.asp (last visited 26 May 2011). See also 'Bring Private Sector under Lokpal Bill' *The Hindu* (15 April 2011), available at http://www.hindu.com/2011/04/15/stories/2011041555360700.htm (last visited 26 May 2011).

[23] Baxi, *Liberty and Corruption.*

[24] Heilbrunn, 'Anti-corruption Commissions'.

In the Indian context, it is important to recognize that there have been various institutional approaches to fight corruption that have not met with success. If a new approach is formulated, it should encompass, within its fold, all aspects of the process relating to investigating and prosecuting allegations of corruption, in addition to educating and empowering people in the fight against corruption. The Hong Kong model and certain tenets of the Singaporean model with a certain degree of adaptability to the Indian context can be more suitable for India.[25] Heilbrunn has also commented on two other models:

... the *parliamentary model* includes commissions that report to parliamentary committees and are independent from the executive and judicial branches of state. The parliamentary model is epitomized by the New South Wales Independent Commission Against Corruption that takes a preventive approach to fighting corruption. Finally, the *multi-agency model* includes a number of offices that are individually distinct, but together weave a web of agencies to fight corruption. The United States Office of Government Ethics with its preventative approach complements the Justice Department's investigative and prosecutorial powers in a concerted effort to reduce corruption.[26]

The Parliamentary model that prevails in Australia and the multi-agency model in the United States are not suitable for India. Both these models presuppose a certain degree of credibility of democratic institutions.[27] Unfortunately, the Indian institutions suffer from a large credibility crisis and will not able to function in an independent manner unless this independence is provided under the Constitution or by way of legislation. There have been huge challenges to maintain the independence of democratic institutions.[28] While electoral democracy has been strongly established in India, we are far from

[25] For a similar argument for establishing the ICAC in Japan, see C. Raj Kumar, 'Corruption in Japan: Institutionalizing the Right to Information, Transparency and the Right to Corruption-free Governance', 10 *New Eng. J. Int'l & Comp. L.* 29 (2004).

[26] Heilbrunn, 'Anti-corruption Commissions'.

[27] Ibid.

[28] Ibid.

developing a democratic culture that respects the autonomy of institutions.[29] In the Indian context, it needs to be recognized that democracy does not in itself provide an effective antidote for corruption.
In this regard, Susan Rose-Ackerman has observed: 'Democracy is
not a cure for corruption, but democratic structures can provide the
conditions needed for anti-corruption policies to succeed.'[30]

The legal system of a country needs to play an important role
in strengthening the institutions and the rule of law that is the
cornerstone of a democracy.[31] In this regard, Claes Sandgren has
observed, 'The role of the legal system is to provide the institutional
framework—rules as well as institutions that apply the rules—for
good governance... The legal system is the warrant for this type of
governance that counteracts corruption. Criminal law has a role to
play, even though it is not as prominent as one may assume.'[32]

The accountability of anti-corruption institutions is vital in India,
given the fact that a large number of institutions and law enforcement
agencies have been politicized and their decisions have been marred
with controversy.[33] Due checks and balances need to be provided so
that the ICAC does not become an all-powerful institution. Claes
Sandgren has further observed,

In addition, the legal system also has the vital role of overseeing the institutions that fight corruption and to hold them accountable. Only if this task is
accomplished in an effective way, and is seen as being effective, it is possible
to gain and maintain the confidence of the public. Without such confidence,
citizens cannot be expected to reject corruption and abstain from using
bribes. In the end, the attitude of the public at large is crucial to the prospect
of success for any effort to fight corruption.[34]

---

[29] Harms, 'Holding Public Officials Accountable in the International Realm'.
[30] Susan Rose-Ackerman, 'Political Corruption and Democracy', 14 *Conn. J.
Int'l L.* 363 (1999).
[31] Ibid.
[32] Claes Sandgren, 'Combating Corruption: The Misunderstood Role of Law',
39 *Int'l Law.* 717 (2005).
[33] Baxi, *Liberty and Corruption*.
[34] Sandgren, 'Combating Corruption'.

The need for establishing an Independent Commission Against Corruption in India is based upon two factors:

## Lack of Faith among the Citizenry in the Government's Anti-corruption Initiatives

Even though there is massive corruption in India and people readily acknowledge the ill effects of it, there is little faith in the ability of the government and many of the existing institutions to fight corruption in an impartial and unbiased manner.[35] Investigations relating to corruption have, by and large, suffered due to political intervention or other forms of biases that affect the integrity of the criminal justice process.[36] The legal system is also marred by huge problems of delay and unpredictability, which have also affected anti-corruption efforts.[37] While police and law enforcement agencies are at the vanguard of anti-corruption efforts, their role and functions need to be subjected to intense scrutiny, given the history of abuse of power, corruption, and other problems that police as an institution faces in India.[38] This has resulted in a situation where the existing police system is not in a position to successfully carry out anti-corruption investigations and prosecutions. This is the case even with regard to one of India's highest investigative bodies, the Central Bureau of Investigation (CBI). The Supreme Court of India in *Narain* v. *Union of India* noted:

The sum and substance of these orders is that the CBI and other government agencies had not carried out their public duty to investigate the offences disclosed . ... Even after this matter was brought to the court complaining of the inertia of CBI and the other agencies to investigate into the offences because of the alleged involvement of several persons holding high offices in the executive, for quite some time the disinclination of the agencies to proceed with the investigation was apparent ... The continuing inertia of the agencies to even commence a proper investigation could not be tolerated any

---

[35] Baxi, *Liberty and Corruption.*
[36] Ibid.
[37] Baxi, *The Crisis of the Indian Legal System.*
[38] Ibid.

longer. In view of the persistence of that situation, it became necessary as the proceedings progressed to make some orders which would activate the CBI and the other agencies to at least commence a fruitful investigation.[39]

The judgment of the Supreme Court in this case is a reflection of the lack of independence of the investigative agencies in the fight against corruption. Further, citizens have little faith in the criminal justice system, given its inability to provide justice in timely, fair, and efficient manner.

Civil society activism in fighting corruption has significantly expanded in the recent years.[40] The Global Integrity Report published by the Centre for Public Integrity has noted in relation to India:

Citizen groups and civil society initiatives are today carving out a space for themselves in the fight against corruption and misuse of authority ...The police have traditionally enjoyed tremendous power and patronage from the political elite. Among the various public institutions, the police are rated as having the lowest credibility by the general public. The politicization of the police force is a matter of serious concern often resulting in the high-handedness, corruption, and arbitrary behavior on the part of the police force. While some efforts are today being made to improve the image of the police, the public perception of the police remains largely unchanged.[41]

The effectiveness of anti-corruption initiatives is significantly dependent upon an active and vibrant civil society.[42] But for the civil society to play a dynamic role in the government's efforts to fight corruption, it should have confidence that the government and its anti-corruption institutions are not only serious about fighting corruption, but also have a properly devised plan and strategy to do

---

[39] AIR (1998) SC 889.

[40] Sondhi, 'Combating Corruption in India'.

[41] Sandeep Shastri, 'Integrity Assessment', in Center for Public Integrity (ed.), Global Integrity: An Investigative Report Tracking Corruption, Openness and Accountability in 25 Countries: India 7 (2004), available at http://www.globalintegrity.org/reports/2004/docs/2004/2004India.pdf. (last visited June 20, 2009).

[42] Sondhi, 'Combating Corruption in India'.

so.[43] At each stage of the investigative process, there may be a need for input from the citizenry, and this information cannot be generated through coercion or undue influence. The Indian citizenry ought to feel socially obligated to share whatever information they may have in relation not only to assisting the investigative process, but also to reducing the incidence of corruption in the future.[44]

Community involvement in anti-corruption initiatives is the least apparent in India. Corruption is a problem that cannot be addressed solely by the law enforcement machinery or, for that matter, the ICAC. There needs to be a multi-pronged and participatory strategy for fighting corruption, and only that will ensure that the anti-corruption efforts of the ICAC are duly supplemented by the support of the public at large. Successful anti-corruption institutions have engaged with the community and have recognized the role of civil society as a vital mechanism in the fight against corruption.

## Separating Anti-corruption Initiatives from Other Police Functions

Police and law enforcement agencies are themselves perceived to be corrupt in India.[45] Thus, any anti-corruption strategy, including the establishment of a separate specialized institution to investigate and prosecute crimes relating to corruption, ought to focus on the nature of the institutional framework that needs to be created. Corruption in the police at all levels of their interaction with the public has left the latter with little faith in this institution, which is supposed to be the protector and guardian of the security of the people.[46] The nature and extent of corruption in the police is observed by Arvind Verma: 'The elitist nature of the police leadership, the politicization of the department, the unaccountability to the people and outdated management practices have all combined to make corruption endemic and even

---

[43] Ibid.
[44] Ibid.
[45] Baxi, *The Crisis of the Indian Legal System*.
[46] Ibid.

acceptable within the organisation. The persistence of open corrupt practices by officers is clearly indicative that the organisation itself has become deviant...'[47] Therefore, the need for totally separating anti-corruption initiatives from policing is essential to maintain the independence of the anti-corruption institution.

In the Indian context, the pool of officers who are drawn for anti-corruption work are people who, either before or after their tenure in this work, will be engaged in policing. This approach poses a number of problems for pursuing serious anti-corruption work. First, the work relating to anti-corruption has become much more specialized, and officers involved in this work may need to have knowledge of not only the law, but also in many cases knowledge of finance, as well as training in investigation relating to money laundering. Corruption today is not confined to petty corruption where even the proceeds of corrupt transaction are negligible and confined to India. While all cases relating to corruption ought to be pursued, it is important to develop a dedicated civil service mechanism with officers who will be trained and vested with the responsibility of fighting corruption. This is critical for the success of the institution.

Second, while policing involves a range of activities related to protecting law and order ensuring that persons who have committed crimes are brought to justice, the nature of corruption is such that there is an important element of abuse of power inherent in any corrupt transaction. The persons who are engaged in public corruption, besides violating the law, are also abusing the power that is vested with them by way of them being government officials. A sound understanding of anti-corruption law, the rules and regulations of the civil service, the techniques of investigation, collection of evidence, and development of a fool-proof case for conviction of the accused are all essential and can be done effectively only if there is a dedicated team whose sole responsibility is to take these matters to their logical conclusion.

---

[47] Arvind Verma, 'Cultural Roots of Police Corruption in India', 22 *Policing: Int'l J. Police Strategies & Mgmt.* 264 (1999).

Third, the prosecution needs to be assisted by the investigating team in an effective manner so that the cases relating to corruption are brought to justice. If there are vested interests that work at this stage, there is good reason for anti-corruption efforts to fail. This is a real danger particularly when the incidence of police corruption is as high as it is in India.

Given the extent of police corruption in India, the anti-corruption institution may be frequently involved in the investigation of cases relating to corruption against police officials.[48] There is thus a need for fundamental reforms in policing, and this should take place regardless of the anti-corruption mechanisms being created independent of the policing functions. In this context, Arvind Verma has observed:

The role and function of any police department is adversely affected if the prevailing norms and traditional ways of doing things encourage corrupt practices. Accordingly, the way to control corruption and reform system is to make change in the way things are being done. This calls for a major transformation of organisational structure, management prac-tices, supervision procedures, decentralisation of power, creation of local accountability system, even a change in role and functions of the police in the society...[49]

A major policy change needs to take place for anti-corruption initiatives to be effective in India. Under the current system, the work relating to anti-corruption is pursued by the police and other law enforcement agencies, and in many cases there is a sufficient degree of overlap between these two functions.[50] Further, the people involved in this work may simultaneously be involved in other aspects of policing. If fighting corruption is to take serious priority, as it should, then it is important to differentiate all efforts to fight corruption from other equally important and responsible ways of maintaining law and order, and the investigation and prosecution of all other crimes. At the state level, the Department of Vigilance and Anti-corruption that

[48] Ibid.
[49] Ibid.
[50] Ibid.

is currently under the administrative system of the director general of police needs to be re-examined. In India, there are both central- and state-level agencies that are entrusted with the task of fighting corruption. Given the vastness of the country, this is inevitable, but there is an urgent need to re-examine the nature, scope, functions, jurisdiction, composition, and overlap of powers of these bodies with a view to infusing a greater degree of accountability, autonomy as well as effectiveness in the fight against corruption.

## TOWARDS ESTABLISHING AN INDEPENDENT COMMISSION AGAINST CORRUPTION

The institutional approach to fighting corruption is an attractive proposition its the focused approach. When there are too many insti- tutions responsible for undertaking similar tasks, there is bound to be confusion and, in many instances, turf wars between the institutions as to who is more powerful in dealing with cases relating to corrup- tion. The fundamental rationale for establishing a separate institution for dealing with corruption is to bring together the functioning of certain institutions, which are already working in the field of cor- ruption, and to create a single nodal institution with all the powers, function and responsibilities to investigate and prosecute cases relat- ing to corruption.

Establishing an ICAC in India could be one of the most effective ways to fight corruption.[51] Hong Kong, as stated earlier, provides a useful model for an ICAC. The OECD[52] has explained the procedure for investigation and prosecution in the Hong Kong ICAC Model thus:

[51] For an analysis of the establishment and working of the ICAC in Hong Kong, see Jean A. Yeung, 'Fighting Corruption: The Hong Kong Experi- ence', presentation paper for the seminar on International Experiences on Good Governance and Fighting Corruption (17 February 2000) (on file with author).

[52] OECD, 'Specialized Anti-corruption Institutions: Review of Models' (2006), available at http://www.oecd.org/dataoecd/7/4/39971975.pdf.

(1) ICAC Report Centre receives a complaint (by individuals, legal persons, ICAC Regional Offices or by other governmental departments) about corruption;

(2) The complaint is examined by ICAC and categorized with a view to pursue or not pursue further action;

(3) For complaints with further action recommended, investigations will be carried out by ICAC's Operations Department;

(4) For complaints with substantiated evidence, relevant details will be submitted for the institution of prosecution to the Secretary for Justice, head of the Department of Justice of the Hong Kong Special Administrative Region Government;

(5) Prosecution of corruption will be conducted by the two ICAC sections (public sector and private sector corruption) of the Commercial Crime and Corruption Unit, Prosecutions Division, Department of Justice. It advises ICAC and handles its prosecutions.

(6) Report will be subsequently made to ICAC's Operation Review Committee.[53]

## Framework

The proposed ICAC in India should be a stand-alone autonomous institution and should not be under any ministry of the government, including the Prime Minister's Office. The ICAC should be established as an institution akin to the Election Commission of India. In fact, it would be appropriate for its establishment to be made through an amendment to the Constitution of India, which will provide a constitutional status to this commission. If that is not possible, given the political complexities of amending the constitution, it may be established by legislation. But the powers, functions and level of independence of ICAC should be in conformity to the guarantees that are provided to the Election Commission of India. Historically, anti-corruption institutions that have been established in India have not enjoyed institutional independence or functional autonomy. All investigative bodies, including police and law enforcement agencies, have come under one or more ministries of the Government of

---

[53] Ibid., p. 35.

India or the state government. This has made the independent and autonomous functioning of these institutions dependent upon the leadership and the integrity and impartiality of the heads of these institutions. While this is necessary and critical for the success of the ICAC, it is important to develop a more sustainable, process- and procedure-oriented institutional mechanism for ensuring independence. In the past, independence of the law enforcement agencies and the individual officers has been dependent upon two factors.

## Honesty and Integrity of the Individual Officers and Heads of Anti-corruption Institutions

The problem with this approach is that it never helps to build a culture of institutional integrity as it depends far too much upon the individual officers who assume such positions. For anti-corruption efforts to be successful over a period of time, there is a need for a sustained approach to fighting corruption at all levels.[54] Institutional integrity and the trust and confidence of the citizenry in the institution cannot be built overnight. The institutional apparatus, the organizational framework, and the need for maintaining the honesty and integrity of the anti-corruption investigative process ought to be deeply ingrained within the ICAC.[55] Typically, institutions in India that are involved in the fight against corruption are under tremendous pressure from different vested interests, and their independence is only in rhetoric and hardly in practice.

## Honesty, Integrity, and (in Some Cases) Benevolence of Politicians and Bureaucrats

The independence or otherwise of the ICAC should not be dependent upon the personal integrity or the benevolence of politicians and bureaucrats. Political and bureaucratic corruption in India is rampant. It is essential that the ICAC as an institution be established bearing in

[54] Young, 'Fighting Corruption'.
[55] Ibid.

mind the practical problems that are faced by agencies such as the CBI and the CVC, which undermine their independence and efficiency in fighting corruption. There is thus a need to develop an institutional framework that leaves little room for powers to be abused.

## Independence

The ICAC needs to have a legal framework that ensures its independence and helps maintain its autonomy. The independence of the ICAC is the most important aspect relevant for its effective functioning. Police agencies in India are notoriously undermined by political intervention. The independence of the ICAC needs to be legally protected so that it does not depend upon the whim and fancy of the government in power. While the independence of the ICAC is critical, its own institutional accountability needs to be ensured. Independence and accountability are two sides of the same coin. While independence of the ICAC for its effective functioning is essential for it to be able to undertake its functions of investigation and prosecution without any fear or favour from other government agencies and politicians, there is also a need to ensure that it does not become an organization that is accountable to none. A fool-proof system of checks and balances needs to be introduced so that the functioning of the ICAC is independent from the executive, but will be overseen by an Independent Board of the ICAC, the membership of which will be mostly from outside the ICAC. This will ensure that the day-to-day activities of the ICAC are conducted by its officials and officers, but that the broad overseeing of its functions is undertaken by another body whose members include a cross-section of society as well as some ICAC representatives. It is important that the structure and framework of ICAC is diligently drawn so that the powers and functions of this anti-corruption agency fulfil the objectives of fighting corruption.

A number of the best practices that prevail in the world providing operational independence can be of use here. The reporting mechanism and internal oversight procedures should reflect a certain degree of rigorousness that is needed for the ICAC to perform what will be an essentially sensitive set of duties and responsibilities. Along the same lines, the ICAC should have financial independence, and the funds that are needed for its effective functioning ought to be made available by the Parliament and not dependent upon governmental discretion. A useful example relating to financial independence in the context of an institution in India is the ECI. It has been noted, 'It is a mark of ECI's independence that it has not faced any major funding problems ... it is funded by the government through the Consolidate Fund ... The ECI's accounts are subject to audit by the Comptroller and Auditor General and its report is tabled in the Parliament. This ensures the financial accountability of the ECI, and had worked smoothly.'[56] I propose that the ICAC's financial independence should be ensured along the same lines as that of the ECI so that no government in the future can interfere in the working of the ICAC and adversely impact its financial independence.

## Composition

The composition of the ICAC should be similar to that of the ECI. The ICAC should be given a constitutional status so that the level of engagement and interaction of the members of the ICAC is not only deemed to be important, but also perceived to be important. The appointment of the members of the ICAC should be done through the same process that is currently adopted for the appointment of the National Human Rights Commission. This will ensure that there is broad political consensus when it comes to the appointment of the members of the ICAC.

## Powers

The ICAC should be empowered to be a nodal institution for undertaking the investigation and prosecution of all cases relating to

[56] Vijay Patidar and Ajay Jha, 'Case Study: India—India: A Model of an Independent ECI' (Ace Project: The Electoral Knowledge Network), available at http://aceproject.org/ero-en/regions/asia/IN/India%20-%20The%20Embodime nt%20of%20EMB%20Independence.pdf (last visited 21 July 2010).

corruption under the state and Central Government. But it is important that the work of the ICAC be limited to cases of corruption that
are not petty in nature, but amounts to a certain degree of significance
either in terms of financial implications or in terms of their impact
on the administration of justice or nature of the abuse of power. The
ICAC should be empowered to determine its investigative procedures
and processes.

The establishment of the ICAC in India by way of a constitutional
amendment is essential to tackle the problem of corruption. While
passing a constitutional amendment is no easy task, there have been
steps taken by way of passing an amendment to the Constitution on
matters relating to the right to education where there was a certain
degree of political consensus. Political parties invariably raise the issue
of corruption and level charges against each other during election
campaigns. These allegations are made when parties or individuals
need to criticize the opposition. In this process, the importance of
the issue and the need for fair and transparent methods to discover
the truth and to seek the punishment of the perpetrators of the crime
of corruption is undermined. The credibility of the criminal justice
process is significantly affected and crimes relating to corruption
almost never end up in conviction, let alone punishment.

The business of investigating cases relating to corruption and
seeking the prosecution of accused persons is an extremely important
and a serious endeavour for a variety of reasons. There is no doubt
that the criminal justice system in India is facing a huge crisis of
credibility.[57] The rule of law will be protected in India only if it is
ensured that those who violate the law are meted the punishment
that is appropriate for that violation. Rule of law ought to ensure that
the legal system and the institutional mechanisms available treat all
people in a fair and just manner; that acts of corruption committed
by the most powerful and influential persons in the society are also
investigated in a professional manner; and that justice is rendered.[58]

---

[57] Ibid.
[58] Baxi, The *Crisis of the Indian Legal System*.

## Anti-corruption Initiatives and Human Rights Protection

The fact that the activities of the proposed ICAC can potentially infringe upon human rights underlines the need for strengthening the human rights machinery in India. If anti-corruption efforts are not adequately provided with democratic checks and balances, the fairly effective institutional approach of anti-corruption that is being proposed could become politicized.[59] Politicization of the corruption issue does not bode well for law enforcement in India.[60] Selective or partial enforcement of law violates the principle of equality and non-discrimination, and indeed threatens the foundations of the rule of law that is being proposed to be established through the ICAC.

## Creating a Communications Office/ Public Affairs Division

There is a need to create a communications office in the form of a public affairs division within the proposed ICAC. The purpose of creating a professionally organized and fully trained office that is responsible for providing the relevant information to the media and to the larger public domain is to increase the visibility of the commission. The fight against corruption has to involve the widest possible sections of civil society in India,[61] and it is for this purpose that the interaction of the proposed ICAC with local and international media is critical. There should be a system by which cases relating to corruption that the proposed ICAC is investigating, or has completed investigating, are brought to the public domain without breaching any rule of confidentiality, or releasing information that would in any way jeopardize the process of investigation. The information that the communications office or the public affairs division of the proposed ICAC provides to the media through a press conference or other appropriate methods is to keep the people of India informed about

[59] Ibid.
[60] Baxi, *Liberty and Corruption*.
[61] Ibid.

the workings of the proposed ICAC. Another important purpose is to ensure that corruption remains a firm and central issue within the social and political agenda of governance in India.

## Dissemination of the Procedures for Approaching the ICAC

Most of the time, even with a sound legal and institutional frame-work in many countries, little information about the functioning of anti-corruption institutions is disseminated to the wider public. There is a need to publicize the existence of the commission along with the procedure that is in place for receiving complaints, the process of taking cognizance of complaints and the approximate time taken for investigation/response, etc. through the mass media and all channels of communication. A great deal of ingenuity and creativity is required for successfully handling this matter as this will ensure citizens' participation in governance. As discussed earlier, the fight against corruption in India cannot be handled only by the proposed ICAC. It has to seek every possible encouragement and support from all individuals and institutions within and external to the government. In particular, for getting the people involved, there is a need for constant education by using multiple channels of communication. The representatives of the ICAC should be regularly invited to give talks and lectures by educational institutions. Further, a close relationship between officials of the ICAC and academic circles of human rights, constitutional law, administrative law, and criminal justice needs to be established.

## Invoking Strong Political Commitments to Reduce Corruption and Non-Interference in Corruption Proceedings

### People-centred Approach to Anti-corruption Work

This means that the ICAC should pursue anti-corruption cases with a view to empowering the people of India who are actually the victims of corruption.[62] Earlier, it was noted that corruption disproportionately affects the poor and the disempowered. In developing societies like India, there are far too many people who are struggling to fulfil their basic needs. If corruption is brought to the central agenda of governance, it is possible to develop a consensus among the political parties, although genuine change relating to honesty and integrity in politics will take a long time. The need for commitments from politicians at the highest levels in the government can be crucial, particularly when the proposed ICAC is able to achieve key convictions in anti-corruption cases. Also, any form of interference in the proceedings besides violating existing laws and the independence that is guaranteed to the proposed ICAC under the law would also discourage the staff of the ICAC through pursuing these matters with the commitment they would have otherwise had. The credibility of the proposed ICAC will also suffer if there is any form of interference or appearance of impropriety by the officials of the ICAC. Thus, the proposed ICAC has to steadfastly guard against any interference that may affect it in a direct or indirect manner in exercising its duties and obligations.

## Training of Parliamentarians

This is a subject that will take a fair amount of convincing to implement. The proposed ICAC should interact with the secretariat of the Parliament to provide suitable training programmes on issues relating to corruption to the parliamentarians. Political corruption needs to be curbed for developing a good governance framework.[63] While every effort ought to be taken by the proposed ICAC to pursue the investigation, prosecution, and conviction of persons who are corrupt, whether they are politicians, bureaucrats, judges or any other individual or institution[64] in Indian society under the functional

---

[62] Ibid.

[63] See Moshe Maor, 'Feeling the Heat? Anti-corruption Mechanisms in Comparative Perspective', 17 *Governance* 1 (2004).

[64] Ibid.

jurisdiction of the proposed ICAC, equal efforts need to be taken to educate and train people about the ill effects of corruption and how it violates human rights, undermines the rule of law and distorts the development process in India.[65]

## ICAC AND ITS RELATIONSHIP WITH OTHER INSTITUTIONS: FORMAL AND INFORMAL

As discussed earlier, corruption is a multifaceted problem. The response to corruption should also be holistic, and hence the proposed ICAC should work with and engage, to the widest extent possible, with other commissions and institutions in India, including, but not limited to, the National Human Rights Commission, Comptroller and Auditor General of India, and other similar institutions. Obviously, the relationship and interaction that the proposed ICAC expects to establish with each of these institutions will vary and depend upon the institutional mandate of the respective institutions. Nevertheless, there is a good argument that corruption affects the efficient functioning of government and violates the rights of people besides undermining the rule of law. It is in this context that anti-corruption efforts can acquire greater legitimacy both within and without the government and its institutions.

The proposed ICAC needs to work on partnerships with governmental institutions and non-governmental organizations in India and overseas. These partnerships would be of varied nature, with the purpose to engage in capacity building so that the ICAC becomes a truly nodal organization to ensure corruption-free governance. The officials of the ICAC should be in a position to conduct seminars/presentations and other forms of training programmes in government departments in India. The ICAC should also work closely with the private sector, particularly on matters relating to corporate fraud and other forms of corruption that take place in corporations.

[65] Ibid.

## Linkage with the Comptroller and Auditor General's Department

There needs to be a broad level of engagement and interaction between the ICAC and the OCAG with a view to providing support in training. There is a need to institutionalize this relationship so that the interaction is not in an *ad hoc* capacity, but based on shared principles and values of institutions within government workings to ensure good governance.

## Relationship with the Media

The proposed ICAC should constantly work towards aggressively pursuing the anti-corruption agenda and involve the media in bringing information on arrests, indictments, trials, and convictions to the public domain. In free and democratic societies, the media plays an important role in exposing acts of corruption and insisting on transparency in governance and accountability of administrators. Independence of the media is essential for ensuring transparency. If it is not independent, this may hinder the establishment of an open and transparent relationship with the media; the impartial and objective approach of the proposed ICAC can also help in influencing the media organizations. In this context, it is important for the ICAC to maintain its independence and autonomy and to deal with cases relating to corruption in an impartial, objective, and efficient manner. This will generate greater confidence among the media in the working of the proposed ICAC.

## Interaction with NGOs and Civil Society

The proposed ICAC needs to expand its partnership with NGOs and the wider civil society in India for fighting corruption. The empowerment of NGOs and civil society is critical for ensuring that the fight against corruption has the necessary credibility, which is extremely important particularly when corruption is writ large in society and people are generally cynical about government initiatives that intend to eliminate it.[66]

Further, since the institutional credibility of anti-corruption agencies in India has suffered in the past, there is a need to work closely with NGOs and civil society for achieving corruption-free governance.[67] Civil society, including the media, has to be involved in a significant manner in India to ensure that corruption-free governance does not remain a policy goal or an institutional aspiration. Civil society is best suited to perform this role, as it can devote itself exclusively to ensuring that the decisions of the government are made in a transparent and socially accountable manner.[68]

Further, civil society in India is part of the democratic set-up and should be involved in both rural and urban India at the grassroots levels. The problem of most human rights commitments has been the existence of a gap between theory and practice, policy and reality.

Corruption-free governance should be part of civil society activism so that the people are empowered to seek transparency and accountability from decision-makers.[69] Further, in many instances NGOs and civil society will also be whistleblowers, and working closely with the proposed ICAC will provide the right kind of trust and confidence for both. This, however, does not mean that the proposed ICAC needs to accept or condone all approaches adopted by NGOs and civil society.

---

[66] Krishna K. Tummala, 'Regime Corruption in India', 14 *Asian J. Pol. Sc.* 1 (2006).

[67] Ibid.

[68] Ibid.

[69] Jon S. T. Quah, 'Corruption in Asian Countries: Can It Be Minimized?' 59 *Pub. Admin. Rev.* 483 (1999).

## THE WAY FORWARD: A COHESIVE APPROACH TO COMBATING CORRUPTION

The empire of corruption has done the greatest possible damage to good governance and the rule of law in India.[70] We need to view corruption from the perspectives of access to justice and human rights so that public institutions can be held accountable for the abuse of power. We must encourage institutions like the National Human Rights Commission and State Human Rights Commissions in India to begin taking cognizance of corruption cases so as to raise the profile of this linkage with human rights. We must also evolve a new language, including the right to corruption-free governance, as a fundamental and non-derogable human right so that the ideal of constitutional governance is implemented.[71] There are various ways and means by which the judiciary can take measures to eliminate the malaise of corruption in light of inaction or apathy by the legislative and executive branches of the state.[72]

Corruption *within* the judiciary, mainly at the lower levels, ought to be an important target for elimination.[73] Anti-corruption work must involve grassroots civil society organizations along the lines of the MKSS in India. Since corruption is a disempowering force, the most effective way to root it out is through the empowerment of citizens both through popular grassroots people's initiatives and through institutional mechanisms that exist in the legal system.[74] A holistic approach to fighting corruption through legal and social action has been long overdue in India. Until such a movement comes about,

[70] C. Raj Kumar, 'Corruption, Development and Good Governance: Challenges for Promoting Access to Justice in Asia', 16 *Mich. St. J. Int'l L* 475, 568 (2008).

[71] Ibid.

[72] Ibid.

[73] Ibid., p. 569.

[74] Ibid.

corruption will continue to eat into the socio-economic development of India and exact a heavy human toll.[75]

I have argued in favour of a humanistic and liberal reinterpretation of 'sovereignty' in the wake of new thinking and new developments in world affairs. Sovereignty exercised as an untrammelled power with irresponsible government institutions exploiting and disempowering citizens results in the lack of accountability. Sovereignty exercised as the responsibility of the governing power with human development as the desired end is the wave of the future that sadly has not yet gained prevalence in India.[76] The way forward is to spread this notion of responsibility and accountability as imperatives for strengthening sovereignty, simultaneous to large-scale efforts of increasing the presence and participation of civil society in governance issues. A corruption-free state enhances its chances of perpetuation, reduces possibilities of unwarranted external interference, and attracts foreign talent and investments by raising its international stature. A population that is content, well-governed, and not discriminated against confers internal stability—a key requisite for projecting power externally.[77] Roping local civil society into this endeavour, in tandem with non-politicized international interventions, will produce tangible results.

It is possible for India to succeed in the fight against corruption and ensure that transparency in governance becomes the basis for the development of the country.[78] But for this to happen, there is a need, as discussed in this work, for a wide variety of actors playing important roles towards eliminating corruption from society.[79] The whistleblower protection laws that exist in a number of countries will provide a useful framework for India to demonstrate its commitment to ensuring corruption-free governance.[80]

[75] Ibid.
[76] Ibid.
[77] Ibid.
[78] Ibid.
[79] Ibid.
[80] Ibid.

But there is also a need to examine the workings of a number of institutions in Asia and to foster close partnerships with such governmental institutions, non-governmental organizations, and civil society for the fight against corruption to succeed. No doubt, this is a long and arduous struggle, but the struggle is worth it as, along the way, many human rights will be protected and promoted and many people will be empowered.

The following specific suggestions are to ensure that the problem of corruption receives the highest priority and attention for ensuring access to justice and the promotion of development policies:

## Laws

The legal framework for fighting corruption needs to be strengthened as a facet of both legal and judicial reforms. The existing legislative framework for fighting corruption in India needs to be thoroughly examined. Efforts ought to be taken to ensure that laws, rules, and regulations for fighting corruption are in place.[81] But it is important to note that anti-corruption laws will not be effective if the law enforcement machinery and the rule of law culture in a society is weak.[82] Hence, there is a need for taking efforts to protect the rule of law and empowering the law enforcement machinery, including the police, prosecution, and other agencies that may be involved in the fight against corruption.[83]

## Institutions

The legal framework for fighting corruption should be supplemented by establishing and empowering institutions. A number of institutions are involved in varying capacities in the fight against corruption. Since corruption is inextricably connected to creating obstacles in the path of access to justice, and to a lack of effective development

---

[81] Ibid., p. 570.
[82] Ibid.
[83] Ibid.

policies, appropriate institutions should be in place to deal with it.[84] The judiciary and human rights commissions are best suited to deal with corruption as a violation of human rights that inhibits access to justice.[85]

The consequences of corruption on development are profound. It is here that the anti-corruption machinery needs to be strengthened and the need for independent commissions against corruption becomes necessary.[86] Independent anti-corruption institutions, like the ICAC as proposed in this book, have the potential to act as a watchdog for ensuring that corruption does not become a hindrance to development and the resources of the state are distributed in a fair and equitable manner.[87]

## Role of Judiciary and Adjudicative Mechanisms

The judiciary and its adjudicative mechanisms have an important role to play in the fight against corruption. At times, the judiciary may be subject to criticism on the grounds that it is interfering in the affairs of the executive. However, the judiciary in India has not shied away from its responsibilities and remains an institution that enjoys tremendous moral legitimacy and constitutional status to intervene in various human rights issues. It is important to recognize that the role of the judiciary in upholding the Constitution should not be overemphasized and will have its inherent limitations. The judiciary is far more effective when it comes to empowering other institutions than it is when taking upon itself the responsibility of fighting corruption.[88] It is in this context that the interface of corruption and

[84] Ibid.
[85] Ibid.
[86] Ibid.
[87] Ibid.
[88] See Rajeev Dhavan, 'Judicial Corruption', *The Hindu*, 22 February 2002, available at www.hinduonnet.com/2002/02/22/stories/2002022200031000.htm (last visited 25 June 2009).

human rights is useful for the judiciary to take steps to implement human rights.[89]

Constitutions at best may provide the political and institutional venue for promoting a rights discourse. They are also written at a time when momentous political changes take place in a country and the framers objectively attempt to transform society. Constitutional guarantees cannot ensure that protection of human rights unless they succeed in engaging the democratic processes in society, an empowering function that should be the goal of constitutionalism. Corruption of the kind that prevails in India disempowers individuals and institutions.[90] It is important that there are independent democratic institutions that function effectively in ensuring that the governance system adheres to the principle of rule of law and the Constitution. Constitutionalism should be understood as encompassing all such institutions—a principle that encompasses a variety of political theory ideals, demonstrating a framework of governance that is based upon human rights, fundamental freedoms, and human dignity.

The constitutionalization of human rights creates a theoretical framework for their protection and from it flow the various legal, judicial, democratic, and institutional mechanisms that ensure it. The judiciary will be able to best perform its constitutional functions only when the independence of other democratic institutions is guaranteed and the government adheres to certain principles of constitutional governance. Human rights and constitutional freedoms are central principles for liberal democratic societies.

Further, formal mechanisms for the protection of human rights through the constitutional apparatus and their enforcement by the judiciary can fail, particularly when these institutions operate under

---

[89] Ibid.

[90] Prashant Bhushan, 'Judging the Judges', *Outlook* (21 January 2009), available at http://www.judicialreforms.org/files/judging_the_judges.pdf (last visited 25 June 2009); A.G. Noorani, 'Against the Law', *Frontline* (October 2008), available at http://www.flonnet.com/fl2523/stories/20081121252308300.htm (last visited 20 May 2011).

limitations.[91] Greater space should be provided for democratic dissent and resistance to intrusions on human rights. This space is also typically addressed by liberal constitutions both in rights guarantees and democratic commitments. It should also be autonomous, so that citizens take upon themselves the task of protecting and promoting human rights and fundamental freedoms.[92] The right to information that is provided both as a constitutional and a legal right is one such example whereby the focus is on empowering the Indian citizenry to seek transparency in governance.[93] It is possible that resistance from citizens can actually serve as a check upon the democratic branches of the government to ensure that human rights are duly protected,[94] and that violations of any nature, including acts of corruption, are met with serious criticism in the form of democratic dissent. More importantly, there is a need for people's resistance and movements to ensure the protection and promotion of human rights.[95]

While a sound constitutional framework, an independent judiciary, and other democratic institutions are upholding the Constitution of India, the principles of constitutionalism have not yet permeated our political culture. It is here that we have a long way to go in ensuring that human rights, justice, and constitutional empowerment become the *sine qua non* of democratic governance in India.[96]

The role of the judiciary in fighting corruption and improving governance is a central element of constitutionalism in Indian democracy.[97] The dialectical relationship between promoting constitutionalism and the development of judicial governance presents three important challenges for understanding the role of law and institutional politics in India:

---

[91] See Upendra Baxi, *The Crisis of the Indian Legal System*.

[92] Ibid.

[93] See S.P. Sathe, *The Right to Information*.

[94] Ibid.

[95] Ibid.

[96] See S.P. Sathe, 'Judicial Activism: The Indian Experience', 6 *Wash. U. J. L. & Poly* 29 (2001).

[97] Ibid.

## Role of the Judiciary

The judiciary is uniquely placed in the matrix of power structures within the system of governance. Judges are not elected but clearly have the power and indeed the responsibility to check the exercise of powers and actions of elected representatives and appointed officials. The judiciary as an institution is vastly respected, notwithstanding huge challenges in ensuring access to justice, judicial process, and issues of transparency and accountability.[98] It is vested with ensuring that the rights and freedoms of the people are protected and the powers exercised by the government in adopting policies are in accordance with the Constitution and other pieces of legislation.[99]

In theory, if the different branches of the government adhere to the basic principle of separation of powers and function within their limits, it is considered a sound system of governance. In practice, however, a number of issues and challenges have emerged. It is in this context that the three branches of the government—the legislature, the executive, and the judiciary—need to have a certain degree of trust in, and deference to, the actions of one another in matters within their respective jurisdictions.

However, trust and deference in relation to the actions of a particular branch should not undermine the judiciary's responsibility to adjudicate on the constitutional and legislative validity of the actions of the government. Clearly, this delicate balancing act of rightfully intervening when necessary requires a deeper understanding and appreciation of the principles of constitutionalism.[100] Rule of law is about all people and institutions respecting laws and acting in accordance with the law. The legislature and the executive as collective powerhouses are bound by these principles as much as ordinary citizens are. When acts of corruption are brought before the judiciary for adjudication, it is important for it as an institution to take account of all legislative and constitutionally available mechanisms in upholding the right to corruption-free governance. The credibility

[98] Ibid.
[99] Ibid.
[100] Ibid.

of the judiciary as an institution needs to be effectively used, notwithstanding the fact that there have been recent issues of corruption within the judiciary that have undermined its reputation.[101]

## Judicial Governance

The term 'judicial governance' in itself is subject to challenge as the judiciary is not supposed to be involved in 'governance'. However, the effort of the Indian judiciary to infuse accountability in the functioning of government institutions, and the growth and development of human rights jurisprudence has demonstrated the central importance of judicial governance.[102] This has posed critical challenges to parliamentary accountability and executive powers and, more importantly, reinforced the need for improving the efficiency and effectiveness of governmental institutions.

The need for social reform preceded the conferment of the role of guardian of individual rights on the judiciary by the Constituent Assembly. Hence, the protection of liberties within the constitutional framework needed to be balanced with the achievement of social reform. The Supreme Court perceived itself as an institutional guardian of individual liberties against political aggression. In that regard, it went beyond the framers' vision of achieving an immediate social revolution. It took upon itself a role similar to that of the United States Supreme Court as defined by Chief Justice Marshall in *Marbury* v. *Madison* (1803).[103] This perception led the court to develop implied limitations on the powers of the political branch that is analogous to the US judiciary's approach to the separation of powers. The best known of these implied limitations, the 'basic features limitation', precludes the amendment of the Constitution by Parliament in ways that displace its basic features.[104]

[101] Dhavan, 'Judicial Corruption'.

[102] Sathe, *Judicial Activism in India* (2006) (New Delhi: Oxford University Press).

[103] For excellent discussions on this see S.P. Sathe, *Judicial Activism in India*, pp. 25–100.

[104] Ibid., p. 78.

## Civil Society Expectations

Legal provisions relating to human rights as a normative framework provide little guidance and help for the masses in India who are aspiring to fulfil their basic rights, in particular their right to acquire and experience the basic needs of survival and existence. Civil society seeks to enforce good governance so that all human rights are promoted and protected.[105]

Undoubtedly, the wider civil society has embraced the notion of judicial governance, given the fact that it provides certain social expectations for creating accountability. The relaxation of the rules of *locus standi*, recognition of a range of human rights under the 'right to life' provision of the Constitution, and the development of public interest litigation[106] are important milestones in meeting civil society expectations on the working of the judiciary.[107] However, given the range of injustices in our society, institutional responses, including those of the judiciary, need to be further expanded.[108] The Indian experience has demonstrated that the initial judicial recognition of human rights has culminated in the passage of an amendment that guarantees the fundamental right to education.

If democracy is to become meaningful in India, it should be based on two important factors: the enforcement of the rule of law and the reform of the political system—each dependant on the other.[109] The judiciary is well-suited to support both these initiatives.

---

[105] Jon S. T. Quah, 'Corruption in Asian Countries: Can It Be Minimized?' 59 *Pub. Admin. Rev.* 483 (1999).

[106] See Ashok H. Desai and S. Muralidhar, 'Public Interest Litigation: Potential and Problems', in B.N. Kirpal et al. (eds.), *Supreme but not Infallible: Essays in Honour of the Supreme Court of India*, p. 159.

[107] See Upendra Baxi, *Courage, Craft and Contention: The Indian Supreme Court in the Eighties* (1985) (Bombay: N.M. Tripathi).

[108] Ibid.

[109] Sathe, 'Judicial Activism'.

## Information

One of the most effective tools for reducing corruption in the functioning of governments has been the effective use of the right to information,[110] which underlines the importance of transparency and accountability in governmental functioning.[111] While there are bottlenecks in the right to information framework, this approach has great potential for throwing open the institutions of government to public accountability.[112] It ensures that the powers exercised by the state and its instrumentalities are subject to public scrutiny and, more importantly, serious accountability. Accordingly, wide ranges of possibilities are available for using the information to create an accountable and transparent framework of governance.[113]

## Media

The role of media in the fight against corruption is critical. Worldwide, the media has played an important role in bringing the instances of violations of access to justice to the public domain. The media has played a dominant role in raising issues of development and how corruption has contributed to it. This role needs to be further improved and the media needs to take more responsible steps to act as a custodian of India's democracy and rule of law. It is important to promote the role of media as the availability and dissemination of information becomes complex. In many cases, there is a need for experts in different fields to understand the nature of investments made and the financial transactions involved in allegations of corruption.[114] The media has the necessary human and other resources to seek this information, analyse it, and make it available for the public to

---

[110] Sathe, *The Right to Information*.
[111] Kumar, 'Corruption, Development and Good Governance', p. 572.
[112] Ibid.
[113] Ibid.
[114] Ibid.

understand. This role of media is critical for raising awareness and contributing to the empowerment of the wider civil society.[115]

## Civil Society

The role of civil society is central to the fight against corruption. Corruption and the lack of access to justice are symptomatic of a larger problem within societies.[116] The only way to reduce corruption and provide for mechanisms that create greater access to justice is to empower civil society.[117] The role of domestic and international civil society is important as it is the best placed to situate the problem of corruption from the standpoint of access to justice.[118] Once recognized as such, the strategies that may be adopted for fighting corruption may include a variety of democratic measures that will put pressure on governments to deal with the problem of corruption.

## Training of Legal Officers

While the proposed ICAC will be engaged in the prosecution of persons against whom it has initiated proceedings, there needs to be an emphasis on the training of legal officers. In the past, many of the anti-corruption proceedings initiated in India have not resulted in convictions.[119] There numerous factors for this, many of which may be beyond the proposed ICAC's powers and mandate to investigate or rectify. But one of the reasons could be the lack of sufficient expertise and experience of legal officers in handling such cases.

There is a need to provide for a regular, substantive, and sustained training of legal officers by both domestic and international experts with a view to enhancing the substantive and procedural knowledge relating to the legal framework as well as advocacy skills that may be

---

[115] Ibid.

[116] Ibid., p. 572.

[117] Ibid.

[118] Ibid.

[119] See Baxi, *Liberty and Corruption*.

useful to pursuing these cases in the courts. The training programmes should become an ongoing feature and should become institutionalized within the working of the ICAC.

## Training of Judges

There is a need to emphasize the training and sensitization of judges to deal with corruption cases. The judiciary is a very important organ of the government and is entrusted with the responsibility to ensure that the other organs act in accordance with the Constitution.[120] Corruption violates the spirit of the Constitution besides undermining the democratic ideals and principles of the constitution.[121] The judiciary has to play a very important role in India to ensure corruption-free governance.[122] In this context, the proposed ICAC may have to work with the judicial training academy and other members of the judicial fraternity, including senior members of the judiciary, to impress upon them the need for training judges to deal with cases relating to corruption.[123] The exact *modus operandi* of the training, including who will be responsible for the actual training, are details that will have to be decided by the judiciary itself, and independence of judiciary should not be undermined in any way in this process.[124]

## Creating Increased Citizen Awareness

Creating increased awareness among citizens about corruption and its effects is another important element in combating corruption—particularly when this group awareness is accompanied by the public's ability to act as a group against it. The need for creating awareness through a wide range of mechanisms is critical for corruption. The awareness should be focused on all aspects of the problem of

[120] Sathe, *Judicial Activism in India*.
[121] Bhushan, 'Judging the Judges'.
[122] Ibid.
[123] Dhavan, 'Judicial Corruption'.
[124] Ibid.

corruption, including its causes and consequences. The efforts of the government to eliminate corruption and the information relating to the institutional mechanisms that are put in place to investigate allegation of corruption need to be widely disseminated. The purpose of the awareness should be both to inform and to empower citizenry.

## CONCLUSION

The problem of corruption, when examined as a human rights issue, produces an entirely new and indeed important approach to ensure that good governance remains the goal of public administration in India. In the context of Hong Kong (or Singapore), the success achieved in combating corruption may not have been sustained, if it had remained purely within the domain of law enforcement and public policy discourse. Community education and participation of the people in generating an attitudinal change was deemed one of the initial goals of the ICAC's approach. There is a need for the empowerment of the people of India to fight against corruption on the basis of developing certain rights against corruption.

The human rights approach to corruption control mechanism makes the people of India central players in the corruption resistance movement. The law enforcement work of the government to ensure corruption-free governance ought to be perceived as a part of the right of the people of India to seek a corruption-free government. Concomitantly, it then becomes the duty of the government to ensure that all of its affairs are conducted in a manner that promotes transparency, accountability, and integrity in public administration. The human rights approaches of corruption control mechanisms are expected to enhance the institutional approach of the proposed ICAC's fight against corruption in India. Constitutional governance is an important dimension of the rule-of-law framework that needs to be established in India. If this framework needs to work in the context of various social, economic, and political transitions that occur in India, the anti-corruption initiatives should be integrated with the human rights discourse and ensure collaborations with in countries that have successfully managed to curb the menace of corruption to a large extent.

Corruption is a significant impediment to the achievement of good governance in India.[125] While it has been noted that criminal law and public policy approaches to the problem have been met with mixed results, there has not been any serious effort to develop a human rights approach to corruption. The right to information in India needs to be integrated with the right to transparency[126] and the right to corruption-free governance. This approach integrted to handling corruption will ensure that the political and bureaucratic machinery in India is accountable to its people.

Accountability is infused by building legal and institutional mechanisms so that official corruption is not tolerated at any level of the decision-making process.[127] The change of political culture in India is possible only if the right to corruption-free governance is guaranteed through the empowerment of the Indian citizenry.[128] It is in this context that the role of the media and other members of civil society become important. The media should expose the corrupt actions of politicians and bureaucrats. Strengthening of the judiciary should be accompanied by the passage of laws, rules, and regulations that are intended to punish acts of corruption. The problem of corruption has the potential to affect democratic decision-making, and has threatened the rule of law in India. While the foundations of democracy are deeply rooted in India, corruption has undoubtedly sowed the seeds of civic and political discontent. Furthermore, the lack of political and bureaucratic transparency and accountability culminate in a sense of callous indifference among the people. Indeed, these discouraging trends in Indian society must be thwarted by the rights-based approach to fighting corruption, which is one way to extend accountability mechanisms for the promotion of good governance.

[125] Maor, note 63.
[126] Ibid.
[127] Sathe, note 96.
[128] Ibid.

# Postscript

As this book goes to press, Indian civil society activism against corruption is witnessing a major impetus in the form of Anna Hazare's campaign that has proposed the establishment of an independent, powerful, and effective institutional mechanism to fight corruption, in the form of a Lokpal. While this is not the first time that Indian civil society has been galvanized to fight against corruption and seek transparency and accountability in governance, this particular movement has had, unlike the previous ones, a strong acceptance in the popular imagination of the Indian citizenry.

Reasonable people can indeed disagree about the tactics and methods adopted by the Anna Hazare movement for seeking the government's attention for establishing a truly independent Lokpal as an institution to fight corruption and to seek accountability of the people who are engaged in corrupt acts. The civil society movement and its broad acceptance amongst the citizenry has reinforced the growing lack of legitimacy of the government to govern effectively and the increasing levels of trust deficit vis-à-vis the people.

It needs to be recognised that people have begun to lose faith in the ability of parliamentary institutions and the political process to ensure good governance. The efforts to establish an independent Lokpal is important not only because of the need to fight corruption, but also to restore the trust and faith of the Indian citizenry in parliamentary democracy. Corruption has reached such alarming proportions in India that it has undermined the foundations of democratic governance.

There is no doubt about the fact that the institutional design of Lokpal as an independent, impartial, and effective mechanism will be the sole factor for its success. The social expectations generated not just by the Anna Hazare movement, but also by the human rights violations resulting from corruption have left a strong desire among many Indians to fight corruption.

The fast by Anna Hazare, followed by the widespread civil society protests across the country, led the Government of India to appoint a 10-member Joint Committee[1] of ministers and civil society members to draft a Lokpal Bill. The Joint Committee has had a few meetings to discuss the draft; and two separate drafts of the Lokpal Bill have been produced with some degree of overlap in both the versions.

The purpose of this Postscript is to discuss some of the critical and contentious issues in the evolving debates relating to the drafting of the Lokpal Bill, on which at present, there is no consensus between the government and the civil society.

## Principles for Establishing an Anti-Corruption Agency by the Lokpal Bill

The jurisprudential foundations of institutional approach to the fight against corruption need to be understood before any attempt is made to establish an anti-corruption agency. Anti-corruption agencies are vested with three broad tasks: investigation and enforcement;

---

[1] The Committee comprises representatives of both, civil society, as well as the government. The Members of the Committee are: Representing civil society: Mr Anna Hazare, Justice Santosh Hegde, retired Supreme Court Judge, RTI activist Mr Arvind Kejriwal, Senior Advocates Mr Shanti Bhushan, and Mr Prashant Bhushan; Representing the government: Finance Minister Mr Pranab Mukherjee, Home Minister Mr P. Chidambaram, Telecom Minister Mr Kapil Sibal, Law Minister Dr Veerappa Moily, and Water Resources Minister Mr Salman Khurshid. Finance Minister Mr Pranab Mukherjee is the Chairman, with Mr Shanti Bhushan as Co-chairman of the Committee.

corruption prevention responsibilities; and education and building of public awareness relating to corruption. Anti-corruption agencies are defined as '... publically funded bodies of a durable nature whose specific mission is to fight corruption and associated crimes and to reduce the opportunity structures favourable to its occurrence through preventive and repressive strategies.'[2]

The following are some of the critical issues that are being debated in relation to the Lokpal Bill. The proposed consultation of the government with all political parties and the debates in the Parliament are expected to further reflect on these issues.

## Single Institution as opposed to Multiple Agencies

One of the most important and central issues relating to the Lokpal Bill is about whether it establishes a single institution in the form of an Independent Commission Against Corruption (ICAC), as in the manner suggested in this book earlier, or rely upon Lokpal along with some of the existing institutions to fight corruption in a concerted manner. The worldwide experience indicates that countries have attempted to follow different approaches in dealing with this issue.[3] It has been observed that anti-corruption agencies are successful in an environment when other institutions are functioning in an effective manner; and that there is a stronger coordination between them to ensure that different roles and responsibilities are appropriately performed. However, the fact of the matter is that, '... experience worldwide indicates that in most countries, cross-agency coordination remains weak or inexistent. Law enforcement agencies are often not well connected and integrated, due to their wide diversity,

[2] Luis de Sousa, 'Anti-corruption Agencies as Central Pieces in a National Integrity System' 7 available at http://www.idec.gr/iier/new/ CORRUPTION%20CONFERENCE/Anti%20Corruption%20Agencies% 20as%20Central%20Pieces%20in%20A%20National%20Integrity%20Sys tem-Luis%20de%20Sousa.pdf (last visited 27 June 2011). See also OECD, 'Specialised Anti-corruption Institutions Review of Models', (Paris, 2007).

[3] This comparative perspective has been included in the book in Chapter 3.

overlapping mandates, competing agendas, various levels of independence from political interference and a general institutional lack
of clarity....'⁴

There have been a number of·institutions in India, which have been
involved in the fight against corruption. We have, in the prevalent
environment in the country, an unparalleled opportunity to create
an institution that can be vested with this responsibility by bringing
together some of the existing institutions within its ambit, which are
already performing this role and responsibility. However, given our
past experience of police and law enforcement agencies engaging in
serious acts of abuse of power, care should be taken in the institutional design to ensure checks and balances. At the same time we
need to recognize that a single institution in the form of the Lokpal
is indeed the need of the hour. Examples of specialized institutions
with multiple competencies are the ICAC in Hong Kong, CPIB in
Singapore, NSW ICAC in New South Wales (Australia), the Directorate on Corruption and Economic Crime in Botswana, the Special
Investigation Service in Lithuania, and the Corruption Prevention
and Combating Bureau in Latvia.⁵

In this regard, it is useful to refer to the experience of Hong Kong
and Mainland China and how the institutional approach to fighting
corruption was a big success in Hong Kong, but similar measures in
Mainland China did not meet with much success. In the context of
Hong Kong's experience, Melanie Manion has rightly observed:

First, by creating a powerful independent anti-corruption agency, the government clearly signalled its commitment to anti-corruption enforcement.
Second, the anti-corruption agency achieved major enforcement successes
quickly and publicized them widely to consolidate its reputation. Third, it
accompanied enforcement with broad public education, reaching out to
the community in innovative ways. Fourth, it studied government work

⁴ Marie Chêne, 'Coordination Mechanisms of Anti-corruption Institutions' (Anti-corruption Resource Centre, Transparency International,
September 2009).
⁵ Luis de Sousa, note 2,

procedures and proposed measures to reduce incentives for corruption in institutional design.[6]

The proposed Lokpal Bill needs to consider this broad-based approach to fighting corruption, as opposed to focusing only on the culpability of the accused, or the investigation of acts of corruption leading to their prosecution.

The experience of China may not be relevant for India as democracy has indeed taken deep roots within India; and this country is governed through a Constitution and there are a number of independent institutions including the courts, which are involved in upholding the rule of law and promoting access to justice. The democratic process in India provides for opportunities to seek political accountability, but issue relating to the rule of law and transparency in governance are indeed challenges that both India and China face. There is no doubt that both India and China have witnessed high levels of corruption; and both countries are attempting to redress this problem. Melanie Manion has compared the experience of Mainland China and Hong Kong in the context of anti-corruption reform and has noted that the political establishment in mainland China has responded to corruption with ambivalent signals, establishing two anti-corruption agencies with overlapping jurisdictions and an unclear division of labour. This is further exacerbated by routine enforcement handicapped by agency design, where the government has launched intensive anti-corruption campaigns that denigrate the law at the same time as they emphasize 'punishment according to law'.[7]

## Composition and Selection of Members

The composition and selection of the members of the Lokpal is crucial for ensuring the legitimacy and credibility of the Lokpal as an independent and effective anti-corruption agency. This is one aspect

---

[6] Melanie Manion, Lessons for Mainland China for Anti-corruption Reform in Hong Kong, 42 *China Review* 81 (2004).
[7] Ibid.

of the Bill that deserves the most careful examination. India has the experience of a number of institutions losing its credibility because of the members who have been appointed to the particular institution. The composition and selection of the members should consider the diversity of the country, the enormity of the tasks involved, and the social expectations that the Lokpal as an institution has generated within the country. While the composition of most commissions and selection processes in India have historically included politicians, bureaucrats, and judges, I would strongly urge that the composition and selection of members of the Lokpal should be far more broad-based than what has been attempted in the past.

Another aspect that is worth considering is developing a three-tier structure for the selection of the members of the Lokpal. For example, the Independent Commission Against Corruption of New South Wales of Australia is different from many other anti-corruption agencies, and has created a new structure in the form of a Parliamentary Joint Committee that needs to approve the appointment of the commissioner.[8]

In the proposed Lokpal Bill, it is worthy to consider this option. In the first stage, there should be an Independent Search Committee, which identifies possible members of the Lokpal and recommends their appointment as members to the Selection Committee. After the Selection Committee recommends the appointment of the members of the Lokpal, it goes to a Parliamentary Committee, which further endorses the recommendation of the Selection Committee. It is possible to create this structure with some degree of flexibility, whereby the Parliamentary Committee returns the recommendation to the Selection Committee once for further review, but shall accept it at the second time. This is similar to the system of Presidential assent for Bills passed by the Parliament in India. This could bring a broader

[8] Independent Anti-corruption Agencies: Basic Trends and Implementation in International Practice 11 (Corruption Research Centre, Tbilisi & Constitutional and Legal policy Institute, Budapest, 2000). For further information on the New South Wales ICAC, see also http://www.icac.nsw. gov.au/about-the-icac (last visited June 27, 2011).

parliamentary oversight to the selection process of members of the Lokpal. Our past experience has demonstrated that the appointment of members to important institutions of governance requires a lot of attention. Recently, the validity of the appointment of the Central Vigilance Commissioner by the Government of India was challenged in the Supreme Court of India. In *Centre for PIL & Others* v. *Union of India*[9], the Supreme Court of India held, 'it is declared that the recommendation dated 3 September 2010 of the High-powered Committee recommending the name of Mr P.J. Thomas as Central Vigilance Commissioner under the proviso to Section 4(1) of the 2003 Act is non-est in law, and, consequently, the impugned appointment of Mr P.J. Thomas as Central Vigilance Commissioner is quashed.'[10]

The Lokpal Bill should also focus on the inclusion of distinguished members of civil society, including academics, media and professional bodies. Corruption is a serious issue that affects all stakeholders in our society. Independent institutions like the Lokpal should not only have people who hold some form of state power, be it political, bureaucratic, or judicial, but should also seek to expand its membership to bring together other members of the society who also have an equal and important stake in establishing a corruption-free society in India.

## Inclusion of the Prime Minister within the Jurisdiction of Lokpal

One of the issues that has come to the forefront of the debate relating to the establishment of the Lokpal is whether the Lokpal should be empowered to investigate allegations of corruption against the Prime Minister while he is in office.[11] There is a strong opinion within the government that the Prime Minister is too important an

[9] Writ Petition No. 348 of 2010. The text of the judgment is available at http://www.indiankanoon.org/doc/310431/ (last visited June 27, 2011).

[10] Ibid.

[11] One of the main areas of contention in the current meetings being held between the civil society and government members of the committee is this issue.

institution for it to be covered by the jurisdiction of the Lokpal; and that the inclusion of the Prime Minister will lead to unnecessary, unwarranted, and even vexatious and frivolous litigation undermining the stability of the government.[12] There is some justification in this argument—since the Prime Minister is not only the most important face of the government within India, but also he represents the people of India in the international community. Any investigation of allegations of corruption against the Prime Minister would undermine the effectiveness of a pivotal institution of the government, both domestically as well as on the international plane. However, it is all the more important to recognize that nobody is above the law; and if India truly wishes to establish a society based on the rule of law, nobody, including the Prime Minister, should be excluded from the purview of any anti-corruption investigation. As far as the fears relating to frivolous cases of corruption instituted against the Prime Minister are concerned, the Lokpal Bill could ensure adequate checks and balances so that such incidents do not occur. The Bill can envisage a separate process for seeking the investigation and prosecution of the Prime Minister by adding a higher level of scrutiny and review mechanism that will limit the possibility of the misuse of this provision.

It seems to me that there should not be any doubt about the fact that the Prime Minister should very much be within the jurisdiction of the Lokpal's investigation as far as allegations of corruption are concerned. The Constitution of India has provided a very strong framework to ensure the right to equality and the equal protection of the laws. It is important to recognize that there have been instances in the past when the Prime Minister of India and his actions have come under serious scrutiny, including the leveling of allegations of corruption. We have an opportunity to establish an institution in India that will not only address the issue of corruption, but also more importantly, seek to restore the faith of the Indian citizenry in democracy

[12] See Kapil Sibal 'Political scene not right for PM's inclusion under Lokpal', *The Economic Times*, 21 June 2011, available at http://articles.economictimes. indiatimes.com/2011-06-21/news/29683690_1_prime-minister-lokpal-bill-kapil-sibal (last visited 27 June 2011).

and the rule of law. Rule of law in India cannot be protected if corruption is not addressed with all sense of honesty and integrity by the government. The Lokpal Bill, in my view, should take into account the fact that this institution of the Lokpal has the ability to transform the governance paradigm in India and even inspire other institutions to work more effectively. While the inclusion of the Prime Minister within the Lokpal's jurisdiction will ensure due empowerment of the institutional machinery to fight corruption, the very exclusion of the Prime Minister will affect both the credibility and legitimacy of the institution. The Lokpal's jurisdiction should not be in any way limited by excluding the Prime Minister when we have the past experience of the Prime Minister playing a critical role and having the Chair of the Cabinet in the decision-making processes relating to the government's functioning.

## Inclusion of the Judiciary within the Jurisdiction of the Lokpal

Another deep concern regarding the Lokpal, is that corruption in the judiciary has affected the judicial process and shaken the people's faith in the Indian legal system to deliver justice. It is important that serious efforts ought to be taken to infuse transparency and accountability in the functioning of the judiciary. There have been numerous incidents of members of the judiciary alleged to have been engaged in acts of corruption. Since the existing institutional machinery does not provide a robust framework for seeking accountability of the judiciary, there is a case for establishing an institutional framework for the fight against corruption. However, the Lokpal will not be a suitable institution for investigating allegations of corruption against the judiciary. The nature of judiciary as an institution under the existing scheme of constitutional governance in India puts it in a special situation, since it has the power to adjudicate on the constitutional validity of all legislation and the powers exercised by the government. Further, it will also be involved in adjudicating on the constitutional validity of the powers exercised, and the decisions taken by the Lokpal under its statutory obligations. The inclusion of judiciary within the

Lokpal Bill would then weaken the proposed institutional framework in its effort to seek transparency and accountability in governance. It would also result in the Judiciary ending up being a Judge in its own cause with respect to adjudicating on the Lokpal's exercise of its powers regarding corruption in the judiciary. More importantly, the context of corruption in the judicial process as well as the members of the judiciary involved in acts of corruption deserve a separate but equally effective process, which ensures that accountability is institutionalized. There is a case for strengthening the anti-corruption provisions of the Judicial Accountability Bill (as has been proposed earlier in this book); and all efforts need to be taken to ensure that there is no sense of tolerance or for that matter indifference when it comes to acts of corruption in the judiciary.

## Accountability of the Lokpal as an Anti-corruption Institution

The fundamental issue relating to the functioning of Lokpal as an anti-corruption institution is its ability to function in an independent, transparent, impartial, and effective manner. One of the shortcomings of institutional approaches to fighting corruption is the possibility of that institution wielding power and authority that is beyond its legal mandate.[13] The legal framework that establishes the Lokpal should, therefore, ensure that sufficient checks and balances are evolved, so that the Lokpal is accountable in some manner (in a manner similar to the accountability of the ICAC proposed in this book). The accountability of the Lokpal as an institution is critical in the context of its functioning as issues relating to corruption have almost always taken political dimensions in the past. There is a need for ensuring a rigorous investigative process that does not in any way

[13] The Government has been opposed to Mr Hazare's draft's recommendation of having no governmental checks on the Lokpal, along with sweeping powers being given to it. See Sibal, 'Hazare seeks Parallel Government without Accountability', RediffNews, 24 June 2011, available at http://www.rediff.com/news/slide-show/slide-show-1-hazare-seeks-parallel-govt-without-accountability-sibal/20110624.htm (last visited 27 June 2011).

undermine the faith and the trust that citizens need to have in the Lokpal as an institution. Anti-corruption efforts are most successful when there is civil society support for these initiatives. Civil society support for the Lokpal will be there only when it is able to ensure accountability. The principle of accountability of the Lokpal as an institution includes the full and complete disclosure of all information relating to the members of the Lokpal as well as procedures for removal for misconduct.

Given the enormity of tasks ahead in fighting corruption in India, and the challenges of establishing an independent commission against corruption in the form of a Lokpal, the civil society and political discourse on this issue is of great contemporary significance. India has a unique opportunity to address corruption at a time when every institution, including every exercise of power or responsibility, has come under the scanner for serious scrutiny in relation to allegations of corruption. The Indian political system including the government, opposition, and Parliament needs to respond decisively to establish the Lokpal, so that corruption could be eliminated, rule of law could be upheld, and the human rights of the Indian citizenry protected and promoted.

# Index

ン ゆ

*A. Wati* v. *State of Manipur*, 26
abuse of discretionary powers and
    rule-of-law, 37–8, 101–2
access to justice
    relationship with corruption,
        49–53, 67–8
    right to, 7, 12
accountability
    in government institutions, 121
    National Human Rights
        Institutions (NHRIs), 142–4
    of anti-corruption institutions,
        183
    principles of, 162–70
'active' bribery, 5
Administrative Vigilance Division
    (AVD), 132
Anand, Justice A.S., 101
Anna Hazare campaign, 180,
    214–15
Ansari, M.M., 169
anti-corruption agencies, defined,
    216
arbitrariness and corruption, 35–6
Article 21 of the Constitution, 23

Article 142 of the Constitution of
    India, 102
Asia, corruption in, 38–9
    Cambodia, 41
    China, 69–70
    in the context of culture,
        85–8
    difficulties of promoting
        human rights, 88–93
    and governance framework,
        82–3
    Hong Kong, 67, 74–7
    India, 72. *See also* India,
        anti-corruption framework
        in; reforms, for corruption-
        free service in India
    Indonesia, 81–2
    and institutional frameworks,
        83–4
    judicial corruption, 67
    linkages between violations of
        human rights and, 80–93
    models for combating
        corruption, 71–80
    Mongolia, 72

non-state actors, role in human
    rights activism, 90–1
Philippines, 68
and policies relating to
    governance, 64–5
political will, role of, 70–1
Singapore, 67, 78–80
South Korea, 84
Thailand, 88
Asian Development Bank (ADB),
    4–5, 65
Asian Human Rights Commission,
    Hong Kong, 15
'Asian values' and corruption, 85–8

Bangkok Declaration of 1993, 85
Baxi, Upendra, 129
Blair-Kerr, Sir Alastair, 74
bribery
    definition, 5
    in India, 97

Central Bureau of Investigation
    (CBI), 110, 150, 160, 184
Central Information Commission
    (CIC), 6, 135
    good governance approach,
        163–71
    scope of powers and
        jurisdiction, 169–71
Central Vigilance Commission
    (CVC), 18, 110, 116–17, 133,
    150, 159–60
Centre for PIL v. Union of India,
    117, 220
Chapter IX of the Indian Penal
    Code, 108
Chatuthai, Maneewan, 88

Civil Law Convention on
    Corruption, 124
Code of 1868, 19
Code of Criminal Procedure
    (CrPC) (1973), 19, 128
    Section 170, 22
    Section 190, 22
    Section 197, 129
Commission on Human Rights and
    Administrative Justice (CHRAJ)
    of Ghana, 152–3
Committee on Economic,
    Social and Cultural Rights
    (CESCR), 40, 153
Common Cause v. Union of India,
    115
constitutional empowerment of the
    citizenry, in India, 106
constitutionalization of human
    rights, 142, 204
Constitution of India, 112–13
contemporary international law, 58
Convention on Combating Bribery
    of Foreign Public Officials
    in International Business
    Transactions, 123
Corruption
    and discretionary power of
        government officials, 36–7
    and discrimination in
        administration, 36
    as a crime under international
        law, 126–7
    at higher level of judiciary in
        India, 118–20
    gratifications, accepting, 109–10
    human rights implications, 2,
        7–8

impact on sovereignty, 61–3
implications for rule of law,
    30–7
legal systems' ineffectiveness
    and judicial indifference,
    19–23
negative consequences, 17–18
overview, 15–28
penalties imposed, 18
perceived as societal
    imagination, 23–8
ranking, 17–18
relationship with human rights,
    28–30, 160–2
and safeguarding public
    servants, 21–2
and unpredictability in law
    enforcement, 37–9
as a violation of human rights,
    105
corruption-free governance, 156–8
    and right to information, 162–70
    judicial enforcement of, 112
corruption-free service, in India,
    103–7
CPRs, 155
Criminal Law Amendment
    Ordinance (1944), 108
Criminal Law Convention on
    Corruption, 124
cultural values and corruption,
    85–8
CVC Act (2003), 117

Davis, Michael, 86
Declaration Against Corruption
    and Bribery in International
    Commercial Transactions, 122

Declarations made by the first
    Global Forum on Fighting
    Corruption, 124
Delhi Special Police Establishment
    (DSPE), 131–2
democratic governance, 60
development
    link between corruption and,
        55–7
    right to, 53–5
Dinakaran, Justice, 120
Dinesh Trivedi v. Union of India,
    116
discrimination in administration
    and rule-of-law, 36
Domingo, Mike, 68

Economic, Social and Cultural
    Rights (ESCRs), 153–4
effective democracy, 125–6
Election Commission of India
    (ECI), 177
empowerment of citizenry, 6
Enforcement Decree of the Act on
    Contracts, 36
Enforcement Directorate (ED), 114,
    133, 150

Fiji Human Rights Commission,
    151
Freedom of Information Act (2002),
    167
fundamental right to corruption-
    free service, 103–7, 131
fundamental right to education,
    106, 130–1

Ghai, Yash, 87

Global Corruption Report (2009),
    17
global human rights movement, 40
Global Integrity Report (2004), 97
globalization and human rights, 58
good governance
    Linda C. Reif's views, 96
    policies for, 64–5
    principles of transparency and
        accountability, 162–70
    strategy to achieve, 91–3, 96
    UN Development Programme
        (UNDP) views, 96
Goodpaster, Gary, 82
governance, definition, 13
governance and corruption, 6
    effect of arbitrariness in
        decision-making, 35–6
    national institutions, role in
        anti-corruption effort, 92–3.
        See also National Human
        Rights Institutions (NHRIs)
    policies for good governance,
        64–5
    strategy to achieve good
        governance, 91–3
Government Procurement Act, 36,
    78
Government Procurement
    (Challenge Proceedings), 78
Government Procurement
    Regulations, 78
Group of States against Corruption
    (GRECO), 124

Harms, Brian C., 177
Heilbrunn, John R., 179–81
Heymann, Philip B., 27

Hong Kong, 67
    corruption in police force, 74
    establishment of the
        Independent Commission
        Against Corruption (ICAC),
        67
    historical perspectives about
        corruption, 73–4
    Independent Commission
        Against Corruption (ICAC),
        75–7
    legal framework for tackling
        corruption, 75–6
human development, conception
    of, 54
    impediments to, 55–7
Human Development Index
    (HDI), 55
human rights approach, to fighting
    corruption, 9–12
human rights framework.
    See also National Human
        Rights Institutions (NHRIs)
    Cambodia, 41
    as a challenge to sovereignty,
        57–63
    developing a theoretical
        framework, 42
    link between corruption and
        development, 55–7
    recognizing corruption as a
        human rights violation, 42–9
    right to access to justice, 49–53
    right to human development,
        53–5
    in South Asia, 43
human rights implications, of
    corruption, 7–8

human rights violations, 8
  cases decided by NHRC on, 160
  investigation of, 159

impeachment cases, 118–19
Independent Commission Against
  Corruption (ICAC), 131, 171–2,
  216
  anti-corruption initiatives,
    183–8, 194
  commitment of, 179
  composition of, 192
  creating a communications
    office/public affairs division,
    194–5
  dissemination of procedures for,
    195
  empowerment of NGOs and
    civil society, 198–9
  establishment of a separate
    specialized institution to
    investigate and prosecute
    crimes, 185–8
  framework, 189–92
  honesty and integrity of
    anti-corruption investigative
    process, 190–1
  independence of, 191–2
  in India, 188–97
  leadership of, 177–83
  level of engagement and
    interaction with OCAG, 198
  media relation, 198
  people-centred approach to
    anti-corruption work, 195–6
  political and operational
    independence to investigate
    cases, 175

political backing and
    accountability of the
    government, significance of,
    173–4
  powers of, 176, 192–3
  proposal to establish an ICAC,
    171–2
  relationship with other
    institutions, 197–9
  resources needed for initiatives,
    174
  training programmes to
    parliamentarians, 196–7
  user-friendly laws, developing
    of, 176–7
Independent Commission Against
  Corruption of New South Wales
  of Australia, 219
'independent' institutions, in India,
  7
India, anti-corruption framework
  in, 6. See also management
  of corruption; reforms, for
  corruption-free service in India
  approaches, 108
  Central Bureau of Investigation
    (CBI), role of, 110
  constitutional approach,
    111–12
  governance machinery, 110–21
  judiciary system, 112–21
  jurisprudence developed by
    the Supreme Court of India,
    117–21
  law enforcement machinery of
    the state, 110
  need for an independent
    commission, 7

Prevention of Corruption Act,
    1988 (PCA), 108
Proposed Judicial Standards and
    Accountability Bill, 2010,
    120–1
right to information, 115–16
Santhanam Committee
    recommendations, 110,
    132–3
whistleblower protection,
    legal and institutional
    frameworks for, 134–8
Indian governance system, 112–13
institutionalized corruption, 38
international anti-corruption
    instruments, 123–5
international anti-corruption treaty
    mechanisms, 60
International Code of Conduct for
    Public Officials, 123
International Covenant on Civil
    and Political Rights (ICCPR),
    40
International Covenant on
    Economic, Social and Cultural
    Rights (ICESCR), 40, 153
International Criminal Tribunals,
    59
International Monetary Fund, 58

Joint Action on Corruption in the
    Private Sector, 124
Joshi, Abha, 163
Judges Inquiry Act (1968),
    119–20
Judicial Accountability Bill, 223
judicial activism, 101
judicial governance, 207

judicial system, impacts related to
    absence of a case of India, Vohra
    Committee Report, 33–4
    case of Laos, UNDP study, 33
    public interest litigation (PIL),
    99–103

Kalshian, Rakesh, 97
Kenya National Commission on
    Human Rights, 151
Kofele-Kale, Ndiva, 126
Kpundeh, Sahr J., 71

law enforcement machinery,
    of state, 111
legal framework, for fighting
    corruption, 202–8
    in India, 108–27
Liann, Thio, 88
Limburg Principles on the
    Implementation of the
    International Covenant on
    Economic, Social and Cultural
    Rights, 156
Lokpal, 68, 117, 180, 214–15
    accountability of, 223–4
    composition and selection of the
        members, 215, 218–20
    important and central issues
        relating, 216–18
    inclusion of judiciary, 222–3
    Independent Search Committee,
        219
    Parliamentary Committee, 219
    Selection Committee, 219
Lord Nolan Committee, on
    Standards in Public Life in the
    United Kingdom, 114–15

Maastricht Guidelines on Violations
of Economic, Social and Cultural
Rights, 156
management of corruption
anti-corruption treaty, 121–2
civil society expectations and
role in, 208, 210
constitutional framework, 94–8
creating awareness, 211–12
customary law norm that treats
corruption as a crime under
international law, 126–7
fundamental right to corruption-
free service, 103–7
international anti-corruption
instruments, 123–5
judicial governance, 207
judiciary and its adjudicative
mechanisms, 203–8, 211
legal framework, 108–27,
202–7
media role in, 209–10
Public Interest Litigation (PIL),
98–103
right to information, 209
training of legal officers and
judges, 210–11
Mander, Harsh, 163
Manion, Melanie, 217–18
Mansukhani, H. L., 110
Maor, Moshe, 177–9
Marbury v. Madison, 207
Mazdoor Kisan Shakti Sangathan
('Labour Farmer Strength
Organization'; MKSS), 164–6
McLean, Gary N., 86, 88
millennium development goals
(MDGs), 56–7, 62

Model Code of Conduct for Public
Officials, 125
Moon, Yong-Lin, 86

National Human Rights
Commissions (NHRCs), 62
National Human Rights Institutions
(NHRIs)
academic learning, role of,
145–6
accountability aspects, 142–4
anti-corruption efforts as part
of human rights protection,
159
business houses, role of, 146–7
cases decided by, 160
empowering the judiciary and
other institutions, 157
functions of, 147–8
fundamental rights, 140
galvanizing social consciousness,
role in, 157–8
Human Rights Commissions
(HRCs), 141–4
human rights education, 144–5
in India, 141–50
investigative division of, 159
protection and promotion of
human rights, 140
recognition of the right to
corruption-free governance,
156–7
research practices, 160–2
revamping the mandate of, 158
rights-based approaches to
governance, 150–8
right to corruption-free
governance, 157

State Human Rights
    Commissions (SHRCs), 141
National Judicial Oversight
    Committee, 120–1
nongovernmental organizations
    (NGOs), 59
non-state actors, role in human
    rights activism, 90–1
Noorani, A. G., 133

'passive' bribery, 5
People for Empowerment and
    Truth, 69
People's Republic of China, and
    democratic governance, 69
Philippines, and graft, 66
police and law enforcement
    agencies, 186–9
political will and anti-corruption
    efforts, 70–1
Presidential Commission Against
    Graft and Corruption (PCAGC),
    68–9
Prevention of Corruption Act
    (PoCA) (1947), 26, 132
Prevention of Corruption Act
    (PoCA) (1988), 19, 21, 108
    Sections 7, 8, and 9 of, 109–10
Principles to Combat Corruption
    in African Countries of the
    Global Coalition for Africa,
    125
Procuratorial Division of Graft and
    Bribery (1989), 70
Proposed Judicial Standards and
    Accountability Bill (2010), 120
Protection of Human Rights Act
    (1993), 147, 150, 158–9, 177

public integrity index, of India,
    97–8
The Public Interest Disclosure and
    Protection of Informers Bill
    (2002), 134
Public Interest Disclosure and the
    Protection of Persons Making
    the Disclosure Bill (2010), 52
Public Interest Litigation (PIL),
    in India, 98–103

Quah, Jon S.T., 38–9, 66, 71–2
quan-xi practice, 88

Ramaswamy, Justice, 120
Rao v. Vasudeva, 103
reforms, for corruption-free
    service in India. See also
    Independent Commission
    Against Corruption (ICAC);
    National Human Rights
    Institutions (NHRIs)
    domestic anti-corruption legal
        framework, 131–8
    institutional measures, 139–71
    legislative measures, 128–38
    rights-based strategies, 129–31
responsibility to protect, 14
rights-based approach, to fighting
    corruption, 9, 93, 129–31,
    150–6
right to equality before the law
    (Article 14), 164
right to equal protection of laws
    (Article 14), 164
right to freedom of speech and
    expression (Article 19[1][a]),
    164

Right to Information Act (2005), 63, 148, 168
  Central Information Commission, 168–9
  constitutional foundation of, 164–5
  preamble, 168
  of public affairs, Supreme Court views, 116–17
  relevance of, 166–8
right to life and liberty (Article 21), 164
'right to life' jurisprudence, 130
Rose-Ackerman, Susan, 182–3
Roy, Aruna, 165
rule-of-law, 206–8, 222
  abuse of discretionary powers and, 36–7
  arbitrariness in decision-making and, 35–6
  as the basis for criminal justice, 38
  conceptions according to modern theorists, 34
  discrimination in administration and, 36
  need for, 38–9
  unpredictability in law enforcement and, 38–9
Rule of Law Project, 34
rule-of-law society, 2

Sandgren, Claes, 182
Sen, Justice Soumitra, 119
Sengupta, Arjun, 89
Senior Experts Group on Transnational Organized Crime, Recommendation 32, 123

Singapore
  corruption in colonial Singapore, 78
  Corrupt Practices Investigation Bureau (CPIB), 78
  experience in fighting corruption, 77–80
  judicial corruption, 67
  legal framework for tackling corruption, 78–80
  Prevention of Corruption Act (POCA), 78
S.N. Bose v. State of Bihar, 109
Sovereignty
  as state responsibility, 14, 63
  dimensions impacted by corruption, 61–3
  goal of, 61–3
  impact on globalization, 58
  in human rights framework, 59–60
  understanding of, 12
state, role in curbing corruption, 12
State Information Commissions (SICs), 6
Statement of Object and Reasons in the Prevention of Corruption (Amendment) Bill, 2008, 21
State of West Bengal v. Union of India, 12
Summit of the Americas Declaration of Principles and Plan of Action (1994), 125

Tenth UN Congress on the Prevention of Crime, 123
Thomas, P. J., 117, 220
transnational civil society, 59

transparency, principles of, 162–70
Transparency International (TI)
    Report, 67
    *TI Source Book 2000,* 173, 176
Treatment of Offenders, 123
Tummala, Krishna, 32
Twenty Guiding Principles for the
    Fight against Corruption, 123

'Uncle Judges' syndrome, 119
UN Convention Against
    Corruption (UNCAC), 3, 122
UN Decade for Human Rights
    Education (1995–2004), 145
UN Declaration Against
    Corruption and Bribery in
    International Commercial
    Transactions, 125–6
UN Development Programme
    (UNDP), 55, 60
UNDP's Human Development
    Report (2000, 2006), 54–5
UN Economic and Social
    Commission for Asia and the
    Pacific (UNESCAP), 91
UN General Assembly (UNGA),
    145

UN General Assembly Resolution
    54/128, 123
UN General Assembly Resolution
    'Action against Corruption', 126
UN Human Rights Committee
    (UNHRC), 40
Universal Declaration of Human
    Rights (UDHR), 40

Varela, Amelia P., 66
vexatious prosecutions, 21–2
*Vineet Narain* v. *Union of India,*
    102, 114, 133, 183
Vittal, N., 106
Voluntary Disclosure of Income
    Scheme (VDIS), 24
*V.S. Achuthanandan* v. *R.*
    *Balakrishna Pillai,* 115

whistleblower protection, legal and
    institutional frameworks for,
    134–8
World Bank, 58, 60
    definition of corruption, 4
World Trade Organization, 58

Xiaoping, Deng, 69